The Ancient Egyptian "Tale of Two Brothers"

The Oldest Fairy Tale in the World

Oklahoma Series in Classical Culture

Oklahoma Series in Classical Culture

The Ancient Egyptian "Tale of Two Brothers"

The Oldest Fairy Tale in the World

by Susan Tower Hollis

University of Oklahoma Press: Norman and London

Published with the assistance of the National Endowment for the Humanities, a federal agency which supports the study of such fields as history, philosophy, literature, and languages.

Library of Congress Cataloging-in-Publication Data

Hollis, Susan T.
The ancient Egyptian "Tale of two brothers" : the oldest fairy tale in the world / Susan Tower Hollis. — 1st ed.
p. cm. — (Oklahoma series in classical culture)
A revision of the author's thesis (doctoral)—Harvard.
Includes bibliographical references (p.) and index.
ISBN 0-8061-2269-2 (alk. paper)
1. Two Brothers (Tale) 2. Fairy tales—Egypt—History and criticism. I. Title. II. series.
GR75.T93H65 1990
398.21′0932—dc20 90-50236
CIP

The paper in this book meets the guidelines for permanence and durability of the Committee on Production Guidelines for Book Longevity of the Council on Library Resources, Inc. ♾

The Ancient Egyptian "Tale of Two Brothers" is Volume 7 in the Oklahoma Series in Classical Culture.

[redacted]

Contents

Foreword

If history can be said to be the recounting of human achievements, then literature can surely be said to be the sum of human thoughts and ideals. In ancient Egypt, literature was used to entertain, educate, and edify. Writing and eloquence were well respected throughout Egypt's history, and in fact played an important role in the development and education of its young people. As the future king Merykare was instructed: "Truth comes to [the wise] fully prepared, in what the ancestors have said. So copy your fathers, those who have come before you. See, their words endure in writing. Open them, read them, and copy their knowledge."

For us today, the recognition that their literature was an important part of the ancient Egyptians' social fabric is paramount to a proper understanding of pharaonic Egypt, as well as a healthy antidote to the popularly held view that the ancient Egyptians were so obsessed with death and the afterlife that they produced little that was not connected to funerary concepts.

But literature comes in a broad spectrum, and we must then differentiate between the various genres of writings, from belles-lettres to autobiographical inscriptions and religious compositions to political texts. For sheer entertainment value, many of the tales that have come down to us from ancient Egypt are as exciting today as they would have been three thousand years ago. The Egyptians were masters at creating plots with enough drama and pathos to captivate their audiences and move their stories along at a good pace. Another genre of writings were the "instructional" pieces, as the ancient Egyptians called them. These were set in the guise of a father teaching his son the proper ways of the world, and their homilies were a veritable blueprint to good social and moral conduct. Literature could also serve as a vehicle for the partial telling of myths. By having their divinities act out various adventures, or even mixing the world of gods with the human world, the storytellers were able to recount wondrous mythical tales, which were in themselves explanations of the world as the Egyptians perceived it. Another literary device was to weave political propaganda in the middle of an exciting narrative, a subtle device often used by the royal house, which had itself commissioned the stories.

The tale of the two brothers Bata and Anubis, the subject of the present book, encompasses many of these facets and therein lies much of its fascination. Its plot moves along at a rapid pace, and the author makes us genuinely feel for the characters. We do care about the fate of the young protagonist Bata through his various adventures. From the attempted seduction by his brother's wife (reminding us of the Biblical story of Potiphar's wife as well as the Greek legend of Phaedra and Hippolytus from the Theseus cycle), to his self-imposed exile and mutilation, through his magical transformations and his eventual triumph, Bata remains the central figure of the story, around whom most of the action revolves.

His older brother Anubis, although deceived at first, turns out to be faithful and unceasing in his efforts to restore his brother's life and is rewarded in the end with fame, fortune, and eventually the kingship itself. If the happy ending seems somewhat abrupt, this is also a feature of ancient Egyptian literature, almost as if the outcome was a foregone conclusion, something that seemed fated from the start.

The story also contains a good number of mythical allusions, all of which would have been clearly understood by an ancient Egyptian audience. The latter would of course have known about the gods and goddesses who inhabited Egypt, their personalities and attributes, as well as the various tricks they were capable of, and they would have responded warmly to the kindnesses shown by the gods, as much as they would have frowned when a particularly dastardly deed had been perpetuated.

The last few decades have brought us a number of excellent translations of ancient Egyptian texts. These have offered fresh renderings as well as up-to-date scholarly resource material, and the present book can be better appreciated in the context of these new studies. A scholar's duty is not only to elucidate the grammatical and lexical difficulties of a given text, but also to place it within its proper historical, social, and religious context. In this respect, Dr. Hollis has accomplished her task with great success. Her painstaking study has explained a number of difficult allusions that would have been obvious to the original audience but may escape a modern reader. By scrutinizing every detail of the text, she has managed to extrapolate as much information as possible from the story, and thus explain it in better detail.

By investigating the particular names given to the two main protagonists, she has demonstrated a deeper, religious level for these characters. The young hero Bata can be said to be an actual divinity who had long been connected to the mortuary cult. As for Anubis, the older brother, he is of course a manifestation of the mortuary god of the same name, whose divine function of royal embalmer and regenerator mirrors the character's ultimate role in the story. This theme of revivification is also reflected in some of the terminology used in the tale: for example, the persea trees that magically grow out of palace doorposts have a religious significance in their connection to solar rebirth, and thus symbolize the hero's own subsequent rebirth.

A consideration of some of the other characters' attributes also repays investigation, as the author points out that the two wives, who can hardly be said to be described in flattering ways, are actually representations of the goddess Hathor in her various guises. Indeed, Hathor was known to the Egyptians both as a warm goddess of love and music, and as a destructive lionness who could wreak havoc among humankind. This type of mythical dual personality was one of the means by which the Egyptians could explain the range of human behaviour, and thus the women portrayed in the tale were simply meant to represent different aspects of human conduct.

In the end, then, the "Tale of Two Brothers" can be seen to be more than just an ordinary story. It is a fairy tale indeed, with many of the characteristics of that genre. But it is also a "story with a message," that of a rite of passage from shepherd to king, which also contains many mythical allusions. This book not only succeeds in revealing all of these aspects, but also does it in a manner that will be readily accessible to the modern reader.

RONALD J. LEPROHON

University of Toronto

Acknowledgements

Many people, both knowingly and unknowingly, contributed to the generation of this work. When it was in its original form as my doctoral dissertation, such people included my fellow students in the Department of Near Eastern Languages and Civilizations and my colleagues and students in the Department of Folklore and Mythology at Harvard as well as my children, Debbie and Harry. Professor Albert B. Lord of Harvard, under whom I did my first teaching and from whom I began to learn about oral traditional narrative, and Professor Hugh M. Flick, Jr., formerly of Harvard and now of Yale, with whom I taught folklore for over eight years, both deserve extra thanks for stimulating the development of my thought.

My parents hold a very special place in this revision because of their providing me with a hard disk for my computer to facilitate it. Annemarie Whelan of the computer services at Harvard Medical School assisted by transferring the material from my ancient eight-inch Wang disks to the necessary three-and-a-half-inch disks in ASCI so I could accomplish the revision without reentering the whole, and Diane Terp of Harvard's Office of Information Technology helped to make sure that I received those disks in good order. Finally, thanks go to Nancy Makl, head of technology services in academic computing at Pomona College, who enabled me to have scanned into the Macintosh computer text figures 6, 7, 13, and 28.

I greatly appreciate the thoughtful comments of the various outside readers who evaluated the manuscript for the University of Oklahoma Press as well as the willing ear of Professor Tova Meltzer of the Claremont Graduate School, who assisted in the long job of proofreading. Finally, special thanks go to Wolfgang Schwarz, a longtime confidant and special friend, and to Thomas O. Lambdin, my professor of Egyptian and dissertation advisor, whose advice, patience, and skills as a teacher remain as a model for all aspiring teachers. Needless to say, I alone am responsible for the ideas and opinions expressed in this work.

SUSAN TOWER HOLLIS

Claremont, California

The Ancient Egyptian "Tale of Two Brothers"

The Oldest Fairy Tale in the World

Introduction

Fairy tales have delighted young and old for ages, but until 1852 no one imagined that a narrative with fairy-tale-like elements existed as long ago as the time of the Egyptian pharaohs. Yet such is the case. Although many question whether the "Tale of Two Brothers"[1] is truly a fairy tale, there is no doubt that the tale contains materials present in narratives generally called *Märchen,* or fairy tales.[2] It also incorporates elements of myth and relates what seems to be the earliest variant of an attempted seduction episode seen in the well-known story of Joseph and Potiphar's wife in Genesis 39. Thus, the narrative has fascinated not only Egyptologists and folklorists but also biblical scholars and various others, many of whom have examined the tale over the years. Recent advances in studies in all related fields as well as the publication in 1960 of the Papyrus Jumilhac,[3] dating from Ptolemaic times, have served to maintain scholarly interest in the narrative, thus justifying a reexamination of its origins and structure, and a search to understand its meaning, purpose, and place in Egyptian society.

It is the aim of this study,[4] using the tools of modern scholarship from a variety of disciplines such as folklore and anthropology, to place the narrative in its cultural and historical context and to attempt to elicit the meaning and raison d'être of the tale for its own time. At the same time, the study seeks to provide a model for the examination of diverse narratives from this and other ancient cultures.

The approach begins with a survey of the issues[5] which previous students of the narrative have raised. Generally such studies have reflected the scholarship of the day,[6] as this study surely does. Following a rather technical but important examination of the tale's protagonists and their respective places in ancient Egyptian thought, it continues with a minute examination of each episode, as well as of some specific Egyptian words present in the tale, and seeks to set each individually within the wider context of the world of the ancient Egyptians. The conclusion draws the whole together, suggesting that the tale is indeed a unity telling of the accession of an Egyptian king, essentially a rite of passage. The apparent fairy-tale motifs are rooted firmly in Egyptian thought. Furthermore, the seemingly problematic divine nature of the main characters is not only appropriate but necessary given the subject matter of the tale.

Behind this approach lies the understanding that when an audience comes to a tale, each member brings a personal history, culture, and background, all of which affects his or her understanding and enjoyment.[7] If audiences for written or narrated works did not bring these experiences, then the writer or performer would be burdened with having to explain every reference or symbol.

In the case of ancient materials such as the "Tale of Two Brothers," the time, place, and historical context, not to mention language, culture, and religion, are so divorced from the present day that to understand the richness present in the material is nearly impossible. For this reason, in addition to attending to the needs of scholarship, this study seeks to unlock that richness for the modern audience.

The Tale of Two Brothers

Papyrus d'Orbiney

The following translation represents a fairly literal rendering of the story as it is found transcribed in Alan H. Gardiner's *Late Egyptian Stories.* The text incorporates several conventions common to translations from the ancient world. The small capitals represent words the Egyptian scribe wrote in red ink, so-called rubrics. The numbers in parentheses show the page and line number of the papyrus itself. Parentheses, (), in the text surround words inserted by the translator for clarity; square brackets, [], show restorations; and angle brackets, <>, enclose words omitted by the Egyptian scribe.

(1,1) ONCE UPON A TIME THERE WERE two brothers of one father and one mother. Anubis was the name of the older; Bata was the name of the younger. Now Anubis had a house and a wife, his younger brother being with him in the manner of a son. He[1] used to make clothes for him, and he used to follow after his herd to the fields. It was he who did the plowing, and it was he who harvested, and it was he who used to do all the affairs of the fields. Indeed his younger brother was a beautiful young man, there being none of his form in the whole land. Indeed the strength of a god was in him.

NOW MANY DAYS AFTER THIS, his young brother (1,5) followed his cattle in (his) daily custom, and he returned to his house every evening, and he was loaded with every plant of the field, with milk, with wood, with every good thing of the field, and he laid (it) before his older brother, he being seated with his wife. He used to drink, he used to eat, and he used to [sleep] in his stable in the midst of his cattle.

NOW AFTER THE LAND WAS LIGHT and a second day dawned, [he took foods] which were cooked and he placed them before his older brother, and he[2] gave to him loaves for the field, and he[3] drove his cattle to allow them to eat in the fields, he going after the cattle, they telling him, "The herbage is good in such-and-such place." And he used to hear all which they said, and he took them to the good (2,1) place of herbage which they desired, the cattle before him becoming very beautiful. They multiplied their offspring very much.

NOW AT THE TIME OF plowing, his older brother said to him, "Have ready for us a span [of oxen] for the plowing because the high land has gone forth, it being good to plow it. Likewise go to the field carrying seed because we will begin to plow tomorrow. AND THEN his (2,5) younger brother did all the things which his older brother said to him, "Do them."

NOW AFTER THE LAND BECAME LIGHT AND A SECOND DAY DAWNED, they went to the field carrying their seed and they began to plow. Their hearts were very pleased because of their work at their beginning of work.

NOW AFTER MANY DAYS, they being in the field and waiting for seed, THEN HE sent his younger brother saying, "Hurry, bring us seed from the town." And his younger brother found the wife of his older brother (with) one sitting braiding her. AND THEN HE said to her, "Stand, get for me seed that (3,1) I may hasten to the field because my older brother waits for me. Do not make a delay." THEN SHE said to him, "Go, open the storehouse and bring yourself what you want.[4] Do not make me abandon my hair dressing."

AND THEN the young man entered his barn and he brought one of the large jars, he desiring to take much seed, and he loaded himself with barley and emmer and he went forth carrying them. THEN SHE said to him, "How much weight is what is on your shoulder?" And he said to her, (3,5) "Three sacks of emmer and two sacks of barley, five in all are those which are on my shoulder." He said (thus) to her. AND THEN SHE spoke with him saying, "Strength is great in you, for I see your strength daily." And she desired to know him as to know a young man. AND THEN SHE stood, and she seized him, and she said to him, "Come, let us spend an hour lying down. It will be beneficial for you. Then I will make beautiful clothes for you." THEN the young man became angry like an Upper Egyptian leopard because of the evil word which she said to him, and she was very frightened. AND THEN HE spoke with her saying, "Now see, you are like a mother to me. Further, your husband is like a father to me. Now the one older than I, he has raised me. What (4,1) is the great wrong which you said to me? Do not say it to me again. Further I will not speak (of it) to anyone, and I will not cause it to go forth from my mouth to any people." And lifting his load, he went to the field. AND THEN he reached his older brother, and they started to work (again) in their work.

NOW WHEN IT WAS EVENING, his older brother returned to his house, his young brother being behind his cattle, and he was loaded with everything of the field, and he brought his cattle (4,5) before him to have them spend the night (in) their barn in the village.

Now the wife of his older brother was afraid of the word which she said. AND THEN she brought fat and grease, and she became like one who was beaten, saying to her husband, "It was your young brother who beat (me)." When her husband returned in the evening in his daily fashion, he found his wife lying ill of guilt, and she did not put water over his hand in his <daily> fashion. And she did not make a light before him, his house being in darkness, because she was lying down vomiting. And her husband said to her, "Who had words with you?" Then she said to him, "No one spoke with me except your (5,1) young brother. When he came to fetch seed for you, he found me sitting alone, and he said to me, 'Come, let us spend an hour lying down. Loosen your hair.' Thus he said to me. I did not listen to him. 'Now am I not your mother? Further, your older brother is like a father with you.' Thus I said to him. He was afraid. He beat (me) in order that I not give to you a report. Now if you let him live, I will die. See, when he comes [do not let him live] because I suffer the evil thing which he did yesterday."[5]

AND THEN his older brother became (5,5) like a leopard of Upper Egypt, and he had his spear sharpened, and he put it in his hand. AND THEN his older brother stood behind the door of his stable to kill his young brother in his coming in the evening to have his cattle enter the stable.

When the sun went to rest, he[6] loaded himself with all the herbage of the fields in his fashion of every day, and he came, and the foremost cow entered the stable. And she said to her shepherd, "Behold, your older brother stands before you carrying his spear to kill you. Flee before him." AND THEN he heard the speaking of his lead cattle and (6,1) another entered and she said the same. And he looked under the door of his stable, and he saw the feet of his older brother as he stood behind the door with his spear in his hand. And he put his load down, and he raised himself to run in order to flee, and his older brother went after him, carrying his spear.

AND THEN his young brother prayed to Pre-Harakhty (6,5),[7] saying, "My good Lord, it is you who judges between the guilty and the innocent." Pre heard his whole petition, and Pre caused a great water to become between (them) to separate him from his older brother, it being filled with crocodiles. And one of them was on the one side and the other on the other, and his older brother struck his own hand twice for not killing him.

AND THEN his young brother called to him on the side, saying, "Stand here until the dawn. When the disk shines, I will (7,1) contend with you before him in order that he give the guilty to the just, because I will not be with you forever, and I will not be in the place in which you are. And I will go to the Valley of the Pine."

NOW WHEN THE LAND WAS LIGHT AND A SECOND DAY BECAME, Pre-Harakhty arose and one saw the other. AND THEN the young man spoke to his older brother, saying, "What is your coming after me to kill falsely, not hearing my mouth speak on the matter? And further I am still your young brother, and (7,5) also you are with me in the manner of father and also your wife is with me in the manner of a mother. Is it not so when you sent to bring seed for us, your wife said to me,

'Come, let us spend an hour lying together.' Further, see, she turned it about for you into another thing." AND THEN he[8] caused him to know all the happenings with him and his wife. AND THEN he swore to Pre-Harakhty, saying, "As for your coming to kill me wrongfully, carrying your spear on the word of a filthy whore," and he brought a reed knife and he cut off his phallus, and he threw it to the water, and the wels fish swallowed it. And he was (8,1) weak and he became feeble. And his older brother was very sorrowing in his heart, and he stood and wept loudly for him, and he was not able to (be) where his young brother was because of the crocodiles.

AND THEN his young brother called to him, saying, "Indeed, if you recall an evil, do you not also recall a good or something I did for you? Now go to your house and care for your cattle because I will not stand in the place in which you are. And I will go to the Valley of the Pine. Now as to what you will do for me <it is> your coming to care for me when you know that something has happened to me. I will have cut out my heart and placed it on the top of the blossom of the pine. When the pine is cut and it falls to the (8,5) ground, you will come to seek it. If you spend seven years seeking it, do not let your heart show dislike, and when you find it, put it in a bowl of cool water and I will live and I shall avenge the transgressions against me. Further you (will) know something has happened to me (when) you are given a jug of beer to your hand and it foams. Do not wait, because already it has happened with you."

AND THEN he went to the Valley of the Pine, and his older brother went to his house, his hands on his head, he being covered with dirt. He reached his house and killed his wife, and he threw her to the dogs and he sat in mourning for his young brother.

NOW MANY DAYS AFTER THIS, his young brother was in the Valley of the Pine, no one being with him and he spending the day hunting small game in the hills, and he came to spend the night under the pine on top of whose blossom was his heart.

NOW MANY (9,1) DAYS AFTER THIS, he built himself a house with his hands <in> the Valley of the Pine, and he filled (it) with every good thing of (his) desire to furnish for himself a house. He went out from his house and he met the Ennead[9] as they were going out to administer the whole land. AND THEN the Ennead spoke, one of them to another, saying to him, "Ho, Bata, bull of the Ennead, are you here alone, you having escaped your town because of the wife of Anubis, your older (9,5) brother? See, he killed his wife. Now you are avenged by him upon all the transgressors against you."

Their heart was very sore for him, and Pre-Harakhty said to Khnum,[10] "Now make a wife for Bata that he not live alone." AND THEN Khnum made for him a companion. She was more beautiful of body than any woman in the whole land, the fluid of every god being in her. AND THEN the Seven Hathors[11] came <to> see her, and they spoke as one, "She will die of a knife." AND THEN he desired her very very much, and she sat in his house while he spent the day (10,1) hunting small animals in the hills and bringing (them) <to> lay before her. And he said to her, "Do not go out lest the sea seize you because I will not be able to save you from it because I am a woman like you. Further my heart is placed on the top of the flower of the pine. When another finds it, I will fight with him." AND THEN he reported his heart to her in its entirety.

NOW MANY DAYS AFTER THAT when Bata went out to hunt as customary, (10,5) the young woman went forth to stroll under the pine beside her house. She saw the sea surge up after her, and she rose up to run before it, and she entered her house. AND THEN the sea called to the pine saying, "Catch her for me." And the pine brought one plait of her hair. AND THEN the sea brought it to Egypt, and he put it in the place of the washermen of the pharaoh. AND THEN the odor of the plait of hair happened into the clothing of the pharaoh, and the king fought with the washermen of the house, saying, "The odor of tallow is in the clothes of the pharaoh." And the <king> became quarrelsome with them daily, and (11,1) they did not know what to do. And the head washerman of the pharaoh went to the bank, his heart being very pained after the quarrelling with him daily. AND THEN he determined for himself he was standing on the land opposite the plait of hair which was in the water, and (he) had one go down, and it was brought to him. And an extremely sweet odor was found, and he took it to the pharaoh.

AND THEN the scribes-who-knew-things of the king were brought, AND THEN they said to the pharaoh, "As for the plait of hair, (11,5) it belongs to a daughter of Pre-Harakhty with the fluid of all the gods in her. Now it is a greeting of another land. Cause messengers to go to every land to seek her. As for the messenger who is for the Valley of the Pine, have many people go with him to bring her." Then his majesty said, "What you have said is very good." And they were caused to hurry.

NOW MANY DAYS AFTER THIS, the people who went to the foreign land came to tell report(s) to his majesty while the ones who went to the Valley of the Pine did not come because Bata killed them. And he left one of them to report to his majesty. AND THEN his majesty had people, many bowmen, go, likewise chariotry, to bring her back, and (12,1) a woman was with them, and every beautiful ornament was put in her hand. AND THEN the (young) woman came to Egypt with her, and there was shouting for her in the whole land. AND THEN his majesty loved her very much and he appointed her to (the position of) Great Noble Lady. AND THEN he spoke with her to make her tell the manner of her husband, and she spoke to his majesty, "Have the pine cut and have it destroyed." And the people were (12,5) made to go, carrying their weapons to cut the tree, and they reached the pine, and they cut the blossom upon which was the heart of Bata. And he fell dead in the evil hour.

NOW AFTER THE LAND WAS LIGHT AND A SECOND DAY BEGAN, when the pine was cut, Anubis, the older brother of Bata, entered his house, and he sat to wash his hands, and he was given a jug of beer, and it foamed, and he was given another of wine, and it made an offensive smell. AND THEN he took his (13,1) staff and his sandals, likewise his clothes and his weapons of combat, and he rose up to make an expedition to the Valley of the Pine, and he entered the mansion of his young brother. And he found his young brother lying dead upon his bed, and he wept when he saw his young brother lying in death. And he went to seek the heart of his young brother under the pine under which his young brother lay in the evening. (13,5) And he spent three years seeking it without finding it. When he began the fourth year, his heart wished to go to Egypt, and he said, "I go tomorrow." Thus he said in his heart.

NOW AFTER THE LAND WAS BRIGHT AND ANOTHER DAY BEGAN, he began and went under the pine and he spent the day seeking it again, and he returned in the evening, and he spent time to seek it again. And he found a bunch of grapes, and he returned carrying it, and there was the heart of his young brother. And he brought a bowl of cool water and he put it in it, and he sat as was his custom.

NOW WHEN EVENING CAME, (14,1) his heart swallowed the water, and Bata trembled in every limb, and he began to look at his older brother, his heart being in the bowl. And Anubis, his older brother, took the bowl of cool water with the heart of his young brother in it, and he caused him to drink it, and his heart stood in its place, and he became like he had been. AND THEN one embraced the other, and one spoke with his companion. AND THEN Bata spoke to his (14,5) older brother, "See, I will become a great bull with every beautiful color and none knows his nature, and you will sit on my back. By the time the sun rises, we will be in the place where my wife is in order that I avenge myself. And you will take me to where the king is because he will do for you every good thing. Then he will raise you with silver and gold for you brought me to the pharaoh because I shall be a great marvel and I will be praised in the whole land and you will go to your village.

NOW WHEN THE LAND WAS LIGHT AND (15,1) ANOTHER DAY BEGAN, and Bata became in the form which he told his older brother. AND THEN Anubis, his older brother, sat on his back. At dawn he reached where the king was, and his majesty was made to know of him, and he saw him and he became very joyful because of him. And he made for him great offerings, saying, "A great miracle has happened." And there was rejoicing because of him in the whole land. AND THEN (15,5) he was raised, rewarded with silver and gold for his older brother, and he lived in his town. And the king gave to him many people and many things, and the pharaoh loved him very much, more than any people in the whole land.

NOW MANY DAYS AFTER THIS, he[12] entered the kitchen, and he stood where the noble lady was and he began to speak with her, saying, "See, I am alive again." And she said to him, "Who then are you?" And he said to her, "I am Bata. I noticed when you had one destroy the pine for the pharaoh on account of me that I not live. See, (16,1) I have been made alive again. I am a bull." AND THEN the noble lady was very afraid of the word her husband told to her. AND THEN he went out from the kitchen.

And his majesty sat and made a feast day with her and she poured for his majesty and the king was very happy with her. AND THEN she said to his majesty, "Come, swear an oath by the god, saying, 'As for what I[13] say, I will hear it because of her.'" And he heard all which she said. "Allow me to eat from the liver of the bull (16,5) because he will not do anything." Thus she said to him. And he suffered very much because of what she said, and the heart of the king was very very ill.

NOW WHEN THE LAND WAS LIGHT AND A SECOND DAY BECAME, the king invoked a great offering in the offering of the bull. The king had one of the head royal butlers of his majesty go to make ready the bull. When he had been slaughtered, when he was upon the shoulder of the people, he quivered in his neck and he made fall two drops of blood beside the two door posts of his majesty, the one happening on the one side of the great door and the other upon the other side. And they grew into (17,1) two great persea trees, each one being ou-standing. AND THEN one went to tell his majesty, "Two great perseas are grown as a great marvel for his majesty in the night beside the great portal of his majesty." And there was shouting because of them in the whole land, and the king made offerings to them.

NOW MANY DAYS AFTER THIS, his majesty appeared in the window of lapis lazuli, a wreath of every flower at his neck, and he was upon a chariot of fine gold, and (17,5) he went forth from the royal house to see the perseas. AND THEN the noble lady went forth upon a team after the pharaoh. And then his majesty sat under one of the perseas <and the noblewoman under the other persea. AND THEN Bata> spoke with his wife, "Ha, traitor, I am Bata. I am living despite you. I noticed that one <was caused> to cut the pine for the pharaoh, <it was> because of me, and I became a bull. And you caused me to be killed."

NOW MANY DAYS AFTER THIS, the noblewoman stood to pour for his majesty, he being happy with her, and she said to his majesty, "Make an oath to me by the god, saying, 'As for what the noblewoman says to me, I will hear it for her,' you shall say." And he heard (18,1) all which she said, and she said, "Have the two perseas cut and have one make them into beautiful furniture." AND THEN all that she said was heard.

AND NOW AFTER A SMALL MOMENT, his majesty had skilled craftsmen go and the perseas of the pharaoh were cut (while) the royal wife, the noblewoman, watched it. AND THEN a splinter flew and it entered the mouth of the noblewoman. AND THEN (18,5) she swallowed it, and she became pregnant. IN THE COMPLETION OF A SHORT WHILE, the king had made all that she desired from them.

NOW MANY DAYS AFTER THIS, she gave birth to a son, and one sent to say to his majesty, "A son has been born for you." And he[14] was brought and he was given a *mnʿt*-nurse and *ẖnmw*-nurses,[15] and there was rejoicing for him in the whole land. And the king sat and made a feast, and he[16] began to be caressed, and his majesty loved him very very much from the hour. And the king appointed him (19,1) Royal Son of Kush.[17] Now many days after this, his majesty made him as *iry-pʿt*[18] of the whole land.

NOW MANY DAYS AFTER THIS, when he completed many years as *iry-pʿt* in the whole land, then his majesty flew to heaven.[19] AND THEN the king[20] said, "Have brought to me my great officers of his majesty so I can make known all (19,5) the past affairs with me." AND THEN his wife was brought and he judged her before them and a "yes" was made from them, and his older brother was brought to him and he made him *iry-pʿt* in the whole land. And he was thirty years as king of Egypt, and he went out to life, and his older brother stood in his place on the day of his death.

Colophon: It has come well to a conclusion by the spirit of the scribe of the treasury, Ka-geb of the treasury of the pharaoh and the scribe Heri-Merimipet. Made by the scribe In-na, the lord of the papyrus-roll. Whoever speaks against this papyrus roll, to him will Thoth be a hostile adversary.

Appendix: The short memoranda of Papyrus d'Orbiney.[21]
(20,1) The fan bearer of the king, secretary of the chief, the elder royal son, Seti-Merneptah.[22]

Verso on back of recto p. 1.[23]

great loaves—17
sets of provisions—50
loaves for the temples—48

On the back of the recto p. 19.[24]
The fan-bearer of the king on the right of the royal scribe, the chief of the army, the elder royal son.

1
Historical Issues

The Beginnings

In 1852, Emmanuel de Rougé announced to the world the discovery of the "Tale of Two Brothers," an ancient Egyptian work of pure imagination, a type not previously known to have existed in that culture[1] and which W. Mannhardt designated *"Das älteste Märchen"* (the oldest Märchen) in 1859.[2] De Rougé's partial translation, résumé, and discussion of the narrative inaugurated the study of this tale, a study which has not ceased. The tale's fascination derives not only from its use of the marvelous but also from its apparent parallels with well-known narratives from ancient and modern cultures and its portrayal of Egyptian life in New Kingdom times.

The papyrus, known as the Papyrus d'Orbiney, BM 10183,[3] was written in hieratic in Late Egyptian dialect[4] and published in facsimile in 1860 by Samuel Birch.[5] Its language and grammar interested Egyptologists, especially in the early years, but it was thirty years before the translation was declared certain, thereby implying a solid control of the hieratic script, the grammar and vocabulary, and the restoration of the lacunae, especially those of the first five damaged pages.[6] Nevertheless, it was its parallels with narratives of other cultures which attracted general notice to the tale. Its close parallel with the story of Joseph and Potiphar's wife found in Genesis 39 is so striking that in 1895, when Charles Moldenke published a translation and accompanying notes for the papyrus, he suggested that Moses, the then perceived author of the biblical work, certainly knew and studied the story of Bata at the University of Heliopolis and must have had the wording in mind while writing the Joseph story.[7]

Although Genesis 39 is not the only biblical parallel[8] and the tale's relation to the Bible was a significant justification for its study in the early years,[9] scholars took a very great interest in its nonbiblical parallels. One such parallel was that of the gods walking to inspect the land in Bata's valley with the gods of Homer who walked to the Ethiopian land to receive hecatombs (*Ody.* 1, 22–25), cited by Mannhardt in 1859.[10] Mannhardt also noted a "surprising correspondence" of the Egyptian narrative with European tales. In his discussion he spelled out specific tales according to what are currently called tale types[11] and motifs,[12] noting particularly a comparison with the two successive transformations in the tale of the two gold children.[13] He concluded that the Egyptian folk tradition had the same "naïve character" as the European tradition, but he felt unable to state what historic dependencies might have existed between the traditions.[14]

In 1868, in *Aegypten und die Bücher Mose's,* the Egyptologist Georg Ebers[15] raised the question of whether the author of the d'Orbiney drew on the Joseph story as his source or whether each is completely independent of the other.[16] He tended to favor the idea of independence because he had observed parallels with the attempted seduction theme in Greek sources, in the stories of Phaedra and Hippolytus, Peleus and Astydamia, and Phineas and Idaa, as well as in the Persian story of Sijawusch and Sudabe and in the German Genovefa-Golo-Geschichte.

The Nineteenth-Century Search for Origins

It is clear that by Eber's time, even Egyptologists were affected by the search for origins inaugurated in 1856 by Max Müller with his publication of a long essay on comparative mythology.[17] Hence one finds the students of the Papyrus d'Orbiney asking the origin of the narrative at the same time that they are pointing out various parallel narratives and themes.

In 1874 François Lenormant, who devoted a considerable space to the "Tale of Two Brothers" in his publication, *Les premières Civilisations,*[18] expressed the view that it was the only Egyptian text representing fabulous fiction.[19] He thought, however, that this story was merely an Egyptian transformation of a popular story in general circulation and expressed in three parallel myths of three different peoples, myths introduced into Egypt with the Asiatic conquests made by the kings of the eighteenth dynasty. The myths in question are those of Attis, a myth of Phrygian origin; of Adonis, from Syro-Phoenicia; and of the Orphic mysteries of Eleusis, each of which was supposed to be drawn from a common source to be sought in Asia. In fact, in his opinion, "Tale of Two Brothers" was a rendition of the Attis myth clad in Egyptian clothing, even down to the parallel of the seduction scene in which Cybele expressed jealousy over Attis.[20]

Lenormant did not completely neglect Egyptian sources in his discussion, although he felt the story to be closer to the Phrygian and Syrian stories than to anything Egyptian. He saw the Osirian overtones, particularly in the respective resurrections and the throwing of the severed phallus into the water to be swallowed by a fish. He opined, however, that while the Osirian story was independent in origin and contained the core of the Egyptian religious system, it too had Asian sources. He then pointed to the various castrations and self-castrations of Agdistis, Attis, infernal Zeus, and Adonis. The Attis myth was invoked again when Lenormant discussed the motif of the heart on the tree, for both trees involved were the pine, and he related them to the tamarisk and Osiris's coffin. He saw a parallel between the gods' creation for Bata of an extraordinarily beautiful woman, a woman replete with evil, and the creation of Pandora, and he saw another between the Nile's carrying the lock of hair and the consecration of hair to river gods in general in Asia Minor and Greece. The death of Bata because of his wife's desire to espouse the king was compared to Eriphyle's delivering her husband Amphiaraus to death, while Anubis's search for Bata's heart was reminiscent of Isis's search for the parts of Osiris. In this last, however, he noted that the Osirian story with a woman in the saving role contrasts sharply with d'Orbiney, in which it is a male who saves. He mentioned other search motifs, such as Aphrodite's finding Adonis's head at Byblos, Cybele's attempts to revive Attis, and Apollo's collecting of the parts of Zagreus's body. The swallowing of the heart is likened to Semele's becoming pregnant by swallowing the heart of Zagreus in a drink from Zeus, while Zagreus, as a bull-formed god, is similar to Bata as bull as well as to Osiris, who is both Dionysus and a bull. Lenormant also compared the growth of the persea trees from the two drops of blood with parallels in Zagreus, the Corybante, Agdistis, Rimmon, and, finally, Attis metamorphosed into a pine. Finally, he related the wife's impregnation by means of swallowing a splinter to the tale of Agdistis's rebirth through eating the fruit grown from his severed male organs. In this fashion, Lenormant showed that the tale emanated from Asian sources, with even the Osirian aspects viewed as a fusion between Adonis of Byblos and Osiris.

The year 1874 also saw Hyacinthe Husson, another Frenchman, discuss the "Tale of Two Brothers." In *La Chaîne traditionnelle*[21] he commented extensively on the actions in the story and on its similarities to other stories. The parallels he noted were basically similar to those already cited, although he observed a similarity of the external heart and the eating of it in the yet unmentioned story from the Panchatantra about the monkey and the crocodile[22] as well as in a Breton story in which an external heart appears. In his consideration of the cedar, the ʿš-tree of the narrative, he felt that the presence of both a blossom and a fruit referred to the Egyptian tree *lebbeck acacia,* and that the Egyptians knew the ʿš-tree only from hearsay. Expanding on the parallel seen by Lenormant between the creation of Bata's wife by the gods and the creation of Pandora by Hephaistos, Husson noted that both were extremely beautiful and both were extremely deadly, though the former was deadly only to her spouse while the latter was deadly to the whole human race. Further, he considered that the prophetic role of the Hathors was basically analogous to that of the Vedic Ushas and Homer's Eos, the latter a personification of the double gleam of morning and evening, recalling the Vedic Aurora, who also appears in multiple form and is called Seven Sisters. Similarly he likened the amorous behavior of the Nile[23] to other sources when he looked to Hellenic parallels of amorous rivers, especially the Xantho of the *Iliad* as it left its bed in pursuit of Achilles (*Il.* 21, 254–72). In his opinion, this reference fits the story more nearly than do the normal conceptions of the Nile as a nourishing power.

Many of Husson's other parallels cited later European materials of the type reflected in modern folklore typologies. He did note an African parallel in a Hottentot story from South Africa in which a child, eaten by a lion, is revived by putting her heart, recovered from the killed lion, in a vessel of water. In other parallels from older sources, he related Bata's transformations to those of Adonis and Attis as well as to those found in Ovid's *Metamorphoses.* Finally, Husson directed his readers' attention to Indian doctrines on the subject. For him, the main Egyptian aspect of the story lay in the figure of Osiris who, on the one hand, was on the earth as the Apis Bull and, on the other, was present as the vegetable Osiris in the tree, Osiris being the god who eternally engenders himself.

In the end, Husson saw the tale as resulting from ancient Aryan emigrations, infiltrations from later India, some Hamitic sources, and perhaps some Turanian races. He also concluded that in poetic conception and the domain of the imagination, man is less apt to be inventive than to repeatedly modify, remodel, and combine the same elements.

In 1877 Emmanuel Cosquin began to question seriously whether India served as the point of origin for this tale,[24] contrary to the then-current idea that tales generally originated there.[25] In his article "Un problème historique à propos du conte égyptien des deux frères," he discussed the European and Asian parallels in popular tales at some length, even more than Husson had done. He considered Bata's transformations, the external heart, the magic sign of Bata's death, and the lock of hair, complete with European and Slavic parallels. He also made reference to Ebers' observation of the parallels with the seductive-wife-chaste-young-man theme in Classical, Phrygian, Syro-Phoenician, and Persian sources. But he was greatly perplexed by how the story came to be, since the European and Asian tales were derived from India and yet the Egyptian tale was three thousand years old, thus predating the Indian sources. What could be the relation between India and

Egypt? Theodor Benfey had suggested that possibly the Indian concept of the transmigration of souls originated in Egypt, since the oldest sources from India lack it. Both these scholars troubled themselves with the problem, but neither found a solution, as may be inferred from the fact that nine years later Cosquin's article was included intact as an appendix to his famed *Contes populaires de Lorraine.*[26]

In 1889 Renouf[27] published a folkloristic comparison of the story similar to that of Cosquin in 1877, being particularly provoked by Spitte-Bey's work on Arabic stories and Duluc's publication of Arabic tales. Renouf mentioned many variants of the separate soul wherein its owner is invulnerable unless or until it is damaged or destroyed. His examples ranged from *One Thousand and One Nights* through Russian and Norse stories. Renouf's point was that the fundamental notion that "a person's life depends upon something external to his body"[28] exists in its oldest form precisely in the Egyptian "Tale of Two Brothers" and in the Greek story of Meleager.[29] Each of these stories focuses on the hero, a positive figure, who has this external feature, while more recent stories show the character with the external feature to be a fiend such as a giant or an ogre. In every case, the life object is concealed, and Renouf even noted the Egyptian tale of Setne,[30] in which the magic book is hidden, as being the complex modern type of concealment. The subject of successive transformations, as found in the story of the two gold children mentioned in 1859 by Mannhardt,[31] whose article Renouf had not seen, was repeated and expanded. He also noted parallels for the life sign, in the end observing that every incident in the "Tale of Two Brothers" shows a counterpart in one or more popular tales current in Europe or Asia, although he carefully noted that no modern Egyptian tales or portions thereof go back to ancient Egyptian origin.[32] He accounted for these parallels through a threefold means of historical transmission: Buddhist missionaries in Asia, Jewish migration, and European gypsies. Nevertheless, he felt that not all stories were Indo-Germanic and that the mix was impossible to sort out at the time. Thus, like Cosquin, whose article he also had not seen, he raised, but did not answer, the question of origins.

In summary, by 1900 the narrative's translation was well established, and various scholars, both Egyptologists and non-Egyptologists, had ranged far and wide to seek parallels to, and possible origins for, this work. Some took note of the Egyptian context of the tale, and thus its reflections of contemporary life, but the much larger issues of its origins and narrative parallels appear to dominate in accordance with general narrative study in the last half of the nineteenth century.

Twentieth-Century Ancient Near Eastern Scholars

The first half of the twentieth century saw something of a hiatus in discussions of parallels. When such discussions recurred, they tended to do so in what one might call an ancient Near Eastern context, since those who wrote were generally scholars of the Hebrew Bible or a closely related field. For instance, in 1965, Michael Astour discussed the Potiphar's wife motif in his *Hellenosemitica,*[33] suggesting that the d'Orbiney borrowed the topic from the Phoenician tale of the pursuit of Eshmun, the young healer-god, by the goddess Astronoe/Astronome (=*ʿAstart-naʿma*) and the Syrian tale of Kombabos related in *De Dea Syria.* Astour equated Kombabos with Humbaba of the *Epic of Gilgamesh,* whom he understood as the counterpart of Bata in light of the cedar-forest locale. Likewise, he viewed the attempted seduction of Baal by Asherah and of Gilgamesh by Ishtar as parallels to Bata, "a typical 'vegetable spirit,' slain and revived, embodied in trees (cedar/pine and persea) and in a bull."[34]

Three years later John D. Yohannan devoted a whole book to the consideration of the ancient, medieval, and modern parallels of the seduction motif,[35] noting two not previously mentioned: the Muslim version from the Koran, Surah XII, verses 21-54, concerning Yusuf and Zulaikha, and the Buddhist account of Kunala and Tishya-rakshite. In his discussion he explained that although the parallels are look-alikes, only some of them are so because of a common source or origin while others are so despite an independent creation.[36] The basic motifs common to all consist of temptation, the chasteness of the youth leading to his refusal of the temptation, and an unfair punishment, though not generally death, which was followed by vindication. From his viewpoint the Egyptian story is the archetypal version, "if 'archetypal' is indeed to mean the oldest."[37]

When Theodor Gaster wrote a commentary on the myths, legends, and customs in the Old Testament in 1969, he mentioned further parallels. Among his citations are the Indic Jataka, the body of the Sindbad cycle in the medieval "Tales of Seven Masters," the Persian *Tutti Nameh,* a Chinese tale, the *Daredevils of Sassoun* from Armenia, Boccaccio's *Decameron* ii, 8, the North American Indian tale of the Jealous Father related by Thompson, and a version in reverse where the male attempts to seduce a female from *One Thousand and One Nights.*[38]

In 1970 the Egyptologist Donald Redford also looked carefully at the Egyptian tale in *A Study of the Biblical Story of Joseph.*[39] To the parallels of what he designates "the motif of the spurned wife" already noted, he added that of Tenes, related in Pausanius x, 14. Like Yohannan, he mentioned that typically the hero escapes the death penalty. He felt, however, that in the episodes from Genesis and the d'Orbiney the escape was shoddy, the latter effected by means of a deus ex machina: Pre produced water filled with crocodiles.[40] Furthermore, to his thinking, both versions reflect "a common motif eminating [*sic*] originally from Egyptian folklore which became very popular all over the Levant."[41] It is this motif into which the figure of Joseph is inserted to behave as a folktale hero (*Märchenheld*).[42]

The reasons for the resurgence of this search for parallels are not so clear for the third quarter of the twentieth century as for the earlier period. Some certainly derive from the theories of oral narrative and oral transmission present in biblical and folklore scholarship. Perhaps the strengthening of folklore as a scholarly discipline also helped, but definite answers to the question are elusive at this time.

One or Several Tales?

Although the search for parallels apparently dominated the study of the narrative in its first half century, the occasional commentator took note of the structure of the tale, variously seeing it as a combination of separate tales or as a unity. The first of these was Gaston Maspero, whose four editions of *Les Contes populaires de l'Égypte ancienne,* along with an English translation in 1915,[43] appeared throughout the last quarter of the nineteenth and the first years of the twentieth century. While taking note of the comparative studies done by others, it was he who first stated succinctly that the tale is composed of two stories, both romances (*romans*).[44] In one of them, the servant is slandered by his mistress whom he has rebuffed, and in the other, the husband is betrayed by his wife.[45] By the fourth edition, Maspero had included the idea of "popular imagination" that a third motif joins the two, that of a man who hides his heart and dies when the enemy discovers it.[46] Previously he had described this link by saying, "the solder (*la soudure*) between the two stories is very coarse (*grossière*)."[47] In presenting the comparisons, however, he left open the question of its origin,[48] merely noting that some Egyptian versions of motifs are far older than those of other nations and that the habits and customs portrayed in the tale are indigenous to Egypt.[49]

In 1906 Alfred Wiedemann contrasted the two independent tales which he felt constituted the story.[50] The first tale, which goes through the betrayal of the secret of Bata's heart to the king by his wife, had to do with the farmer and simple man, while the second, in which the deceased Bata lives again and finally becomes king, shows the hero as a "half-god" (*Halbgott*).[51] In an earlier publication, he,[52] like those before him, had reiterated that the tale was Osirian, came from Asia Minor, and was told for pure enjoyment. He also observed that its significance within Egyptian literature lay in the fictitiousness of the characters and the anonymity of all the other characters, the king included.[53]

In 1907 Hermann Schneider, an intellectual philosopher in Leipzig with a longtime interest in Egyptian culture, included a lengthy discussion of "Tale of Two Brothers" in *Kultur und Denken der alten Ägypter.*[54] He aligned the tale with the myth of Osiris as a modernization of the latter, especially in a moral sense. While acknowledging the heterogeneity of its elements when isolated, he stated that a real unity lay behind the tale, that of divine purpose and predetermination. Bata suffered, as did Osiris, and, like him, was avenged and transformed. Anubis played a mixed role, evil when angry, but good when aiding his brother, while the females were evil personified and had to die. Thus Schneider considered the basic view propounded by the story to be that the simple, good man must reach his divinely decreed heavenly goal. As a modern version of the old Osirian tale, this story revealed Osiris in human form as a sufferer who eventually attained his predetermined end. Finally, Schneider reemphasized his sense of the tale's unity by suggesting that there was a didactic nature to the tale: in this world as well as in the other, good will win out despite the duality of all happenings.

In 1927 Max Pieper[55] postulated a unity with a slightly different twist when he stated that in this tale "a whole series of originally independent folktales is worked into one another."[56] The ingredients which were included were the sundering of the brothers' relationship by a slanderous woman, the hiding of the heart, the entrance of a god-created, beautiful woman who behaves evilly towards him, the Cinderella motif,[57] and finally the juniper tree (*Machandel*) motif.[58] In his opinion, however, "the whole is ruled by a single idea: the wickedness of the wife,"[59] constituting "a firm unity."[60]

More than fifty years later, Leonard Lesko reiterated the unifying device of the evil woman, albeit indirectly.[61] Discussing the tale in conjunction with two other Late Egyptian tales, "Truth and Falsehood"[62] and the "Contendings of Horus and Seth,"[63] he felt each expressed a contemporary negative attitude toward queens. Lesko links this attitude to a reaction to the series of strong queens in the early eighteenth dynasty.[64]

Walter Scherf described the tale as showing how a swineherd became king, analyzing the narrative as AaTh 318 with AaTh 569.[65] By implication he viewed the tale as a unity—a typical approach for folklorists.

Twentieth-Century Ideas on Structure and Origins

The discussions of parallels and origins with respect to the "Tale of Two Brothers" reflected similar discussions of folktales generally.[66] One result of the many debates was the emergence of a clear need for a basic classification of folktales. Instigated by Kaarle Krohn, furthered and contributed to by Antti Aarne, and realized by Stith Thompson, the study of folk tales, indeed of folk narrative in general, now has two basic classification systems to assist its work: *Types of the Folktale* by Aarne and Thompson[67] and *Motif-Index of Folk-Literature* by Thompson.[68] Other classifications do exist[69] and in some cases supplement these, but these two are the most commonly used and provide a standard for discussion in the field. Thus it is not surprising to find that they are regularly employed to aid in the classification of the motifs and tale-types present in the "Tale of Two Brothers," given the parallels for the tale already noted.[70] It has been noted that as early as 1877, Cosquin had identified five common motifs,[71] and by 1931, J. Bolte and G. Polivka had identified two more.[72]

The latter two commentators asserted that there was no valid argument against an Egyptian origin for the story since the setting, the names of the brothers, the Osirian parallel for the phallus, the presence of the Ennead, the Hathors, and Khnum, and the transformations all point to Egypt. In this assertion, they went contrary to the discussion of parallels seen so far, while virtually contemporaneously, Carl Wilhelm von Sydow expressed a very different opinion. Although he had earlier acknowledged the presence in the tale of some purely national motifs,[73] in 1932[74] he suggested that in the Egyptian narrative there are two tales derived from *oikotypes*[75] that are extra-Egyptian in origin but common in eastern Europe and the Slavic areas. The oikotype found in the Slavic areas deals with the transformations while the other has to do with the sign of life, itself the result of two oikotypes: the external heart and the talisman of life. The latter was a theme which he felt to be foreign to Egyptian thought. As he explained,[76] a nucleus K existed in the Satem language which branched off into oikotype K with motifs a, b, and c in the Indo-Persian area and oikotype K with motifs d, e, and f in the Slavonic area. These two later merged in Asia Minor or Syria and were brought by merchants or soldiers to Egypt, where Egyptian motifs x, y, and z were incorporated to make the story now known from the Papyrus d'Orbiney. He dated the development in Egypt to about 1300 BCE, although he felt there had been a lengthy development prior to this date. He confirmed his belief in this thesis again when he discussed the development of fairy-tale research and philology in 1948.[77]

In the 1940s the expatriate Russian Egyptologist Vladimir Vikentiev published numerous articles on the folkloristic aspects of Egyptian tales. Initially, in 1917, he had published a monograph in Russian on the Papyrus d'Orbiney,[78] and in 1931 he had dealt with some of its specific motifs and questions.[79] From 1940 on, however, he published articles not just on the individual motifs and their parallels but on whole stories, comparing Egyptian material with non-Egyptian sources.[80] In a 1949 article specific to "Two Brothers," he compared the d'Orbiney and the *Epic of Gilgamesh,*[81] outlining episodes from both texts. He concluded that *Gilgamesh* is the "more ancient and violent (of the two) . . . and [t]herefore, it is 'Gilgamish' [sic] which is able to have served as the prototype for the 'Two Brothers' and not the reverse."[82] He also suggested the possibility that the two works drew from a common, even older source that did not derive from Egypt. This type of wide-ranging comparison typified his later writings, certainly from 1948 on, and was not generally acceptable to other scholars, as is shown by Lefebvre's discussion of Bata and Ivan in 1950[83] and by his comment, written in 1972, that "(Vikentiev's) later work is often characterized by eccentric theories and concepts which mar its value."[84]

Myth or Folktale? The Folklorists' Views

The classification of tales by motifs and types was fueled by the historical-geographic search for origins, a model of which was Kurt Ranke's 1934 publication of the well-known monograph *Die zwei Brüder.*[85] In *Die zwei Brüder,* Ranke collected, analyzed, and discussed 770 "Two Brothers" tales, including that from the Papyrus d'Orbiney, showing that the only link between the general corpus and the tale from the d'Orbiney was the life-sign. Even that was different in the Egyptian story, for usually the sign was a personal one, a gift (e.g., a knife), but in the d'Orbiney it is a drink. Because only this one element binds the story with the other *Brüdermärchen,* Ranke considered that essentially it was not of the same order. He also commented tersely, "The Egyptian story is certainly no folktale (*Volksmärchen*) but rather a work of literature,"[86] although it did not lack Märchen-like elements. Later in 1965 and again in 1978, he analyzed the tale as containing three specific motifs: the love of the wife for Bata; the golden hair carried by a bird or a wave with the owner of which a foreign king falls in love, sight unseen; and the indestructible life of the hero.[87]

In 1953, when Friedrich von der Leyen surveyed the range of Egyptian literature in *Die Welt der Märchen,*[88] he observed both the presence of ideas from what he termed the "primitive world" in the "Two Brothers," ideas such as the belief in magic birth, transformation, and difficult wanderings, and, at the same time, ideas of the inseparable brothers, the relation of man and animal, and the relation of tree and river. These elements combined with Egyptian parallels such as Si-Osire's magic birth[89] and signs of danger as well as the Osiris-phallus relation made it possible that the story could embody a myth of brother pairs such as sun and moon or day and night, and so he was troubled by its usual identification as a folktale or fairy tale.

Jan de Vries, writing in 1954,[90] was bothered both by the story's fairy-tale identification and by von Sydow's theory of its origin. In his discussion, de Vries detailed the discrepancies between the usual fairy-tale form of a motif and that which the d'Orbiney tale shows, such as the life-sign[91] and the obstacle flight.[92] In his opinion the flight is not the true Märchen obstacle flight, in which the pursued throws objects behind him that then magically become obstacles in the path of the pursuer, for in the Egyptian story the obstacle results from a prayer. Thus the so-called obstacle flight falls into the realm of divine wonder rather than magic. Furthermore, both parts of the tale relate the story of an unfaithful wife, which he does not consider true *Wundermärchen,* especially since revenge is visited on each. The presence of this last theme reminded de Vries more of an Icelandic-type saga than of a Märchen. He also questioned why Bata had to be born through the faithless wife and why her cruelty became so great that he finally killed her. In the end, he concluded that the "Tale of Two Brothers" is not true Märchen despite the motifs, and its classification must be sought in the realm of the mythic.

In this regard, de Vries saw the revival of Bata as like that of the Horus-Osiris myth and the hiding of Bata's heart in a tree as similar to the growth of the tree around Osiris after his death. He surmised that the self-castration was a Phrygian import, since it is not found in Egyptian tradition, but he considered the whole to be Egyptian.[93] He particularly felt that the "Tale of Two Brothers" showed clear relationships to an old Egyptian royal rite, even to the reflection of thirty years as the amount of time to reign. Indeed, de Vries decided that the text was written with Seti's name twice because Seti viewed it as significant to the myth of god-kingship, and thus it is more appropriate to view the tale as myth than as a fairy tale. In the end he dispatched von Sydow's theory about its origin "because it is just not a folktale."[94]

When Karol Horálek wrote on the Egyptian "Two Brothers" tale for the *Enzyklopädie des Märchens* in 1978,[95] he described it as "a well-composed whole," a Märchen but one whose author has mythologized "the Märchen-like patterns." Nevertheless, he pointed out some discrepancies, such as the kidnapping of Bata's wife while he remained well and whole, and his self-revelation when he was transformed rather than his being recognized, as was usual. In this same article, Horálek also described modern parallels to the various parts and motifs, concluding that the tale is

> a literary composition of three different folktale types, which still live in later tradition: AaTh 870 C*, 302 B,[96] and 318. The original form is especially well preserved in the third part. The influence of other types of folktales is not able to be excluded, but only concerns insignificant details. It is also necessary to reckon with a secondary mythologizing (apparently through the Egyptian reviser). In this sense the "Tale of Two Brothers" can be valued as a testimony of ancient Egyptian mythology.[97]

Myth or Folktale? The Egyptologists' Views

Between the World Wars the Egyptologists expressed varied ideas on the classification of the "Two Brothers"; as a group, however, they presented no clear-cut characterization. In 1927 Pieper felt it was in no way to be viewed according to the old theory of "weakened myth," despite the divine names, for the fact is that divine names served as names of persons at the time and the basic motifs are pure Märchen motifs, unrelated to myth. Three years later, he suggested that perhaps there may have been a myth, probably Asiatic, at the base of the present fairy tale, as suggested by Bata's castration and by the brothers' divine names, although he noted again that in Ramesside times, it was common practice to give divine names to deceased persons. By 1935, Pieper asserted that the only mythic element in the story lay with the severed phallus thrown to and swallowed by a fish. Otherwise he felt the story to be a Märchen in which Bata, the younger and more proficient of the brothers, left and set himself up in the Valley of the Cedar as a typical Märchenheld.[98]

In the English translation of his 1923 collection, *Die Literatur der Aegypter,*[99] Adolf Erman wrote, "This delightful story is certainly based on a myth, as is shown by the names of the two brothers . . . a myth belonging to (Saka) that the storyteller has here transferred to the sphere of human activities."[100]

In 1933 Hermann Kees briefly discussed the d'Orbiney in *Kulturgeschichte des alten Orients.*[101] His opinion was that divine history generally shaped the background of Egyptian Märchen, so "old stories of the gods are stuck in the best known folktales of the New Kingdom, the narrative of the two brothers . . . but what changes the myths have made through the mouths of the folk when one compares the dark tone of the preserved piece from the religious literature."[102]

Authorship and Style of Composition

Among Egyptologists there is a general consensus that the tale as it is known to the modern world had at least a compiler if not an author, rather contrary to the concept of the anonymous folktale. The name of the scribe, In-na, is known from the colophon, but there is no agreement on the purpose of its composition and writing. For instance, in 1874 Lenormant expressed the view that it was a story of pure imagination, invented by its writer. To him, the purpose appeared to be that of distraction and entertainment of the young prince who would later become Seti II, and in writing it, its author, like the seventeenth-century French author Perreault, gave decisive and literary form to a popular story previously circulated in a purely oral form, being, like most stories, a degenerated myth stripped of its religious character.[103]

On the other hand, Petrie[104] stated that while parts of the story were likely to be older than the nineteenth dynasty, the colophon *ir n sš*, "written," suggests a new composition in Ramesside times. Not only did he point to the contrast between the idyllic, simple opening and the marvel-upon-marvel nature of the last part, but he also noted the conciseness of language and lack of superfluous words in the first part as compared with the "pointless profusions" in the language of the second part. In fact, he felt that the opening was "out of harmony with the forced and artificial taste of the nineteenth dynasty" and that some "inartistic compiler" had lengthened the story on the basis that "longer is better."[105]

For his part, because of the writing of Bata's name, Erman considered the story to be of "late origin" but believed it went back to an older form of the legend, perhaps represented on the ostracon from Edinburgh.[106]

Returning to Pieper's 1927 comments, one finds that he considered the tale to be a literary work because of the unifying device of the evil wife, and so he categorized the tale of the Papyrus d'Orbiney as "the oldest preserved short story of world literature."[107] When he compared the opening and the closing of the story, he showed that the former relates a lengthy, unfolktale-like, technical description of peaceable living while the latter expresses a terse finality, one sentence about the wife's behavior and judgment. The one was literary, the other in the true style of *Volksmärchen*. He finally concluded that the tale is an artistic composition.

Concern with style also appears in Pieper's 1930 article[108] with his discussion of the additions and exaggerations of its author (e.g., Bata's self-emasculation as witness to his chastity). Another example of the author's tendency toward exaggeration is found in Anubis's three-year search for Bata's heart and the last-minute discovery of it. Pieper further believed that the juxtaposition of Bata's statement that he was a woman with his action in killing the Pharaoh's troops suggests an addition by the author. In the end, Pieper felt this story rather clearly reflected the stamp of the author's personality.

Following Pieper, both Ranke and de Vries removed the tale from the folktale classification. In 1935 Ranke identified the narrative as a "work of literature" despite its fairy-tale-like elements, though he did not discuss the issue beyond this statement,[109] and as de Vries pointed out in 1954, the presence of the name of the crown prince Seti on the papyrus suggests that it was the court society that was interested in this tale rather than the more ordinary people,[110] the usual audience for the folk tale.

The Egyptian Context

Despite the early concern with parallels for the story in other cultures, Egyptian scholars did not overlook strictly Egyptian parallels. Goodwin[111] noted the Grimms' comparison of it with Herodotus II, 134–35, the story of Rhodopis, and the Cinderella-type theme of love for the unknown owner of an object, resulting in a search for her—a parallel also noted by Mannhardt. The latter added another parallel when he suggested that the story of Nitokris and her guile in Herodotus II, 100 was analogous,[112] while Ebers noted a parallel in Herodotus's story about King Pheros (Herod. II, 111; cf., Diodorus Siculus I, 59) in which adultery resulted in the woman's death by burning.[113]

As well as narrative parallels, the early commentators discussed the tale's relation to actual life in ancient Egypt. De Rougé mentioned the enormous size of women's coiffures in eighteenth- and nineteenth-dynasty Egypt.[114] He also discussed lapis lazuli and the king's collar, the accoutrements of the king at the window.[115] In concluding his commentary on the text, de Rougé observed the curious role of the gods as well as the transformations of Bata. He believed these transformations were related to an Egyptian belief in the transmigration of the soul in which the justified soul had the power of taking the form it wished and transporting itself where it willed.

Goodwin's contribution to the Egyptian context lay in his suggestion that the separation of the heart from the body was a theme familiar to the Egyptians, and furthermore that the author of the tale, should he have assigned a time to the tale, would have placed it in the prehistoric times when the dynasties were of demi-gods and heroes.[116] After Goodwin, Mannhardt mentioned that the persea tree, the dwelling place of the sun-cat, was sacred to the sun, which was worshipped in Heliopolis. Ultimately, for him, the core of the story was very old, rooted in the being and fate of the soul which, when justified, returns to the sun, itself the light of Osiris. He was convinced that it is the soul to which the Egyptian word for heart, *ḥ3ty*, refers, and further, that Herodotus was not wholly mistaken in II, 123 concerning the cycle of the soul, for the German scholar felt that the tale rested on a belief in the wandering of the soul. In sum, Mannhardt felt that Bata lived on as spirit in the light of Osiris, undergoing his transformations in order to be born again as man.[117]

When Samuel Birch published the facsimile edition of the papyrus, he included various comments, one of which suggested that the story is "a mythical legend of the life of Anubis and Typhon," clearly an Egyptian theme. Birch also stated that the idea of the transmigrations of the soul, the connection of the soul and the heart, the speaking of animals, and the "direct interposition of the gods in human events" were all familiar to the ancient Egyptians.[118]

In the last quarter of the nineteenth century, the question of Bata's several transformations figured in a number of discussions. For instance, Deveria felt that pure corporeal resurrection belonged mainly to popular belief, although renewal of different corporeal parts formed a part of ancient doctrine. Maspero, however, understood that the justified soul could take the form of a hawk of gold, a lotus, a Bennu bird, or a crane, but such a transformation marked the passage of the soul alone and nothing more. Pierret, who cited the sarcophagus of Seti I, felt that the transformations expiated faults that were not serious enough to warrant annihilation.[119]

When Petrie wrote on the tale in 1895,[120] he demonstrated its nature as Egyptian. He felt that the first section resembled the typical pastoral scene of the eighteenth dynasty, although the work about the house done by Bata, particularly the making of bread, seemed to him to be more properly the work of Anubis's wife. When he discussed Anubis's gesture of striking his hand twice, Petrie observed that it resembled a gesture made by the modern Egyptian when a thing is worthless, though in the story it represented positive anger.

When, like the earlier commentators, Petrie discussed parallels, his strongest contribution lay in his explanations of various motifs and situations of the story. He placed the Valley of the Acacia[121] by the sea, and probably in Syria, and he explained that the nine gods represent one of the cycles of divinities that were variously composed in different places. He viewed Bata's god-created wife as totally lacking in affections in accordance with her non-natural formation. She was ambitious, however, and attacked Bata out of fear that he would remove her from her high station, for she craved only power—what Petrie called the "Lilith motif." The seven Hathors represented the fates and lacking names, unlike the four birth goddesses in the Westcar Papyrus, were generic, as the word "hathor," goddess,[122] suggests. Furthermore, the Hathors played the role of "seer" rather than that of controller of destiny. While he suggested that the role of the sea might be likened to a pirate raid, he conceded that this was unlikely. He also noted that the offerings made to the bull prior to the sacrifice likened it to all sacred slayings, and the wife's desire to eat the liver was an attempt to destroy the soul by eating it. The falling of the drops of blood was unintentional and should not have happened, but the fact that they became two persea trees recalls ancient Egyptian tree worship. Finally, he observed that the expression that the king "flew to heaven" was quite typically Egyptian, and so he found the tale to be a mixture of indigenous Egyptian material and Asiatic beliefs, interwoven with myth and folk belief, the whole not separable into parts.

Pieper raised questions of considerable interest when he discussed the Egyptian aspects of the tale.[123] For instance, he noted that the Ennead which spoke to Bata was not the Heliopolitan Ennead, since Pre was present. Also, although the Ennead addressed Bata as "Bull of the Ennead," it brought his ruin by creating the young woman, an act reflecting true Märchen style. In addition, he related the removal of Bata's heart to Egyptian practice, identifying it with belief in sympathetic magic.[124] Earlier, Maspero had suggested that this concept governed the hair episode,[125] an idea reiterated by Pieper.

That the hair reached the Residence (the king's palace) via water suggested to Pieper that the story originated at a time when the Residence lay near the sea—that is, the Ramesside period. He also noted the apparent discontinuity in Bata's ability to kill the soldiers who sought his wife, when earlier he had asserted to her that he was a woman like her. When she finally arrived in Egypt, she effected Bata's death through her knowledge of his hidden heart, for "naturally she was anxious in front of her husband."[126] At this point, Pieper raised the question of why the soldiers had not taken Bata's heart. Further, Anubis's lengthy search suggested to him that the tree must not have been in the expected place. Finally, as before, he reiterated that the whole is ruled by the evil adulterous wife.[127]

An Allegorical Approach

Unrelated to the comparative and structural concerns of these scholars but nevertheless forming a part of the history of d'Orbiney scholarship is the treatment of the work as allegory. The general approach to narrative as allegory[128] has its roots in the Greek world, if not in that of the Egyptians.[129] Philippe Virey stands in a long line of commentators in regarding the "Tale of Two Brothers" as allegory, first in "Influence de l'Égypte ancienne sur les transformations du paganism,"[130] and then in *La Religion de l'ancienne Égypte.*[131] In these expositions he treated the entire narrative, item by item, as an allegory of Egypt, Osiris, and the Nile.[132] In the notes accompanying his summary of the story, he explained the nonallegorical meanings of certain details. He saw Bata's self-castration as "offering himself in sacrifice to Truth,"[133] and he equated the Valley of the Cedar with the celestial valley. The reason Bata could not save his wife from the river lay in the fact that with his heart on the flower, he no longer had free movement; and, finally, the river which carried the lock of hair between the sky and the earth was the "highway of the descending sky" in the "Hymn to the Nile."[134] He also saw a parallel between sending the first unsuccessful mission for Bata's wife, followed by the dispatch of a second successful one with the failure of Theseus and Pirithous to rescue Persephone from the Underworld, followed by Heracles' success at the mission. From this last, Virey suggested the possibility that the Greek tale had an Egyptian origin.

Virey's primary interest, however, lay in giving a minute, allegorical description of the story. The points of it are as follows: Anubis is the horizon, as Virey understands him to be in Plutarch's *De Iside et Osiride* 38, and the sun disappears each evening in him, that is Anubis, and rises from him each morning, "whose course (i.e., Anubis/sun) is the image of human life."[135] It is Anubis of the west whom Bata tells that he is leaving to go to the other world, and it is with Anubis of the east that Bata is transformed into a bull and returns to the land of the living. Therefore Bata-Osiris[136] personifies the principle of life, being at one and the same time the sun, who dies to be reborn, and the Nile, which annually develops the power of fecundation in the form of the Apis bull. It is repulsed by aridity, the enemy of the land, and departs, but leaves fecundity behind.

Anubis's wife represents the mountain slopes of Libya and Arabia, which do not receive the inundation because they are too high; Bata, as the Nile, refuses his fecundity to them. In his flight from Anubis, he is the Nile returning from the flood, and his plea asks the sun to distinguish the real riverbed from the apparent one of the flood. When Bata throws his severed phallus into the water, it represents the destruction of the grain by wetness, the grain entrusted to the land that will eventually emerge into new life. The water filled with crocodiles is the remains of the flood in the dry season.

Bata's wife, the daughter of the gods, personifies the earth itself, the mysterious power, the essence of the gods that gives life, while the heart represents frail new life and new grain which eventually result in new existence. The water following Bata's wife is the high Nile, the celestial flood, reaching the valley, whereas the rest of Egypt represents the messenger of the flood. The king's magicians are the sages who explain the mysteries of renewal of life to the king. The first expedition that failed represents the feminine principle without which all is sterile, showing that the time of fruitfulness is not yet come, while the following successful expedition represents the adorning and greening of earth, as the woman accompanying the expedition gives ornaments to the young woman. The celebration over the wife on her arrival at court equals the feasts celebrated over germination, and the cutting of the tree portrays the harvest.

Anubis's seething pot of beer is the swelling river as inundation approaches. The three years of hunting represent the triple rebirth, and the heart drinking water is like the fruit and grain finding fruitfulness in moisture. Once the heart is in its place, it is equated with the grain in the flood, ready to grow. The bull, long since thought of as Apis, equals the inundation and is celebrated as Hapi. When the wife of Bata recognizes him in the bull, the recognition represents that of land for water, and the bull's death equals the retreat of the inundation. The two drops of blood are the fruitfulness left behind by the Nile, and the resulting perseas signify the transformation of fruitful seed. As the wife, seated beneath the persea, is covered by the shadow of Bata, she is the earth covered by new growth. Finally, the fertilization by swallowing the splinter represents the definitive triumph of life through the union of the two principles.

In his later discussion, Virey added that Bata's swoon after the emasculation represented the last degree of the diminishing flood, and he further explicated his identification of Bata and Osiris by stating that Bata was the Osiris-Nile, the Osiris-Grain, and the Osiris-Vegetation.[137] Finally, he explained the unification of the two principles, the Woman of the West and the Woman of the East, as seen in Rekhmire's tomb. The Woman of the West is the earth as the spouse of the dead grain, and the Woman of the East is the earth as the mother of the plant engendered by this grain. For Virey, this idea sums up the entire Egyptian doctrine: the being who is reborn is the incarnation of the one who is dead.[138]

Psychological Approaches

Not surprisingly, with the rise of psychological theories, various psychological practitioners have taken an interest in the "Tale of Two Brothers." Sigmund Freud's protégé Otto Rank discussed it in a lengthy essay published in 1913,[139] with an additional mention of it in one paragraph of his article "Traum und Mythus," included by Freud as an appendix in the fourth through seventh editions of his *Die Traumdeutung.*[140] Using H. Schneider's 1907 discussion as the source, Rank sought to elucidate his sense of a hidden unity through a psychoanalytic interpretation. Essentially, he found that the solution lay in viewing the story as expressing the longed-for satisfaction of a tabooed wish, in this case the seduction of the mother or mother-figure by the son. Rank viewed the story as a doublet, the second part with the royalty being the socially raised duplication of the first part. For him, the two women are one. Furthermore, he understood the emasculation of Bata as the punishment for his desire to have incestuous relations with his "mother," a motif repeated in the sequential deaths that Bata suffers following the initial emasculation. Rank then related the tale to the Osirian story as told by Plutarch, in which Isis created a replacement phallus.[141] He also sensed a relationship with the brotherhood of Horus and Seth and their battle involving Horus's eye and Seth's testicles. Rank felt this was another marriage-bed situation involving rival brothers.

The work of Bruno Bettelheim also reflects Freud, and when Bettelheim wrote on two brothers tales in general in his book on the uses of fairy tales,[142] he paid special attention to the Egyptian "Tale of Two Brothers." In his opinion, two brothers tales generally present opposite aspects of human nature in which the heroes represent, on the one hand, a striving for independence and self-assertion and, on the other, a desire to remain safely at home, retaining close parental ties. The need is to leave home in order to break an oedipal attachment. He feels, however, that the Egyptian story deviates from this pattern in that it expresses "the undoing of the brother who remained home" and a developing "out and away from the central motif of the destructive nature of oedipal attachments and sibling rivalry."[143] At the same time, Bettelheim wrote, "We can interpret the story as telling either about a mother figure who gives in to her oedipal desires for a young man who stands in the role of a son, or of a son accusing a mother figure of his own oedipal desires for her."[144] He also stated that Anubis's desire to kill his brother shows the motif of sibling rivalry.

The analytical psychiatrist Carl Jung took a wholly different approach to the story, concerning himself basically with the individual motifs and their relationship to the archetype in the collective unconscious, never dealing with the whole tale or even a whole section of the story. For instance, as he saw it, the tree with Bata's heart participated in the "tribe of death trees," and so when the tree was felled, Bata died, to be revived twice, thus playing the role of "an instrument of change."[145] The aspect of the tree as the "altered form" (*Wandlungsform*) of man is represented when Bata was transformed into two persea trees.[146] Water as an animating force was important for Jung, and in connection with Bata, he quoted an Edfu text: "I bring to you the vessel with the parts of the god (i.e., the Nile) for you to drink; I freshen your heart with it so that you may rest."[147]

Writing from a Jungian perspective in 1973, Bernd Sledzianowski approached the tale as a growth of self-understanding, the integration of the *anima,* so the person becomes a "'*mana* personality,' one whom the king represents utterly (*kat'exochen*)."[148] the argument runs that in the house of his brother, Bata first confronts the feminine, that is the contrasting pole of the I-consciousness, the anima as understood by Jung. In this case the anima is projected on the wife of Anubis and as enemy, resulting in disaster and flight into presumed safety. The removal of Bata's heart represents his lack of consciousness (*Bewußtsein*), his life as a half-animal (*Halbtier*), but the creation of the female by the Ennead compels Bata to face the feminine again. As a creation of the gods, the young woman confirms her origin in Bata's unconscious. She meets him outside, and now Bata's relation to her is ambivalent. He does not wish separation, and yet she is still enemy. Through the stages of the metamorphoses, in which he ends as human again, she effects his gain of self-control and understanding, and he is no longer divided but is integrated.

The allegorical and the psychological approaches, the latter occasionally showing a relation to the former, rest on the views of modern interpreters of the narrative. It is rather as if the interpreter, especially in the case of the psychological view, works from a theoretical viewpoint into which he or she sets the material. The difficulty here is that one at best ignores and at worst divorces the narrative from its context, its time, its place, and its people. It is certainly inappropriate to call these approaches wrong, but it cannot be said they really elucidate the tale's meaning for its own time.

Postwar Egyptological Studies

The years since World War II have seen the publication of English, French, and German collections of the literature of ancient Egypt,[149] along with various studies of specific works, one of which has been the "Tale of Two Brothers." They reflect advances in scholarship in various areas, most especially in literary structure, although they do not ignore the questions of origins, context, and genre.

In 1949 Gustave Lefebvre published a new translation and collection of selected Egyptian stories,[150] a work updating Maspero's *Les Contes populaires,* both emending it from later studies and adding material discovered subsequent to 1911. In his general introduction, Lefebvre discussed the different categories of stories, classifying "Two Brothers" as "psychological" (the first part) and "marvelous" (the second part), stating that the themes in this story go far back into antiquity and have many parallels, sometimes direct and sometimes not. He also felt that the Egyptian stories are basically indigenous, with an occasional trait sifting in from elsewhere. For instance, in "Two Brothers," Bata and Anubis are human forms of the age-old Egyptian gods Seth and Osiris, while the hair motif was introduced late. Like Maspero, Lefebvre saw the tale as an amalgam of two stories which a rhapsode of the thirteenth-century BCE had joined together. The first is a banal, classical tragedy, rebuffed woman and chaste young man, the characters carrying the names of divinities, while the second shows a predominance of magic and a sequence of prodigious occurrences—a boon for the folklorists.

At that time, Lefebvre suggested that a hitherto unnoted parallel could be drawn between Bata's transformations and those of Proteus in *The Odyssey* (*Ody.* 4, 456–59),[151] and in 1950 he devoted an article to its similarity with the Russian tale of Ivan, the son of the sacristan, a parallel first mentioned by Alfred Rambaud in 1876.[152] In his 1950 study,

Lefebvre made an item-by-item comparison showing the similarities, beginning with the point where the troops are sent out to get the woman for the king through to the end of the tale. Behind this comparison lay his disagreement with Vladimir Vikentiev over the application of the comparative method to folklore. Only on this particular story would Lefebvre agree with Vikentiev, as he stated in his article.

Spanning the years 1950 to 1952, Fritz Hintze published two volumes analyzing the stylistic approaches of Late Egyptian stories,[153] including the Papyrus d'Orbiney. He accomplished his analysis by means of the use of grammatical formulas, assuming that the preponderance of a given formula in a particular section pointed to one version, and the mix in a particular story showed the number of stories put together. Viewed in this fashion, the d'Orbiney shows five divisions, which correspond to the main motifs: opening and closing, the Joseph-motif, the Nitokris-motif,[154] the heart motif, and the juniper motif.[155] He noted, however, that the tale "does not 'disintegrate' into these segments or single tales, e.g., motifs, but is extraordinarily cleverly interlaced into a unity."[156] Nevertheless, he considered it to be a late compilation of originally independent stories of different origin, as he felt the linguistic, stylistic, and structural distinctions suggested.[157]

When Walther Wolf discussed the Papyrus d'Orbiney in his *Kulturgeschichte des alten Ägypten* in 1962,[158] he reiterated that it interweaves two tales: Joseph and Potiphar's wife and the dying and living again of the bringer of fruitfulness, who is incarnated in the king. Because Anubis's name appears, Wolf considered the story to be a divine history told on the earthly plane, with the sense of the whole representing the drive of a good man for the will of god which he finally attains through luck.

In 1967 Helmut Brunner also discussed the tale,[159] taking special note of the neutral position of the narrator of the story, one who reports facts but takes no moral position: evil is not named evil, nor good, good. Even as he pointed out the many widespread motifs of the tale, he was concerned to emphasize its Egyptian nature, not just in coloring but also in theme. For him, only the frame of Egyptian religion makes comprehensible the themes of generation-incarnation, the mutilation and restoration of generative power, close relation to the cows, and the existence of the artificial (*künstlichen*) woman.

In the *Handbuch der Orientalistik* in 1970, Joachim Spiegel[160] wrote, "the narrative of the two brothers . . . belongs in the type of popular legend, which was represented for us in older times through the 'story of the birth of the kings' of the fifth dynasty."[161] He suggested that the story was built around the age-old myth of the death and revival of the god of fruitfulness, basically of Syrian origin, and behind it lay the nature symbols, whose generative power was incarnated in the king. Peculiar to the "Two Brothers" is that it is clothed in Märchen form and moves from "unlucky" to "lucky."

In 1971, reviewing and expanding on what he had written in 1960 in *De la Divinité du pharaon,*[162] Georges Posener[163] asserted that the "Tale of Two Brothers" is a combination of two stories, one incorporating the story of Joseph and Potiphar's wife, the other adapting "a basic tenet of Egyptian theology, that of the self-creating demiurge." The first half derives from the milieu of *fellahin* with little that is supernatural while the second is "steeped in the strange and the supernatural." Furthermore, Bata has analogies with Seth in the first part, but in the second he is more like Osiris. The whole is joined formally by the continuation of the two brothers Bata and Anubis as the characters and by "the persecution of a righteous man by an evil woman."

At the same time, he noted that no moral opinion is expressed by the narrator, for "in Egypt the tone of the stories is always objective—it is the rule—and only the behavior of the protagonists and their remarks make it possible to distinguish the good from the bad."[164] In his earlier work, he had stated that the Seth-Bata equation, drawn from the Papyrus Jumilhac (Jum. III, 21–22; XX, 18), the anonymity of the preceding king, and the Osirian relationship, which of course relates to the deceased king, make problematical the ultimate succession expressed in the tale. Further, the lack of miracles worked by the king in a miracle-filled tale bothers him.[165] Nevertheless, he views the tale as folkloric, while considering that it encompasses myth as well.

When Emma Brunner-Traut published the first edition of her

Altägyptische Märchen in 1963,[166] she included notes, discussion, and a new translation of the "Tale of Two Brothers" among the forty stories in the volume. In addition, she has mentioned it frequently in other discussions of Egyptian tales and motifs, as in *Enzyklopädie des Märchens*[167] and in *Altorientalische Literaturen,*[168] to mention two. In her summaries, she has included its use of world-wide motifs and has emphasized that in the story Bata remains Bata, even as the son. In this she differs from Eberhard Otto, who refers to "Bata's son in whom he arises again."[169] For Brunner-Traut, the wife also remains the wife, even as the mother. The tale thus has no concern for the passing of time and generations in typical folktale style. Furthermore, although the initial scenes are domestic, as the tale progresses, cows speak, gods intervene, and the younger brother lives separated from his heart. He is also able to rise three times from the deaths[170] inflicted by his wife,[171] whom Brunner-Traut perceives to be the new incarnation of his sister-in-law. Brunner-Traut feels that because both brothers are gods and the wife is a creation of the gods, the story is a myth, one which was localized in the seventeenth nome of Upper Egypt, as shown by the Papyrus Jumilhac, which dates from Ptolemaic times.[172] She made use of this latter work to explain Bata's castration, which she held is mirrored in the castration of the Sethian bull of which it tells, thus elucidating the significance of cattle common to both these papyri. At the end of her discussion, she summarized the story as "the myth of the dying and rising again god of fertility, who is ever reincarnated; the man, animal, and plant with its pervasive divine creative power."[173] Thus, she has considered the d'Orbiney to be a combination of motifs partly from the Osirian myth and partly from a myth with which the Papyrus Jumilhac stands in relation.[174]

In the early 1970s, Elke Blumenthal wrote a major article on the tale,[175] followed in the later 1970s by two studies produced by Jan Assmann.[176] Blumenthal sought to place the story synchronically within the corpus of Late Egyptian stories, the collection of which she then set within the mainstream of Egyptian literature.[177] In the course of her discussion, she questioned what genre the "Tale of Two Brothers" represents above and beyond its fascination for folklorists. She asked, for instance, whether an otherwise unknown myth underlies the story or if it represents "a non-binding play with Märchen-like and mythical elements."[178] Another question dealt with the possible relation between the d'Orbiney and the Jumilhac, the latter containing a "regular myth of the god Bata."[179] Furthermore, she noted that there are those who call it a fairy tale with mythic traits.

She believed that the d'Orbiney itself "played . . . with the elements of theological tradition, bound them to a delightful series of tales, and rooted the whole with a powerful charge of irony, with the result that the reader was magnificently amused at the cost of the highest divine council."[180] Furthermore, a definite sense of the foreign is present in these stories, especially as "somewhere-nowhere," i.e., without having definitive locale, giving it a remoteness. Thus there exists an inextricable interweaving of what is labeled "historical" and "mythical" in modern terminology. Blumenthal questioned whether these terms ought even to be used, especially since there seems to have been no boundary between the two for the Egyptian. Mythical legitimacy coexists with historicizing of the mythic.

Although Blumenthal dated the actual stories of the Late Egyptian collection to the New Kingdom, she felt they were built on an earlier base, albeit exceedingly revised, and their purpose was to amuse and entertain, an idea supported by Brunner-Traut when she wrote again on the tale in 1982.[181] Generally Blumenthal saw no didactic purpose to Late Egyptian stories, save possibly in "Truth and Falsehood,"[182] although she acknowledged that one might find the moral in the d'Orbiney that an innocent one, oppressed by disaster, finally gets his reward. Furthermore, being written in the Late Egyptian dialect rather than the classical Middle Egyptian, it is clear that these texts were not school texts. They were, however, probably connected with a hypothetical, non-literary folk tradition, shown by their use of colloquial speech and their favored folkloristic themes. In addition, their presence on papyrus suggests favor in the upper ranks of society. She concluded the study urging that from an identification of literary genre, a search proceed toward a definition of unity for the Papyrus d'Orbiney.

Assmann's 1977 essay discusses the physical and structural composition of the tale with the partial aim of defining its unity,[183] an essay which certainly reflects developments in structural and folklore studies. He begins with an analysis of the writing on the papyrus, stating that the rubrics physically present in the text, written in red, mark chapter and book divisions. In this way one finds three books, each consisting of eight chapters. Book I presents the initial situation and the attempt at seduction, with the action occurring in an Egyptian province, ending with the separation of the brothers. The second book opens in the Valley of the Cedar[184] and contains the creation of the wife, the loss of the hair, the episode of finding it in Egypt, and the return to the valley where Anubis revives the dead Bata and from which they set out on their return to Egypt. The final book takes place entirely in Egypt and narrates the second and third attempts to kill Bata with his resulting birth from his wife and acknowledgement as crown prince, finishing with his accession, revenge, and rule for thirty years.

After having defined this set of divisions, Assmann analyzed the structure of the story. He worked backward from what he terms the end-situation to the beginning of the story, methodically examining what the situation is and then looking for the preceding action which had culminated in the previously found situation. He was thus able to present a structural progression from the beginning to the end in which each situation is disrupted by an action that in turn results in a new situation. He further analyzed the second and third chapters of the tale according to the morphology of Vladimir Propp,[185] the Russian folklorist, who himself felt the tale would submit to this type of analysis.[186]

In his later article, Assmann discussed the thematic focal points of the story: kinfolk relations, work relations, and male productivity and power. The kinfolk relations first introduces the two brothers by name and the wife of the older brother without a name, and then shows the disruption of these relations through the wife's action. This, in turn, is followed by the older brother's desire to kill the younger, who flees to safety. All these actions upset the initial situation. The theme of work relations concerns the farmer and the shepherd, and Assmann noted especially that the talent of Bata the shepherd touches the wonderful and divine. Though Bata has these characteristics, he is subordinate to the lesser farmer, perhaps intentionally setting up the seduction of the more talented by the wife of the less talented. The third theme of male fertility and power appears in the early description of Bata: "the power of the god was in him" (d'Orb. 1,4), but is negated with the self-castration. Assmann related the three by means of seeing each as evolving into a kind of "adultery" (*Ehebruch*) with broken, shifted contracts.

Assmann perceived these shifts at different points as the story progresses. The initial contractual situation, that is of Bata as "son" to Anubis and then as helper in the farming, turns around as Anubis is bound to Bata through the life-sign motif. Another type of shift is that from the conflict of farmer and shepherd to sexual conflict (over Anubis's wife), and later, that from Bata's sexual weakness to the more general weakness derived from his lack of his heart, thus focusing about the maiden. A contrast also shows between Bata's end-situation of enthronement and the unassuming, socially secondary situation portrayed at the outset. Thus a total shift in the locale and social position of the hero occurs, clarifying other motifs such as *Kamutef* and the theme of departure and return. Assmann likened this shift to the initiation narrative so common in folktale and fairy tale wherein the hero disintegrates in the original familial situation and leaves it, experiencing various tests, a death (or deaths) and resurrection, an unrecognized return followed by identification, and finally a transfiguration and reintegration on ascending the throne and marrying. Although no Egyptian initiation rite can be related to this story,[187] Assmann maintained that this theme unifies the whole, the first book representing the emancipation from the home situation that had become intolerable, while the second book depicts the journey to the other side with a self-chosen death (castration) followed by death due to destruction of his external heart, a condition from which he is resurrected with the infusion of his heart. Finally, the third book presents his unrecognized return, with identifications, confrontations, and resultant transfiguration in his accession to the throne and thus to a higher plane. The turn from the first to the second part derives from an old myth that was interwoven into the tale, itself representing the larger and age-old conflict of the ancient Near East of shepherd and farmer.[188] Brunner-Traut disagrees with this idea, although she reflects the studies of Assmann in his efforts to analyze the text in relation to form and content and espouses his division of the tale into books and chapters.[189]

The Papyrus Jumilhac[190]

With the possible exception of Gardiner's 1905 publication of Edinburgh Ostracon 916, which provided a second example of Bata's name,[191] the publication of the Papyrus Jumilhac in 1961 by Jacques Vandier has been the single most important event to affect the scholarship of the Papyrus d'Orbiney since its discovery. This papyrus, written entirely in hieroglyphics and dating from the end of the Ptolemaic period or the beginning of the Roman period,[192] holds particular interest for a study of the Papyrus d'Orbiney because of its explicit equation of Seth with Bata.[193] The document is devoted to the religious history of an area that coincides mostly with the eighteenth nome of Upper Egypt, an area that was stretched out on the left, or eastern, bank of the Nile, extending north to el-Hibeh and south to Tehneh, and was designated by the falcon standard. The falcon god of this nome, along with those of the twelfth and sixteenth nomes of Upper Egypt, was seen in some way as a warrior god who protected the eastern borders of the land.[194] As Vandier points out, such a god, although anonymous, is known from the Pyramid Texts and has been compared to these three different falcons.[195] Although the falcon of the eighteenth nome was originally independent of Horus, the falcon god par excellence, at some imprecise point in time it became assimilated to Horus, who, in turn, became syncretized to Anubis.[196] Within the nome itself, Horus was master of *Ḥwt-nswt* and Anubis at *Ḥr-dy*, but Anubis had gained the ascendant position by the reign of Merneptah and was called "the master of the nome of the falcon with extended wings."[197]

The content of the papyrus is varied, ranging from lists of towns and sacred items, many with mythological references, to legends about the gods and their activities, most especially

Anubis. Other major gods who are mentioned include Osiris, Seth, Horus, Thoth, Re, Isis, and Hathor. The predominant theme of these legends concerns the rescue of the parts (*ḫt-m-ḫftyw*) of Osiris from Seth, who stole them and fled. Mostly, these parts of Osiris are the *rḏw* or efflux (*humeurs*) of the god, which was the sacred relic preserved in the eighteenth nome and was perceived to be the source of the fertility of the area.[198]

The presentation of the material appears mostly in the form of etiological statements;[199] in fact, the purpose of the papyrus appears to be to provide explanations of the sacred practices, beliefs, and myths of the area. It is this type of statement that was used to express the Seth-Bata equation:

> *ḏd.tw n.f* (=*Stš*)
> *Bṯ m Sꜣkꜣ ḥr.s* (Jum. III,21–22)
> He (Seth) is called
> Bata in Saka because of it;
> *ir Bṯ Stš pw* (Jum. XX,18)
> As for Bata, he is Seth.

The nature and contexts of these statements suggest that Bata was incorporated into a story in which he did not originally belong,[200] although on the political-historical plane they may indicate some hostility between the seventeenth and eighteenth nomes.

2
The Brothers

Anubis and Bata, the two brothers in the Papyrus d'Orbiney, both bear the names of gods, each written with the divine determinative. They thus bring a dimension to the tale which they would not convey were they ordinary people. For Assmann, this fact "is of highest significance both for the question about the types (myth or fairy tale) as well as for the judgement of the coherence of its plot and theme."[1] This is to say that whatever each god has as his own particular traits, actions, fate, and myth will be implicitly understood by the audience and presumably should affect the course of the narrative. Therefore an examination of each of these two gods comprises a necessary preparation for its study.

Although Anubis was a well-known divinity at the time when the tale was discovered,[2] Bata was totally unknown and was even called Sata in the initial publication. The first attempt to identify him did not take place until 1877, when Lauth suggested that Bata is the Bytis of the dynasty of demigods reported in the Armenian version of Eusebius's redaction of Manetho's writings.[3] Since then, there has been a proliferation of efforts to determine who he is, making use of sources ranging from the Early Dynastic period up through the Ptolemaic era and discusssing both orthography and context.

Bata in the Ramesside Period

Bata, written with the *bꜣ*-bird and the *tꜣ*-bread (fig. 1), was known only from the Papyrus d'Orbiney until 1905, when Alan Gardiner published the Edinburgh Ostracon 916[4] (fig. 2), which contained a further example of the name. Since then it has also been found in two other New Kingdom documents, the Wilbour Papyrus[5] and the Cairo Calendar.[6] The striking information conveyed by the Ostracon was Bata's identification as Lord of Saka, a town in the seventeenth nome of Upper Egypt.[7] The orthography of the name on the Cairo Calendar, dated to the time of Ramesses II, lacks the epithet "Lord of Saka" but otherwise is identical with that of the d'Orbiney and the Ostracon, even to the determinative (fig. 3). The same is true, although the determinative is lacking, for the six examples from the Wilbour Papyrus (figs. 4a, 4b, 4c, 4d, 4e, 4f), an economic document dating from the time of Ramesses V. In addition, one of these examples includes the full epithet, "Lord of Saka" (fig. 4f).

Fig. 1[8]

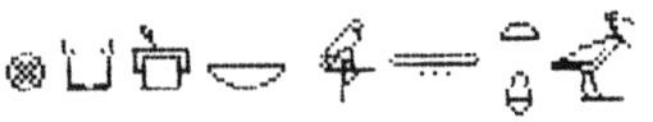

Fig. 2[9]

Fig. 3[10]

Fig. 4a[11]

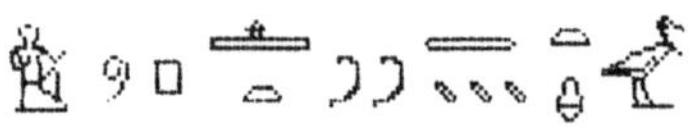

Fig. 4b[12]

Fig. 4c[13]

Fig. 4d[14]

Fig. 4e[15]

Fig. 4f[16]

Although this form of the name, known only in the nineteenth and twentieth dynasties, commonly has been vocalized as "Bata," William F. Albright's work on the vocalization of Egyptian syllabic orthography has shown that the name is more properly read *Bi-ti*,[17] a reading he proposed as early as 1918.[18] The significance of the use of the syllabic orthography in this case is not wholly clear. Albright showed that in general it was used largely for foreign names from Semitic and Hittite and for rare or forgotten Egyptian words, but he also found it was used in native Egyptian words, documented by his list of syllabic values and their use. In a letter to Albright in 1935, Joseph Sturm applauded Albright's work, stressing more strongly the use of syllabic orthography in native Egyptian words.[19] A later essay by Lambdin and Albright documented its use "for the writing of Egyptian hypocoristica . . . from the Middle Kingdom period."[20] Although this orthography was used about equally in the Papyrus d'Orbiney for loan words (table 1) and Egyptian words (table 2), its use in Bata's name implies that a normal, non-syllabic writing of it was not available to the scribe. Thus one surmises that the name was revived from a much older or almost forgotten stratum of Egyptian thought, for it is unlikely the name is hypocoristic or that the god Bata was of foreign extraction.

The use of syllabic orthography precludes any realistic attempt to translate the god's name. Such an attempt is further discouraged by the simple, biconsonantal nature of the writings of *Bt*, the Early Dynastic and Old Kingdom deity who appears to be related to the New Kingdom figure.[21] In its later appearances it is possible to translate Bata's name as "the *bꜣ* of the bread (?)," but one must ask what that means. Maybe "the *bꜣ* of the land" is an appropriate translation, further supporting the chthonic nature shown in the shepherd song, but because of the gap in time between the Old Kingdom appearances and the first sure attestation in the New Kingdom, in addition to the use of syllabic orthography to write the later form, no certain conclusion can be drawn.

1.		*Bi-ti* Bata	Albright, *VESO,* p. 40, V B 15, Dyn. XIX; d'Orb passim.
2.		*'a-ha-ya(t)* barn, stable	Albright, *VESO,* p. 33, II A 14, R. III; d'Orb. *W* I, 118, 5, 9.
3		*ya-m(a)* sea	Albright, *VESO,* p. 36, IV 3, Dyn. XIX; d'Orb. 1 1; 10, 5; 10, 6–7; 10, 8; *Wb* I, 78; *CD,* p. 18
4.	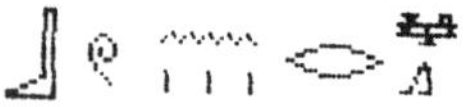	*ba-nra* outside	Albright, *VESO,* p. 39, V A 3, Dyn. XVIII–XX; d'Orb. 10, 1; *Wb* I, 461, 4.
5.		*ni-mu* who?	Albright, *VESO,* p. 46, IX B 5, Dyn. XIX; d'Orb. 4, 10; 15, 9; *CD,* p. 132.
6.		*ha-ru-ru* blossom	Albright, *VESO,* p. 50, X C 14, Dyn. XIX; d'Orb 8, 4; 8, 9; 10, 3; 12, 6 17, 4; *Wb* III, 149, 18; *CD,* p. 176.
7.		*si-mu* herbage	Albright, *VESO,* p. 55, XIV, B 3, Dyn. XIX; cf *NÄG,* §33; d'Orb. 1, 6 1, 10; 2, 1; 5, 7; *CD,* p 225.
8.	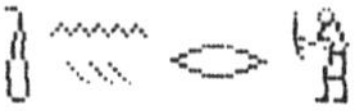	*ta-na-ra* strength	Albright, *VESO,* p. 62, XIX, A 15, Dyn. XIX; d'Orb. 3, 6; *Wb* V, 382 6, 7.

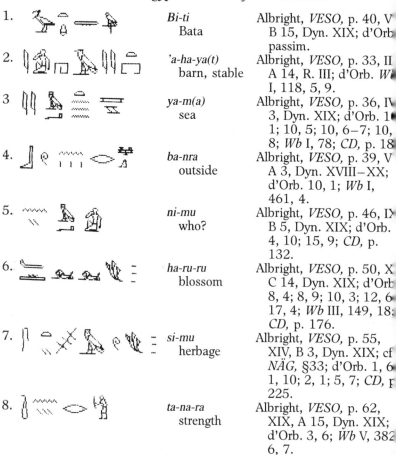

Table 1. Examples of Syllabic Orthography from *VESO* that Appear in the d'Orbiney

Biconsonantal Names Commonly Related to Bata

There are several other writings of names or titles that employ the consonants *b* and *t* which have been associated with Bata, but because even the readings of these names are by no means certain, it is appropriate to consider problems of orthography separately before taking up a study of the contexts in which the names occur. Although nearly all these writings date from

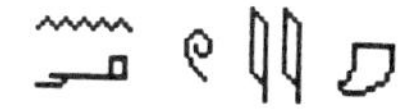	*n-ʿu-ya* javelin	d'Orb. 5, 5; 5, 9; 6, 2; 6, 4; 7, 8; *Wb* II, 202, 15 (Dyn. 19–20).
	*na-ḏa* splinter	d'Orb. 18, 4; *Wb* II, 377, 7 (Dyn. 18–19).
	*ru-'i* side	d'Orb. 6, 7; 6, 9; 16, 19; 16, 10; 7, 8; *Wb* II, 400, 9 (Dyn. 19–20); *CD,* 147.
	*ša-wa-ba* persea	d'Orb. 16, 10; 17, 1; 17, 5; 16, 6; 18, 1; 18, 3; *Wb* IV, 435, 11 (N.K.); *CD,* 263.
	*ga-sa* mourning	d'Orb. 8, 8; *Wb* V, 156, 1 (N.K.).
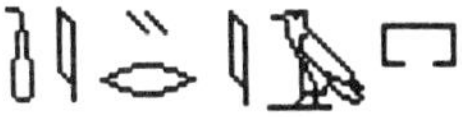	*ta-ar-'i* door	d'Orb. 16, 10; 17, 2; *Wb* V, 318, 15 (N.K.).
	*pú-ya* to fly	d'Orb. 18, 4; *CD,* p. 87.
	*n-ha-mu* to shout, jubilate	d'Orb. 12, 1; 14, 9; 15, 4; 17, 2; 18, 9; *CD,* p. 135.

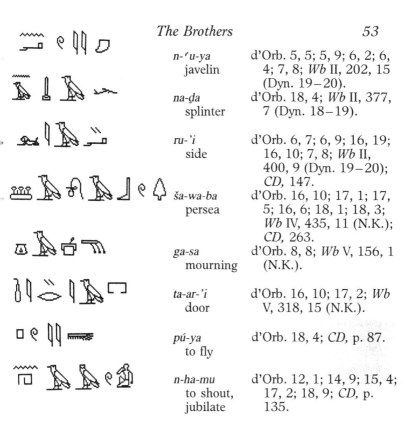

Table 2. Other Examples of Syllabic Orthography in the d'Orbiney

the Old Kingdom, one dates from the Early Dynastic period, one comes from the eighteenth dynasty, and two date from the Ptolemaic period, with a questionable example from the Middle Kingdom. The eighteenth-dynasty example was found in the temple of Tuthmosis IV at Amada (fig. 5), and according to the traditional transliteration, is read *B3-ty, nb S3-k3.* Although it is not impossible to read the standing ram of this period as the syllable *bi* according to Albright,[22] Helck describes such a reading as "a very rare writing."[23] The epithet, however, identifies the god represented by this writing with the Bata of the nineteenth- and twentieth-dynasty documents, and so it may be assumed that this is one of the rare instances in which the standing ram is to be read as *bi*.

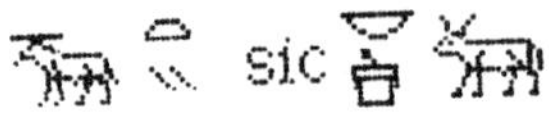

Fig. 5[24]

The Old Kingdom examples are more problematical because they lack vocalization[25] as well as any localizing epithet. An exception may be seen in the example from Niuserre's sanctuary of Re at Abu Gurab (fig. 6), of which there is a twenty-second dynasty copy in the festival hall of Osorkon II (fig. 7). The latter includes phonetic determinatives of the flaming *b3*-pot and the double weak aleph. From this match, the reading is probably *B3-ty*, although syllabically *Bi-ti* is possible.

Fig. 6[26]

Fig. 7[27]

The other Old Kingdom examples have no similar helps, having been written simply with the alphabetic signs *b*[𓃀] and *t*[𓏏]. The most prominent of these are found in the six examples of the *Hirtenlied,* or "Shepherd Song," from fifth- and sixth-dynasty mastabas and tombs at Sakkara (fig. 8), differing from each other only in the determinative used. From the fifth dynasty comes a scribal palette with an identical writing (fig. 9), and a mate lacking the alphabetic signs (fig. 10). An epithet of Wenis also shows the same alphabetic orthography (fig. 11), and the name appears again in a fifth-dynasty papyrus from Abusir. This last example shows it as part of a personal name (fig. 12), where it is distinctive because of its use of the cow's-skin determinative[28] rather than the expected recumbent ram. A final Old Kingdom example, again part of a personal name, was discovered by Lopez among graffiti at Khor el-Aquiba (fig. 13), which Lopez has dated tentatively to the late fifth or early sixth dynasty.[29]

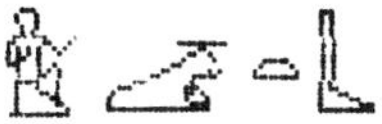
Mastaba of *Ty* (twice), Fifth Dynasty (ca. 2450 BCE)

Mastaba of *Mrrw-kꜣ*, Fifth Dynasty (ca. 2400 BCE)

Chapel of *Sḫm-ʿnḫ-Ptḥ*, Fifth Dynasty (ca. 2450/2350 BCE)

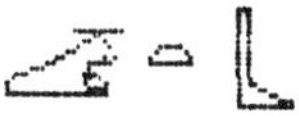
Jeremiah Cloister

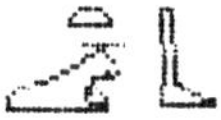
Nbt

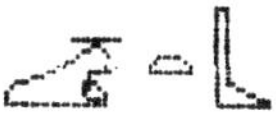
Mḥw

Fig. 8[30]

Fig. 9[31]

Fig. 10[32]

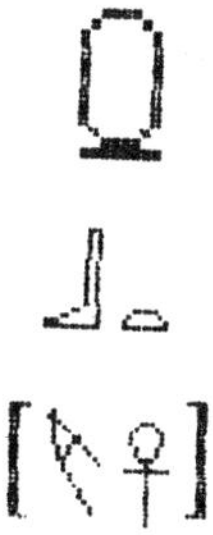
Fig. 11[33]

Fig. 12[34]

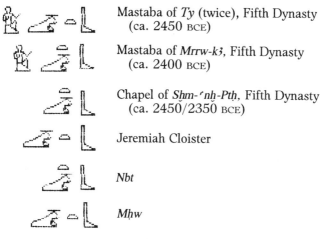

Fig. 13[35]

In the Early Dynastic period, the name appears only in examples of the name of the mother of *Smr-ḫt* from the first dynasty, of which Kaplony has collected five complete examples (fig. 14).

a. 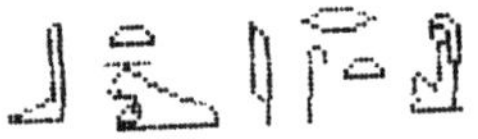 Daressy, *BIFAO* 12 (1915) p. 167.

b. 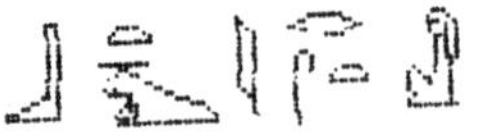 Weigall, *History,* p. 49.

c. 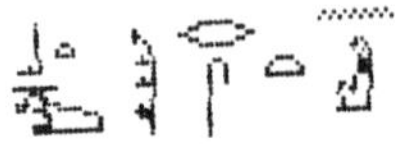 Borchardt, unpub.

d. 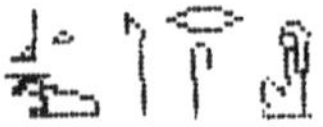 Cerny, unpub.

e.  Edwards, unpub.

Fig. 14[36]

Dating from Ptolemaic times, the Papyrus Jumilhac has three examples of the name, each written as *Bṯ* (fig. 15). The second consonant may be understood as the Ptolemaic rendering of the older alphabetic *t*,[37] thus directly relating this name to the older biconsonantal examples. A fourth Ptolemaic example derives from an Edfu list citing the guardians and locations of the relics of Osiris (fig. 16). Its orthography differs from the Jumilhac examples in the use of the old sign for *ti* to designate *t*,[38] but the most significant difference occurs in its epithet, "is bifaced."[39]

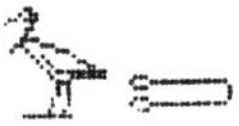

Fig. 15[40]

Fig. 16[41]

The one Middle Kingdom example comes from the Sinai (fig. 17), and in its initial publication by Gardiner, Peet, and Cerny, the name in which it occurs was read as *ḥtp-Ḫrty*.[42] The presence of the flaming pot, which generally assures the phonetic value of *bꜣ* for the standing ram, suggests that a more accurate reading of the name is *ḥtp-Bꜣty*,[43] thus providing a possible example from this period.

Fig. 17[44]

Contexts of the Ramesside Examples

Two of the three "outside" documents from the nineteenth and twentieth dynasties containing the name of Bata specify that Bata was Lord of Saka. Section IV of the Wilbour Papyrus, a section which deals mainly with the Cynopolite nome, i.e., the seventeenth nome of Upper Egypt,[45] shows personal names, two sanctuary nomes, and a place-name, each of which incorporates Bata's name. In addition, the name of a priest of the Temple of Bata, Lord of Saka, was *kꜣ-nfr* (fig. 18), "beautiful bull," which recalls Bata's transformation into

. . . *wʿ n kꜣ ʿꜣ*
iw.f m inw nbt nfr (d'Orb. 14,5)
. . . a great bull,
he being of every beautiful color.

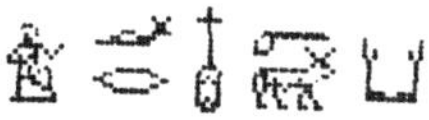

Fig. 18[46]

The Leyden V, 1 stela, dating to the nineteenth dynasty, suggests, however, that this bull need not necessarily have been the Bata of the d'Orbiney. The stela's reference to *kꜣ nb Sꜣkꜣ*, Bull, Lord of Saka (fig. 19),[47] suggests the possibility of a bull god in Saka who was distinct from Bata and with which Bata had become associated by the time of the nineteenth dynasty.

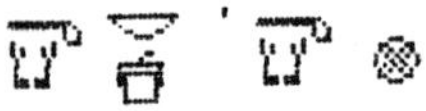

Fig. 19[48]

It was Gardiner who first identified Bata with Saka in Upper Egypt in his brief publication in 1905 of Edinburgh Ostracon 916, the "Poem on the King's Chariot." The relevant part of this text reads:[49]

> *ir nꜣ bꜣti*[50] *n tꜣy.k mrkbt*
> *Biti nb Sꜣkꜣ*
> *iw.f m mꜣwḏ sꜣ*[51] *n Bꜣst*
> *[. . .] hꜣʿ r ẖꜣst*
> As for the *bꜣti* of your chariot,
> they are Bata, Lord of Saka
> when he is in the arms[52] of the son of Bast,
> [. . .] (being) cast away in a foreign land.

Besides the important identification of Bata as Lord of Saka, the paronomasia of *bꜣti* of the chariot and Bata, the association of Bata with the son of Bast, and the reference to a foreign land emerge as significant aspects of the text. The full impact of the paronomasia is diminished because the exact meaning of "the *bꜣti* of the chariot" remains unknown. The word is probably Northwest Semitic **baytu* since the following *mrkbt*, "chariot," is well-attested in Northwest Semitic. Furthermore, *bt.mrkbt* appears in Ugaritic,[53] *bīt narkabti* is found in Akkadian,[54] and a Sumerian word list attests to *giš-é-gigir*,[55] each of which may be translated as "house of the chariot," as Cyrus Gordon actually renders the Ugaritic.[56] This "house" could refer either to a part of the chariot itself, such as the section in which the driver and the warrior ride, or it may allude to the "house" in which the chariot is kept, perhaps a shed.[57]

The description of Bata in the arms of the son of Bast, who is Bastet, would seem to refer to the tale from the d'Orbiney. In reviving Bata, Anubis, who was known as a son of Bastet in the nineteenth dynasty,[58] took Bata in his arms and embraced him (d'Orb. 14,3–4). One need not assume, however, that Bast is not the mother of Bata, for he could be embraced by the son of the same mother, but that is not what the text says. The only way one could see that Bastet is the mother of Bata is when she is in the Bastet form of Hathor, a real possibility, for there is little difficulty in identifying Bata's wife/mother with Hathor, with whom Bastet was equated from the Old Kingdom,[59] or in identifying Anubis's wife, who acts "like a mother" to Bata, with Hathor. Since Bata eventually became king, the Pyramid Text which cites Bastet as the mother of the dead king lends further support to the idea that Bastet is his mother:

> *šdy.n sw mwt.f Bstt* (*Pyr.* 1111a)
> His mother Bastet nursed him.[60]

Thus it appears quite possible that Bastet is the common mother mentioned in d'Orbiney 1,1. There is no question, however, that this is speculative.

The third "outside" document from this period, the Cairo Calendar, contains an apparently etiological reference. It warns that the third day of the fourth month of *ꜣḫt* was considered extremely inauspicious:

> *imi.k ir ẖt nb m hrw pn*
> *hrw pwy n iri sqri*
> *m ʿnḫwy msḏrty n Biti*
> *ḫntt ḥwt.f n štꜣw.f*[61]
> Do not do anything on this day.
> It is the day of the smashing
> in the ears of Bata
> within his places of his secrets.[62]

Because the sense of the passage is explanatory, Abd el Mohsen Bakir suggests that the smashing of the ears is related to the smashing of the ears on portrait heads in the Old Kingdom,[63] apparently assuming a deliberate act of some sort. Recently, however, Nicholas Millet suggested that the broken ears on these heads resulted from their use as sculptors' models,[64] an idea which would mitigate Bakir's suggestion. Although Millet's thought helps with the actual broken ears, the allusion to Bata's ears is puzzling. A partial elucidation is perhaps provided in the calendar from Papyrus Sallier IV, also from the Ramesside period, in which it is Osiris's ears rather than those of Bata which were affected.[65] This reference comes from a damaged portion of the papyrus, however, and H. Altenmüller has recently questioned it.[66] If the reading "Osiris" were correct, the calendars would support the old idea that Bata and Osiris are related in some way, held by many commentators from the earliest days of the study of the tale. As it stands, though, no certain conclusions may be deduced from them.

Contexts of the Biconsonantal Names Related to Bata

The biconsonantal names commonly associated with Bata vary in their usefulness for learning about *Bt*, even before the question of *Bt*'s relationship to Bata is addressed. Of them, both the example from Tuthmosis IV's temple at Amada and the Middle Kingdom example from the Sinai have fuller writings than the Old Kingdom and Ptolemaic examples and perhaps can be related orthographically to the Ramesside examples of Bata more directly. The Sinai example, accepting my revised reading, shows only that *B3ty* was used in a personal name in the Middle Kingdom. Whether the *B3ty* of this personal name was related to Bata of the New Kingdom or even to *B3ty* in the Amada example is questionable. The later example, probably to be read *Bi-ti*, as suggested above, occurs in a list of twenty-one deities inscribed on the sides of six pillars in the king's hypostyle hall at Amada and is one of two which refers to a divinity with a specific locale who appears in a place north of the fourth Upper Egyptian nome. It reads:

> *nfr nṯr ḥq3 ḥq3w Mn-ḫprw-Rʿ*
> *Bity nb S3k3 mr di ʿnḫ*[67]
> Good god, ruler of rulers, *Mn-ḫprw-Rʿ*
> Beloved of *Bity*, Lord of Saka, given life.

The epithet of the god suggests that he is the same god as Bata of the Ramesside documents. One wonders, however, why he should be cited among the deities who love Tuthmosis IV at Amada[68] and be only one of two "northern" deities, the other being Bastet, mistress of *ʿnḫ-t3wy*, the Giza necropolis.[69] It is interesting that Bastet and Bata both appear here, albeit on different pillars, but one cannot draw any certain conclusions from their juxtaposition.

The inclusion of *Bt* in the name of the mother of *Smr-ḫt* from the First Dynasty is problematical. The form of the divine name matches that of the other early examples, but the meaning of the full name is disputed, as is its transliteration. Peter Kaplony transliterates it as *B3t-irjt-s(n?)*,[70] Lana Troy writes it BATIRYTES,[71] and I read it as *Bt ir.st*. Kaplony states that it is untranslatable but nevertheless reads *bt* as "*b3t*, '*Mutterschaft* (sic)'," interpreting the whole "untranslatable" name as "mother sheep (is) her companion."[72] Peter Seibert, on the other hand, reads the hieroglyphs simply as *bt*, suggesting the whole name reads *rwnt-Bt*, "the young cow of *Bt*", or *ni-Bt-irtyw*, "the showy garment of *Bt*."[73] I would translate the name as "*Bt* made her."[74] While there are no grounds on which to assess the value of these suggestions, it is difficult to dissociate the name from the *Bt* of the other texts in view of their virtually identical orthography. At the same time, the most that can be said is that *Bt* appears as part of one theophoric name of the period.

Bt's inclusion in the theophoric name from Khor el-Aquiba of the late fifth or early sixth dynasty is a different matter, however, and may serve to relate Old Kingdom *Bt* directly to New Kingdom Bata. Lopez has read the inscription in which the name occurs as "the governor (?) of the nome of the dog, Khabaoubet [*ḫʿ b3w Bt*], has come with an army of 20,000 men in order to raze Wawat."[75] Because the "nome of the dog" is the seventeenth nome of Upper Egypt, the one in which Saka was located during the New Kingdom, this official's name, "the might of *Bt* appears in glory," suggests that *Bt* of the fifth/sixth dynasties had a cult place in the seventeenth Upper Egyptian nome and can therefore be related to Bata of the New Kingdom, who had temples in the same area.

Bt's name on the two fifth dynasty palettes and in the epithet of Wenis furnishes no information about the relationships or activities of this god. The examples from the palettes occur in lists designating funerary domains and read *irt Bt*, "the work of *Bt*."[76] The epithet of Wenis states merely *mr Bt ʿnḫ Wnis*, "*Bt* wishes that Wenis live,"[77] which should refer to the revival of the king in the Otherworld. Each example attests at least to *Bt*'s presence, and their sum can be interpreted as suggesting that he had some importance to the king at the time and was known outside the seventeenth Upper Egyptian nome.

The example of *Bt* from the Abusir Papyrus occurs in a list of persons cited in an account of brick deliveries brought to the temple storerooms.[78] If one can accept the questionable equation between the cow's skin determinative and the usual recumbent ram determinative, the *Bt* of this scribe is the same *Bt* of the other Old Kingdom documents. In this example, the name, *Bt ḫ*ʿ*(w)*, can be rendered as "*Bt* has appeared in glory" or "may *Bt* appear in glory," like many other theophoric names.[79] The use of *ḫ*ʿ*i*, "to appear in glory of a god or king (esp. of king's accession),"[80] with the name could ultimately be related to the accession of Bata in the d'Orbiney, but this idea is highly speculative.[81] It is also necessary to exercise caution in the use of this name because of the divergent determinative, especially since the largest number of examples employ the recumbent ram.[82]

The contexts of *Bt* in Niuserre's sanctuary of Re at Abu Gurob and *B*ꜣ*ty* in the festival hall of Osorkon II are pictorial rather than inscriptional and are distinguished by the commanding and authoritative position of the person labelled *Bt*/*B*ꜣ*ty*. In the sanctuary of Re, *Bt* is facing right, carrying a loop in his raised left hand, and is preceded by three smaller figures while overlooking at least three prostrate figures.[83] *B*ꜣ*ty* in the later festival hall faces left, this time with a double loop in his upraised right hand and overlooking twelve prostrate figures.[84] Both depictions occur in the larger setting of the royal Sed-fest, the festival of renewal, and the figures were assumed by F. W. F. von Bissing and Hermann Kees to be in the office of *bt*, or shepherd, on the basis of the loop they carry.[85] The lack of any divine determinative, the fact that the ram is standing rather than recumbent, and its appearance in primary position suggest that these examples do not properly belong with the others being considered.[86]

A further example associated with Bata dating from the Old Kingdom was proposed by Edouard Naville in 1906 when he suggested that *B*ꜣ*t* of *Pyr.* 1096b (fig. 20) was related to Bata. Naville identified *B*ꜣ*t* as the two-headed bull attested elsewhere in the Pyramid Texts as well as in some early tombs and on a few palettes.[87] Maspero espoused this suggestion in the fourth edition of *Les Contes populaires,*[88] but in 1912, Kurt Sethe asserted that *Bꜣt* was an old cult symbol of Hathor and thus Naville was incorrect.[89] More recently H. G. Fischer has shown conclusively that *Bꜣt* is a goddess whose home is the seventh Upper Egyptian nome and who was eventually assimilated to Hathor.[90] There is thus no relation between Bata and *Bꜣt.*

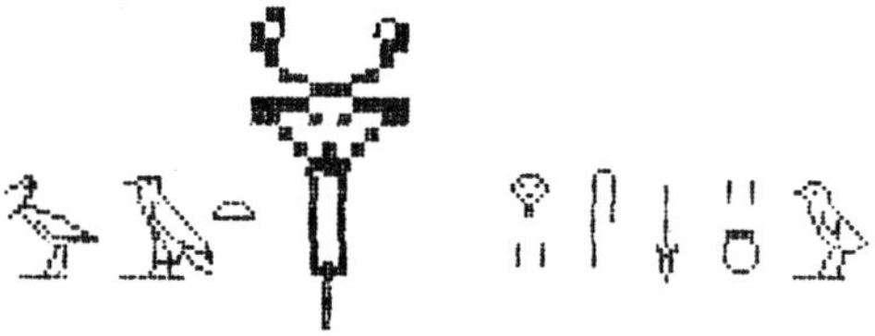

Fig. 20

The remaining Old Kingdom examples occur in the context of the "Shepherd Song." This song, or strophe, known for over a century, reads as follows:[91]

i Imnt iw B[t ṯn][92]
iw Bt m mw mm rmw
iw.f mdw.f ḥnʿ nʿr
  snbb.f ḥnʿ wḥʿṯ
Imnt iw Bt ṯn
  Bt n Imnt
O West, [where] is *B[t]*?
Bt is in the water among the fish.
He talks with the wels
  and greets the oxyrhynchos.
O West, where is *Bt*,
  Bt of the West?

It accompanies a scene of plowing and sowing in the tombs of *Sḫm-ʿnḫ-Ptḥ* and *Ty* and of threshing in the tomb of *Mrrw-kꜣ.* The contexts of the other examples are less precise: the block from the Jeremiah Cloister shows merely the upper parts of the figures,[93] and the examples from *Mḥw* and *Nbt* remain unpublished.[94] In *Ty*'s tomb, four drivers with whips follow seven sheep that are led on by a man feeding them. A sack carrier follows the group.[95] In the offering chapel of *Sḫm-ʿnḫ-Ptḥ*, two sowers precede a herd of long-horned sheep, the second sower coaxing the lead ram along. These are followed by four men each with a stave and the "shepherd's implement"[96] in one hand and a whip in the other. The threshing scene depicted in the mastaba of *Mrrw-kꜣ* shows one driver with a stave and a flail following a herd of long-horned sheep, preceded by a man holding a sheaf in his left hand, while his right is opened to the lead ewe whose head is down near it.[97] The only clear difference between this last and the two earlier examples is the presence of a specifically defined floor and a sheaf of the harvest. Because just the upper parts of the animals and people are extant on the block from the Jeremiah Cloister, either sowing or threshing is possible.[98]

The strophe itself has been subjected to much discussion over the years, from Maspero in 1888[99] to Kaplony in 1969 and 1970[100] and Hartwig Altenmüller in 1973,[101] in the course of which *Bt* is compared frequently with Bata of the d'Orbiney.[102]

First, the actual form of the name *Bt* demands attention. In it, the presence of the final *t* of *Bt* may be interpreted in three ways: as a sign of the feminine, as a defective writing of a nisbe, or as a radical. The suggestion that it indicates the feminine is quickly eliminated because there is no question that the person involved is not male, if for no other reason than the use of the male pronoun within the strophe itself, though it might also be surmised from the two cases in which the male determinative is employed. Maspero suggested that the *t* denotes a nisbe (*-ty*) related to the verb *bi*, "to hoe," and so *Bt*, or *BITI* as he transliterated it, is he who hoes.[103] Hans Goedicke also considered it to be a nisbe,[104] as did Kaplony,[105] who related *Bt* to his presumed **bꜣt*, "herd of holy sheep."[106] Other scholars have simply referred to *Bt* as a god,[107] apparently treating the final *t* as radical,[108] as seems appropriate.

The reading of the initial syllable of the name is problematical. In 1888 Maspero stated, "The recumbent ram is only the determinative of the syllable *BI, BA, BAI*."[109] This interpretation of the recumbent ram easily leads to relating *Bt* to *bꜣty*, in which the standing ram provides the initial syllable *bꜣ*. Thus it is not surprising to find that Adolf Erman used the standing ram as the determinative in place of the recumbent ram in his 1918 publication of the "Shepherd Song," stating at each point, even in his discussion, "The sign is actually a recumbent ram."[110] The next logical step soon followed: the *B3ty* of Niuserre and Osorkon II was defined as a shepherd[111] with reference to the "Shepherd Song," when von Bissing and Kees wrote of *B3ty*, "In him, we have to see the shepherd."[112]

In these examples, however, the use of the recumbent ram and the standing ram differs significantly. Not only do their respective placements in the word diverge, for one is found following two alphabetic signs and the other appears in initial position, followed by one or two alphabetic signs, but also the rams differ in their physical appearance, with one recumbent, having unarticulated hindquarters, and the other standing and fully articulated. The placement of the recumbent ram suggests that it functions as a determinative,[113] just as it does in the name of the mortuary god *Ḫrty* (fig. 21)[114] and in the name of *Ṯ3i-sp.f* (fig. 22), a little-known early god.[115] Both this position and its appearance in these widely varied names militates against its interpretation as a phonetic determinative.[116] Furthermore, the unarticulated hindquarters of this animal recall an idol or mummiform animal. Sethe noted this form and compared it to idol forms of the falcon from Hierakonpolis and of Sobek, along with those of an unnamed jackal god and the cow goddess *Ḥs3t-Ḥr* (fig. 23).[117] Raymond Weill, in a similar comparison, likened it to the "falcon-mummy" of *Ḫnty-irty* and felt it to be an idol which was indicative of the respective god's character, in this case a "dead god."[118] One then surmises that above and beyond its function as a determinative, its form implies that there is a nonliving, or mortuary, character to *Bt*,[119] even as H. K. Jacquet-Gordon states when referring to *Bt*, the mummified ram.[120]

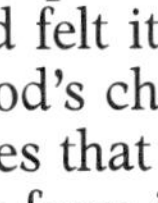

Fig. 21[121]

Fig. 22[122]

Fig. 23[123]

Although the standing ram, fully articulated and thus suggesting vitality, can function as a generic determinative,[124] it also appears in the primary position, often accompanied by a phonetic determinative: either the flaming *bꜣ*-pot or the *nḫnm*-vase for *ḫnm*. The latter is particularly frequent when the name of the god Khnum is written.[125] When this ram appears without any phonetic aid, the exact reading may be uncertain, as is commonly the case with the divine element of a theophoric name.[126] On the other hand, it often appears alone accompanied by an epithet which designates it as the Ram of Mendes.[127] The most common examples are *Bꜣ nb Ḏdt* and *Bꜣ ʿnpt*, clearly denoting the Ram of Mendes, and others include *Bꜣ mnḫ* and *Bꜣ ʿnḫ*,[128] each of which may occur without the *bꜣ*-pot.

Not only does the writing of *Bt* with the unarticulated, recumbent ram suggest a nonliving context for this god, but also the strophe itself conveys the same sense. When the text describes *Bt* as being "in the water, speaking with the fish," it suggests complete submersion, recalling the reference in "The Dispute between a Man and his Ba" in which the Ba tells the man that the fish speak to the dead who died on the riverbank.[129] Peter Seibert even proposes that the condition depicted in the "Shepherd Song" is reflected in the Papyrus d'Orbiney as the *pars pro toto* principle: the phallus thrown into the water by Bata and swallowed by the *nʿr*-fish reflects the whole body in the water, as expressed in the Old Kingdom song.[130]

When Alexandre Moret treated the "Shepherd Song" in the 1926 Frazer Lectures,[131] he related it to Osiris, suggesting that the "shepherd" (=*Bt*) is "the shepherd type, the god who handles the cross of the shepherd and the lash of the cowherd, Osiris-Anzti." He recalled that when the dismembered Osiris was thrown into the water by Seth, his parts were completely recovered except for his phallus, which was eaten by fish,[132] even as the phallus of "Bataou-Osiris" was eaten by the *nʿr*. Moret then concluded that the song was sung by the human shepherds to "the shepherd of the West . . . 'the god who presides in the West,' Osiris-Khentamenti,"[133] at the ritual moment of *ḫbs tꜣ*, "the plowing of the land," a conclusion that appears plausible in light of the activity of the accompanying scenes. Moret's association of *Bt* with Osiris, and therefore with the mortuary realm, as well as with agriculture, planting, and herding, is significant in view of Bata's association with planting, herding, and the mortuary realm in the d'Orbiney.

In a very brief reference to the strophe, Pierre Montet suggests that *Bt* of the West is Osiris and *Bt* in the water is Osiris dismembered,[134] while Kaplony's *Bt*, understood as *bꜣty*, functions as a kind of priestly shepherd, even as the king functions. The god *Bt* thus represents a kind of cult symbol and cult action related to the seed.[135]

H. Altenmüller began his study of the strophe by suggesting that the reading is *Btjj(.j)*, "my-what-belongs-to *Btj*," rather than simply *Bt*. For him, *Btjj(.j)* "can then be only the phallus of the god which was thrown into the water."[136] According to him, *Btjj(.j)* represents a mythological expression for seed, since the phallus is the seed organ as well as the sex organ for the ancients.[137] Thus, he considers *Bt* in the water as representing the sowing of seed, and he concludes that the "Shepherd Song" was sung to *Bt*, a chthonic deity, during the sowing to ensure the fruitfulness of the fields.[138]

In whatever way it is interpreted, the "Shepherd Song" and its accompanying scene clearly impart the sense that *Bt* is related to the mortuary realm as well as to the agricultural sphere of sowing and seed. The two are not so far apart when it is recalled that mortuary gods and seed implicitly carry dual meanings. The seed is "dead" and then becomes alive and grows, as is distinctly shown in the description of the corn divinity Neper in the Coffin Texts: "It is this Neper who lives after death."[139] In a similar manner, the mortuary gods represent death in this world at the same time as they provide the key to life in the other world, and so they are both feared and courted.

From the Ptolemaic period, the Edfu example of *Bt* shows a two-faced ram god as guardian of the right leg at Herakleopolis in the twentieth Upper Egyptian nome.[140] Both the location and the bifaced nature of the god militate against an identification of this god with the Old Kingdom *Bt* or with Bata of the seventeenth Upper Egyptian nome. It is possible, however, that it may be a late misinterpretation of the Old Kingdom *B3t ḥrwy.s snw* of *Pyr.* 1096b cited earlier.

The other Ptolemaic examples appear in the Papyrus Jumilhac, in which scholars have generally equated the Jumilhac's Seth-Bata with Bata of the d'Orbiney.[141] In fact, Altenmüller, who has stated that the d'Orbiney and the Jumilhac provide the main sources of the "Bata-Mythos,"[142] drew up the following diagrammatic comparison to show the similarities between the two:[143]

d'Orbiney 1, 1–8, 8[144]	Jumilhac III, 13–25
1. The brothers Anubis and Bata work harmoniously in field; Bata is sent to get seed and goes to Anubis's house.	Anubis and Seth live in enmity; Anubis goes out, and Seth uses this chance to go to Anubis's house.[145]
2. While Bata is holding the seed, the wife of Anubis seeks to seduce Bata to adultery, but Bata remains chaste.	Seth steals the *ḫt-m-ḫftyw*[146] of the god's body.
3. Anubis, on going home, learns of the "attempted adultery"[147] by Bata and pursues him because of it.	See 5.
4. Bata flees and gets safely to the other side of the water.[148]	Seth escapes and crosses a river.
5. See 3.	Anubis returns home and notes the loss of the *ḫt-m-ḫftyw* and follows him because of it.
6. Anubis and Bata stand on the banks of the water and clarify the situation.	Anubis reaches Seth, who has transformed himself into a bull and takes him captive (Jum. XX, 16).[149]
7. Bata cuts off his phallus and throws it to the wels for food.[150]	Anubis cuts off the phallus and testicles of the bull (Jum. XX, 16–17).
8. Bata departs from Anubis and goes into the Valley of the Cedar (sic).	Seth receives the name *Bt* and is kept captive in the slaughtering place (Jum. XX, 19–20) and afterwards is transferred to the embalming room, the *wꜥbt*.

Although some of the actions, such as the flight and the severing of the phallus, appear similar, the motivation and the actual execution are so utterly different that the identity of the two tales is difficult to sustain. For instance, Bata was sent by his brother Anubis to carry out the task of getting seed, which is a totally different concept from the assumption of Anubis's form by Seth in order to steal the *ḫt-m-ḫftyw:* the one is a beneficial, cooperative effort, while the other is an underhanded, disruptive act. There is no obvious comparison between the attempted seduction of Bata by his sister-in-law, in the face of which he remains chaste, and Seth's intentional theft of the *ḫt-m-ḫftyw,* save that both acts violate or transgress the boundaries of another's territory. Both flee, but the one flees from lies and calumny to save his life, while the other flees from the just results of an evil deed. The necessary clarification of the situation is effected between Bata and Anubis in the d'Orbiney, after which Bata voluntarily severs his phallus, apparently as further proof of his chastity and sincerity; in the Jumilhac, on the other hand, Anubis catches and binds Seth, now in the form of a bull, after which he cuts off the bull's phallus and testicles, presumably as punishment, finally imprisoning him. In the "Tale of Two Brothers," the emasculated Bata goes off freely to the life of a hunter in the Valley, having remained an admirable, honorable person, but in the Jumilhac, Seth remains imprisoned under the custody of Anubis.

The vignette that accompanies the more lengthy version in the Jumilhac (Jum. XX, 1–22) suggests a different tradition. One picture shows a ram god, nude with his arms outspread as a sign of weakness or submission and lacking sexual organs;[151] he is so posed on his socle that this fact is quite apparent, while above the neighboring socle is found a large phallus, which one assumes is that severed from the ram. According to the text (Jum. XX, 16–17; also III, 18–20), one would expect a castrated bull, not a castrated ram. The presence of the ram perhaps reflects a tradition of *Bt* as a ram different from *Bt* as a bull and is more reminiscent of the Old Kingdom *Bt* with the recumbent ram determinative than it is of the tale in the Jumilhac.[152] The Jumilhac depiction also recalls Bata's self-emasculation (d'Orb.7,9), especially since the phallus alone is represented in the neighboring picture.[153] The two pictures together certainly seem to deal with something other than the tale found in the accompanying text.

In the same vignette, on the other hand, the picture immediately to the right of the castrated ram clearly reflects the text it accompanies (Jum. XX,1–22), for it depicts a bull whose hind legs are bound with a rope held by Anubis. A figure of Osiris lies prone on the bull's back, and the bull is identified as *Bt*, that is to say Seth-*Bt*, of the story. Both this picture and the tale itself, in which Seth carries the *ḫt-m-ḫftyw* of Osiris on his back, can be seen reflected as early as the Pyramid Texts, in which Seth as a bull[154] is the carrier of the Osiris-king,[155] is bound,[156] and has lost his testicles,[157] the last in conflict with Horus. Thus this tale from the Papyrus Jumilhac relates a coherent story about the Seth bull[158] that reflects an old tradition dating at least to the late Old Kingdom, much as the "Contendings of Horus and Seth" found in the Chester Beatty I Papyrus from the twentieth dynasty reflects an age-old quarrel previously seen only in brief allusions. Furthermore, it is clear in the Pyramid Texts and in the Jumilhac that Seth as a bull carries Osiris as punishment, a fact which contrasts sharply with Bata's voluntary transformation into a magnificent bull which returns to Egypt carrying Anubis (d'Orb. 14,5–6). This latter is no punishment but rather culminates in a triumphal entry and celebration (d'Orb. 15,1–4). In the end, then, the only real relationship between the tales is that made by the late writer: As for *Bt*, he is Seth.

Finally, there is Bytes of the Manetho's dynasty of demigods, whom Franz Joseph Lauth identified with Bata, a suggestion which Maspero quickly espoused[159] and which Gardiner considered as a "brilliant and even probable, yet wholly unproven, conjecture."[160] More recently, Wolfgang Helck stated that in Bydis "perhaps is to be seen the god *B3t3*."[161] In view of the lack of orthographic and contextual evidence that might confirm or deny the idea, Helck's and Gardiner's restrained interest in the theory is most appropriate.

Anubis: His Home and Relationships

At the time of the discovery of Papyrus d'Orbiney, the ancient god Anubis, in contrast to Bata, was well known to Egyptologists. He was the major mortuary deity of the early dynasties and early Old Kingdom, with strong ties to royalty.[162] In addition, he had close relationships to both the seventeenth and the eighteenth nomes of Upper Egypt,[163] and, in fact, the ancient standard of the seventeenth nome depicts a recumbent jackal that resembles Anubis (fig. 24).[164] His relationship to these nomes derives from the fact that "his" town of Hardai (*Ḥr-dy*), which was located on the eastern bank of the Nile, belonged at different times to each of them.[165] From the time of the sixth dynasty, he was also associated with *Ḥwt-bnw*, a place that is possibly identical with the later town of *Ḥwt-rḏw* and with which he was also identified. Both localities were in the eighteenth nome.[166] In addition, a twelfth-dynasty inscription describes him as related to Henu (fig. 25), a town or area associated with Saka in the seventeenth nome (fig. 26). Finally, in Denderah during Graeco-Roman times, Anubis was identified as Lord of Saka (fig. 27).

Fig. 24

Fig. 25[167]

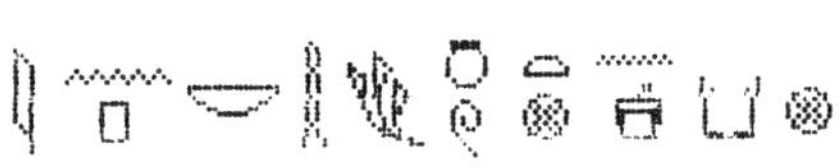

Fig. 26[168]

Fig. 27[169]

The location of Anubis at Hardai and Bata at Saka led Gardiner to suggest that the "Tale of Two Brothers" "seems to reflect a close relationship between the two towns, and from the fact that Bata was the younger brother of Anubis, we ought probably to deduce the further fact that at the time when the tale was composed, Sako (sic) was a place of less importance than Hardai, the nome home (⊓) of Anubis."[170] On the other hand, Anubis's twelfth-dynasty relation to Henu and the Jumilhac reference to Anubis, master of Henu of Saka, led Jacques Vandier to feel that the tale may explain the eclipse of Henu by Saka.[171] At the very least, their common geographical locale makes the identification of the two gods as brothers plausible.

In the d'Orbiney, however, the brothers' relationship was predicated on their common parentage, a fact emphasized by the narrator when he includes it as the first piece of information given about them.[172] It is especially significant because the only other pair of divine brothers with two parents in common was Osiris and Seth. They were the male children of Geb and Nut within the Heliopolitan Ennead.[173] There exists a still older stratum pairing Horus and Seth as brothers, which underlies the more explicit Osiris-Seth relationship,[174] but there are no parents cited for it. Unfortunately, and like the Horus and Seth duo, the parents of Anubis and Bata are not named, although, as mentioned above, New Kingdom sources name Bastet as the mother of Anubis.[175]

In addition to Bastet, the goddesses Hesat, Nephthys, and Isis also appear as the mother of Anubis. Of these, mention of the cow goddess Hesat dates as early as Pepi II's pyramid, where it refers to Anubis in his imiut form:[176]

> *msk3 n imy-wt*
> *ms n Ḥs3t* (*Pyr.* §2080*e*)
> the skin of the Imiut,
> born of Hesat.

Hesat was assimilated to Hathor at times, and she mothered the Apis and Mnevis bulls[177] as well as nursing the crown prince.[178]

Isis appears as Anubis's mother relatively late, with the only certain attestations dating to the Papyrus Jumilhac[179] and to a third-century CE demotic papyrus.[180] In addition, a possible reference comes from a twentieth/twenty-first-dynasty sarcophagus.[181] The examples from the Jumilhac relate Anubis to Isis by means of his equation with Horus, while the demotic example refers to Anubis as the eldest and first son of the king, also implying an equation with Horus.

Anubis's relation to Nephthys is likewise late, though not as late as that to Isis, for it is found in the Magical Papyrus Harris, dating from later Ramesside times:[182]

> *ink Inpw-Spd*
> *s3 Nbt-ḥwt* (Mag. P. Harris VII,7–8)
> I am Anubis-Sopdu,
> son of Nephthys.

This is the only known attestation to Anubis's relationship to Nephthys before Plutarch, who wrote that Anubis was born from an illicit union of Nephthys and Osiris.[183] Thus, it could hardly have been a prominent feature.

The Magical Papyrus Harris also reports that Anubis was the son of Re:

> *ink Inpw-Spd*
> *sꜣ Rꜥ* (VII,8)
> I am Anubis-Sopdu,
> son of Re,

a relationship which dates at least from the time of the Coffin Texts:

> *[Inpw] fdnw n msw Rꜥ*
> *rdy hꜣ.f m pt*
> *r smnḫ Wsir* (*CT* VII, 112*l–m*)
> [Anubis], the fourth of the Children of Re,
> was caused to go down from heaven
> to set Osiris in order.[184]

Other Middle Kingdom sources give Osiris as his father. For example, the "Hymn to Sobek" reads:[185]

> *nḏ.n.k it.k Wsir*
> *ip.n.k n.f ibw nṯrw*
> *ḫpr m Inp*
> You have protected your father Osiris;
> you have allotted the hearts of the gods to him,
> having become Anubis.[186]

This same relationship appears also in the Jumilhac from Ptolemaic times[187] and again later in Plutarch.[188] Both relationships invoke Anubis's mortuary function as regenerator of the deceased, and neither can be connected with a common father for the brothers because there is no known attestation of a father for Bata. Thus the question of common parents must remain open, especially with regard to the father.

Anubis, the Ancient Mortuary God

Anubis, or at least an Anubis-type canid and the imiut associated with him (i.e., the skin of a canid hung on a pole and missing the head with its threatening teeth and the two front paws with their destructive claws [fig. 28],[189]) is known from the first dynasty.[190] Thus he is one of the most ancient Egyptian gods. The recumbent canid that appears in the Old Kingdom mortuary offering formulas (fig. 29) prior to Osiris generally is taken to be Anubis, although it is not specifically named Anubis before the sixth dynasty[191] and may be subject to other possible interpretations.[192] Ursula Köhler observes, however, that basically such a question resolves into the recognition that a general mortuary deity in the form of a recumbent jackal underlies any proposed reading, and the general attribution of Anubis's name to the recumbent canid derives from comparison of the contexts and epithets of the two.[193] Furthermore, Anubis is the jackal to which the Egyptians attached specific functions and ascribed a definite nature based on their observations of jackal behavior: these animals went after the corpse, even when it was buried, eating the flesh and gnawing and scattering the bones.[194] They therefore endangered the deceased's life in the next world, where bodily integrity was deemed necessary. There was, however, a positive aspect to such behavior in that it represented a "second death," a neutralizing of the initial death, because in the incorporation of the deceased into the animal, he was revived and reborn for a new life.[195] The depiction of the jackal as imiut (fig. 28) symbolized this destruction-renewal cycle. The net result was the early and close relation of the Anubis-jackal with burial,[196] a relationship which persisted throughout Egyptian history.

Fig. 28[197]

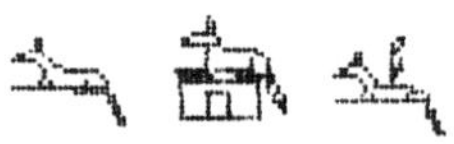

Fig. 29

From the earliest periods, Anubis, as Anubis-imiut and Anubis-jackal, was more strongly related to the king than to a specific local area.[198] The royal relationship was especially strong during the Old Kingdom and remained dominant in the Middle Kingdom.[199] In time, this exclusive connection with the king came to be shared with Osiris, with the effect that Anubis, an independent deity, was incorporated into the Osirian mythological cycle as the Horus-son who avenged his father, pursued his father's enemies, and was active in ritual acts on his father's behalf.[200] His ritual behavior was the strongest point of assimilation, for it represented the renewal of his father, the Osiris-king, who was revived through his actions. One further result of Anubis's regenerative function joined him to the rebirth of the sun, whose cyclical renewal was easily seen in Anubis, the "horizon animal," where a pair of Anubis-jackals represented the total cycle of renewal in swallowing and giving forth.[201]

In a rather interesting development beginning in the late eighteenth dynasty, skins different from that of the jackal, such as the cow skin and the panther skin, began to be used for the imiut. When the cow skin was used, it was interpreted as the skin of the heavenly goddess in cow form, the goddess who swallowed the sun in the evening and gave birth to it the following morning.[202]

The king sought to be identified with the Anubis-jackal in order to gain regeneration and to obtain the capabilities of the god, even if only temporarily.[203] Thus, the mortuary literature contains frequent references to the deceased or to parts of him as Anubis, such as identifying the king's face, shape, and other body parts with the corresponding parts of Anubis:[204]

ḥr.k m Inpw (*Pyr.* §135*b*)
your face is (that) of Anubis,
ḥr.k m s3b Inp (*CT* VI, 103*g*)
your face is (that) of the jackal of Anubis,
r.k m Inp (*CT* III, 358*d*)
your mouth is (that) of Anubis,
spty.i m Inp (*BD* Ch. 42)[205]
my lips are (those) of Anubis,

or stating that the king assumes his name:

ip ibw.sn m rn.k pw n Inp ip ibw (*Pyr.* §1287*a*)
claim their hearts in your name of Anubis, the claimer of hearts.

> *ip.sn ṯw m rn.k pw n Inp* (*Pyr.* §1537*a*)[206]
> they recognize you in this your name of Anubis,
> *ẖw.sn rpw.k m rn.k pw n Inp* (*CT* I 303*h*–304*a*)
> they prevent you from rotting in this your name of Anubis.

When the king assumes the shape of Anubis, he can go to the horizon and have power:[207]

> *pr N*[208] *pn iṯt.f qmꜣ n Inp*
> *N pn sps pr m ꜣẖt.f*
> *N pn nwn pr m sḫm.f* (*CT* VI, 98*c*–99*b*)
> this N will go out and seize the form of Anubis;
> this N is one who is tousled(?),
>   who went forth to his horizon;
> this N is one who is disheveled,
>   who went forth with his sceptre.

Many texts command the king to act as Anubis:

> *ʿḫʿ.k m Inp* (*Pyr.* §793*c*)
> Arise as Anubis;
> *sꜣḫ ṯw N Ḏḥwty is Inp is sr ḏꜣḏꜣt* (*Pyr.* §1713*b*–*c*)
> Glorify yourself like Thoth and like Anubis, magistrate of the tribunal;
> *hꜣ RN pw*
>   *ʿḫʿ ḥms ḫnty ib.k*
>   *Inp is ḫnty imntyw* (*Pyr.* §2198*a*–*b*)
> Ho king,
>   rise up and sit down as you wish,
>   like Anubis, head of the Westerners.

In fact, the stated purpose of Spell 546 in the Coffin Texts is to enable the deceased to become Anubis:

> *[ḪP]R M INP*
> *ink [. . .] [Ḥ]sꜣt*
> *ink ḥr wʿrt wrt*
> *[in]k nb swnw*
> *ink Inp nb sḫm m ꜣbḏw [. . .]*
> *[ink] Inp nb tꜣ ḏsr wr*
> *šsp.i sʿḥ.i*
>   *šsp.i smsw sʿḥ.f* (*CT* VI, 142*g*–*o*)

[TO BECOME] ANUBIS:
I am [. . .] Hesat,
I am at the foot of the Great Lady,
[I am] Lord of the Tower,
I am Anubis, Lord of the Scepter in Abydos, [. . .]
[I am] Anubis, Lord of the Sacred Land, the Great One,
and I assume my dignity,
I assume the eldership of its rank.

At the point where the king assumes the form of Anubis, he is as newborn, which also accounts for him as the young *inpw* jackal and explains the following Middle Kingdom text:

rs rs N pn
rs Wsir rs Inp
tp mni.f (*CT* I, 282*a–b*)
Awake, awake, this N,
awake Osiris, awake Anubis (i.e., newborn king),
upon his death.

The Mortuary Role of Anubis

From very early times, Anubis's function as the regenerator of the dead led to his active role as the mortuary functionary, the Lord of the Burial:[209]

Inp pw N pn nb qrst (*CT* VI, 296*c*)
N is Anubis, Lord of the Burial.

The mortuary offering formulas, his epithets, and his acts as described in the mortuary literature clearly attest to this role. For instance, the Old Kingdom mortuary offering formulas frequently ask him for a *qrst nfr*, "a good burial," often in the *smyt imntt*, "the western desert," and for *prt-ḫrw*, "invocation offerings," and include the request that the dead be permitted to:

iw m nb im3ḫ r imntt
come as Lord of the Glorified to the West.[210]

This last shows up only in the fourth dynasty, but the bid for proper offerings and a good burial occurs in the offering formulas of all periods, appearing also in the corpus of the Pyramid Texts,[211] the Coffin Texts,[212] and the Book of the Dead.[213]

The major epithets applied to Anubis emphasize this role by describing him as being "over" or "head of" the funerary realm or a part of it. In the early periods, he bore four major epithets: *ḫnty imntyw*, "the one who is over the Westerners" (i.e., the dead); *ḫnty tꜣ ḏsr*, "the one who is over the sacred land"; *ḫnty sḥ nṯr*, "the one who is over the divine booth"; and *tpy ḏw.f*, "the one who is on his mountain."[214] The latter three persisted until Graeco-Roman times.[215] Of these three, Köhler considers *ḫnty tꜣ ḏsr*, "the one who is over the sacred land," to be the oldest,[216] an epithet which began to appear as *nb tꜣ ḏsr*, "lord of the sacred land," by the fifth dynasty. The *tꜣ ḏsr*, literally "the land set apart,"[217] has been variously defined as Abydos, the name of a cemetery, and the name of the mortuary realm.[218] According to Gardiner, it meant a place from which one "kept aloof,"[219] while in a subsequent discussion, Helck defined it as the "forbidden land," the area of graves.[220] Both Jurgen Settgast[221] and Altenmüller[222] associated this area with different rituals belonging to the necropolis, and Köhler considered the area as having a special significance for the regeneration of the deceased, actually for the dead king in the older texts.[223] For her, the aura of the *tꜣ ḏsr* was such as to define it as a place to which "neither man nor god can draw near."[224]

The epithet *ḫnty sḥ nṯr*, "the one who is over the god's booth," regularly appears in the oldest offering formulas[225] as well as in the Pyramid Texts.[226] H. Altenmüller defines the *sḥ nṯr* as a place that served as a kind of entry hall to the area of the necropolis. It was distinguished by its *ẖkr* frieze and was located in the valley temple. As the place in which the mummy was briefly laid out, the *sḥ nṯr* functioned as the goal, at least in the later periods, for the first or land part of the "Saite" journey, and it was from this location that the mummy departed on the second part of the journey by boat to the place in the temple mythologized as "Sais."[227] It was also the place in which the embalming ritual occurred.[228]

The third persistent epithet, *tpy ḏw.f*, "the one who is on his mountain," is found only once in the Pyramid Texts,[229] but occurs quite frequently in the private mastabas of the Old Kingdom[230] and also in great numbers on Middle Kingdom stelae from Abydos.[231] It is felt to indicate Anubis's lordship over the necropolis areas in general, areas which are located on non-agricultural lands composed of desert fringe between the edge of the valley and the beginning of the "gebel,"[232] or mountains where canidae and other predatory animals and birds live.[233]

Although each of these epithets indicates Anubis's lordship in the mortuary areas,[234] the texts of the mortuary literature reveal the various functions which Anubis performed in these areas, especially in the *tꜣ ḏsr* and *sḥ nṯr:* he washed entrails,[235] placed his hands on the deceased,[236] embalmed and wrapped him or her,[237] straightened and knit the deceased together,[238] and caused his or her odor to be sweet.[239] All of these functions describe his embalming role[240] and form part of the embalming ritual for which he served as the master of ceremonies.[241] His designation as *ḥry sštꜣ*, "the one who is over the secrets," often written with the sign showing him seated on a chest,[242] also attests to his embalming role. Presumably the chest contains his secrets or the tools of his trade, and therefore it can also be seen as a means of regeneration in much the same fashion as the imiut.

He appears in his role of regenerator as he calls the king forth:

> *pr.k ḥr ḫrw Inp* (*Pyr.* §796*c*)
> You come forth at the voice of Anubis,

and as he commands Osiris (the deceased):

> *rs t(w) n ʿnḫ* (*CT* I, 221*d*)
> Awake to life.

In another text, the deceased is instructed:

> *rs t(w) n ʿnḫ*
> *n mt.k*
> . . .
> *iw n.k ʿnḫ ḫr Inp(w)* (*CT* I, 237*c–f*)
> Awake to life;
> you are not dead;
> . . .
> you will have life from Anubis,[243]

and Anubis is even said to form the deceased so that he may travel about daily:

> *Wsir N*
> *qd.k pw ipn* (sic)
> *wn.k im.f tp t3*
> *ʿnḫ.ti*
> *nmnm.k hrw nb* (*CT* VI, 414*u–v*)
> Osiris N
> Anubis[244] indeed forms you
> so that you may be on earth through him,
> you being alive,
> that you may travel about every day.

The gathering and joining of the god's parts, that is, Osiris's parts, was another of Anubis's functions, both in his embalming and his regenerating roles, but it was not made explicit before the time of the Jumilhac. The Jumilhac mentions Anubis's departure to collect the parts of the god in three places,[245] and one of the vignettes depicts the imiut with the different parts of the body within it.[246] In fact, Anubis's pursuit of Seth after he stole the *ḫt-m-ḫftyw*[247] can also be considered as a seeking and finding of Osiris's parts.

The ancient imiut[248] is where the reconstitution and regeneration of the deceased took place, but there are no early reports that it was Anubis who physically went out to get the parts that were regenerated in it. Rather, these earlier documents tell of seeking and gathering by Isis, Nephthys, Nut,[249] and occasionally Horus.[250] The explicitness of the Jumilhac about Anubis's search may derive from its concern with Anubis, but it may also draw on an old tradition, perhaps implicit in the imiut itself.

Part of the god's role of embalming and regeneration involved purification which occurred in the *sḥ nṯr*,[251] and if Anubis himself did not do it, he commanded it:

> *wḏ.n Inp ḫnty sḥ nṯr*
> *wʿb.t.k m 8.k nmst*
> *8 ʿ3bt prt m ʿḥ (sḥ) nṯr* (*Pyr.* §2012*b–c*)
> Anubis who is before the god's booth has commanded
> that you be purified with your eight *nmst*-jars
> and eight *ʿ3bt*-jars which come forth
> from the god's temple.

His daughter *Qbḥwt* also participated:

> *gm RN pn Qbḥwt s3t Inp*
> *ḫsft im.f ḥnʿ 4.s iptw nmst*
> *sqbḥ(w).s ḥ3ty n nṯr ʿ3 im hrw.f n rs*
> *sqbḥ.s ni ḥ3ty n RN pn im n ʿnḫ*
> (*Pyr.* §§1180*b*–1181*a*)[252]
> This king has found *Qbḥwt*, the daughter of Anubis,
> who met him with these four *nmst*-jars of hers
> with which she purified the heart of the great god
> in his day of awakening,
> and she purifies therewith the heart of this king for
> life.

Purification also formed part of the Ritual of the Opening of the Mouth.[253] The master of ceremonies in this ritual was the *sm*-priest, originally the oldest son of the king and normally distinct from Anubis, although in the Jumilhac, Anubis himself acted as *sm*-priest for this ritual.[254] As *sm*-priest, this son carried out the mortuary cult for his father the king and represented him in relation to the gods, acting as the intermediary between the king and the Otherworld.[255] Although the formal identification of the *sm*-priest with Anubis appears late, the Egyptians perceived Anubis as participating in the Opening of the Mouth as early as the New Kingdom. A number of paintings from this period depict Anubis either presenting the mummy of the deceased in an upright position for the Opening of the Mouth[256] or bending over the supine mummy with the *nw3*-tool in his hand actually performing the Opening of the Mouth himself.[257] The *nw3*, a word which is used to designate tools of many types[258] and which is called the *nw3-Inp* in some cases, was probably brought in from the embalming ritual for use in Scene 26 of the Ritual of the Opening of the Mouth,[259] thus connecting the two rituals and making possible the relation of their respective masters of ceremonies, Anubis and the *sm*-priest.

The Negative Aspects of Anubis

Although the positive aspect of Anubis, that is, his regenerative powers, had become dominant as early as the beginning of the historical period,[260] his negative side was never completely eclipsed and can be detected in texts and pictures throughout Egyptian history, albeit expressed discreetly or transferred to other gods.[261] The graphic depiction of the imiut, the skin of the jackal, can also be found in all periods.[262] Although it symbolized regeneration, its form also recalled the negative side of the god in what it was missing, for the head with its threatening teeth was cut off, as were the two paws with their destructive claws; in other words, the dangerous parts were eliminated (fig. 28).[263]

Anubis's persistent role as embalmer also evoked his dangerous side, for in it he was related to a damaging of the corpse, reminiscent of the gnawing and scattering of flesh and bones typical of the canid. Expressions referring to his relationship to this type of activity include *ḫnty ꜣmm*,[264] "to pound or pack with the fist," *rḫs m dm.wt...m-bꜣḥ Inpw*,[265] "to slaughter with knives before Anubis," *mi r.k r.k mds ḫnt Inpw*,[266] "Come before Anubis, O sharp-knived one." Other references reflect his sharp teeth and nails, clearly delineating the danger that Anubis posed to the deceased.[267] Anubis had a particularly important relationship with knives, which can be seen in his position as the gatewatcher, who is equipped with a knife in numerous New Kingdom depictions.[268] Not only is the knife a necessary tool for the embalmer as he eviscerates the corpse, but it also can be perceived as symbolic of the cutting and scratching claws.

Numerous texts reflect the memory of the canid eating (swallowing) the corpse when they report that Anubis swallowed his father. The fifth hour of the *Book of Gates* states:

> *Inpw sʿm.f it.f*[269]
> Anubis swallowed his father,

and a pillar in the sarcophagus hall of the tomb of Ramesses VI reads:[270]

> *Inp ḫnty imntt*
> *nṯr ʿꜣ*
> *sʿmw it.f Wsir*
> Anubis, head of the West,
> great god
> who swallowed his father Osiris.

Köhler has outlined how this last text encompasses the various roles of Anubis:[271]

1. his role as eater—*sʿmw NN*
2. Lord of Burial—*ḫnty imntt*
3. regenerator of Osiris—*ḫnty imntt . . . sʿmw . . . Wsir*
4. son of Osiris—*ḫnty imntt . . . sʿmw . . . it.f Wsir*

A gloss to Spell 335 of the Coffin Texts concerns the hound-faced one who swallows myriads, apparently referring to Anubis, although Köhler notes that it could be Seth.[272]

The possibility of seeing the hound-faced as Seth demonstrates that over time there occurred a displacement of Anubis's negative aspects onto other gods. In the case of Seth, it corresponds to the mythology of the Osirian story in which Seth was responsible for Osiris's death[273] and, at the same time, it reflects an emphasis on Anubis's positive role. Seth was not the only god who was given the negative side, for other canid gods, like those mentioned in the Jumilhac,[274] and Babi,[275] among other gods, also assumed his negative features. In the Book of Caverns even the Ennead took on jackal form in order to swallow corruption.[276]

The ambiguous picture of Anubis found in this examination is precisely the perception of him which the tale's audience would have brought. One might expect, too, that in some way Anubis's behavior within the narrative will reflect the "outside" portrait—as it does. It is less easy to think that the pictures given of Bata from sources external to the tale will be seen within the narrative because of the less decisive and rather mixed nature of the materials available. Furthermore, the nineteenth-dynasty audience was probably not as intimately familiar with him as with the very prominent Anubis. Nevertheless, the mortuary sense about the early form of *Bt,* as demonstrated both iconographically in the mummiform determinative in the early forms of his name and verbally in the "Shepherd Song" suggest that he too will act within the parameters of his traditional form. Between the two, they truly make a pair: Anubis represents death and new life and Bata portrays the reborn king, revived by the traditional mortuary deity.

3
Rural Egypt

The Brothers at Home

After introducing the brothers, the narrator describes the initial setting of the tale. Scholars generally have viewed it as a description of rural Ramesside Egypt,[1] but in fact it is timeless in terms of ancient Egyptian civilization, depicting a life revolving about herding and agriculture and governed by the rise and fall of the Nile. The family was composed of a husband (Anubis) and wife (unnamed) with the husband's younger brother (Bata) as a virtual son. The narrator interjects the unusual as he describes Bata:

> *istw pꜣy.f sn šriw m ꜥḥ ꜣwty nfr*
> *nn wn qdw.f m tꜣḏr.f*
> *is wn pḥty n nṯr im.f* (d'Orb. 1,3–4)
> Now, his younger brother was a fine young man,
> one without equal in the whole land;
> indeed, the strength of a god was in him.

The noun *pḥty* means both divine creative power and male power in the sexual sense,[2] expressed as a dual form which Wolfhart Westendorf suggests derives from either the loins or the testicles.[3] The epithet *ꜥꜣ pḥty,* "great of power/strength" is a common one for different gods. For example, Seth,[4] Ptah,[5] the Nile,[6] Horus,[7] and the king[8] all bear it.[9] Thus, the term immediately relates Bata to the divine world,[10] serving to emphasize the use of the divine determinative with his name.

Bata's customary occupation was that of cattle herding and shepherding, one that occupied an important place in the agricultural economy of Egypt.[11] His care for his charges even extended to sleeping with them in the stable,[12] and his relationship to them was also unusual, for:

mtw.f thm n3y.f i3wt
  r dit wnmw n sḫwt
iw.f šmt m-s3 n3y.f i3wt
iw.sn dd n.f
  nfr p 3 sty-smw n st ḥmnt
mtw.f sdm p3 dd.sn nb
mtw.f ḥr it3yw r t 3 st nfrt
  n sty-smw nty st i3bw.sn
iw n3 i3wt nty r ḥ3t.f ḥr ḫprw nfr r iqr iqr
  qb.sn msw.sn r iqr iqr (d'Orb. 1,9–2,2)
he drove his cattle
  to allow them to eat in the fields;
he used to go behind his cattle,
and they used to say to him,
  "The grass is good in such-and-such place";
he heard all that they said,
and he would take them to the good place
  with the herbage which they desired;
and the cattle which were before him became very beautiful,
  and they multiplied their offspring many times over.

The speaking by the cattle, which is usually described as a folk motif,[13] actually appears in ancient Egyptian tradition within the worlds of the divine and the dead. It derives naturally from the friendly relations the Egyptian had with his animals, which one can see depicted in the pictures from the Old Kingdom tombs[14] such as those discussed in relation to the "Shepherd Song." Furthermore, there was the sense that man was not lord over the animal since the animal has a power that man cannot control. The Egyptians thus perceived the animal as a manifestation of the numinous.[15] Other examples of speaking animals are found in mortuary literature, both in lamentations and in the mortuary texts proper, in royal inscriptions, and in other tales like the "Doomed Prince."[16] Typical of the lamentations is the following one from the nineteenth dynasty:[17]

iw.tw r ḏd <n> *nꜣ n mnmnt*
itḥw m wrd ibw.tn
ḏd.tn ir n nꜣ[18] *n mnmnt*
iw.n r itḥw wr sp.sn
iw.n ẖr pꜣ ḥsy
itḥw.tn di.t n st (sic) *ḥr nmt.t*
r br[19] *n inr*
r tꜣ pn ẖꜣryr (ẖrr)[20] *im.f*
dmi pn r nḥḥ
It shall be said to these cattle,
"Pull, do not let your heart tire."
Said by the cattle,
"We will pull very much
as we carry this praised one."
"You pull and place him on the way
to the area(?) of stones,
to this land in which are the dead(?),
this place of eternity."

The Coffin Texts[21] and the Book of the Dead[22] also contain examples of animals who speak, and one finds a truly fine example in the speech of Hathor to Hatshepsut in which the Hathor cow acclaims the queen as her daughter.[23] Without exception, all examples occur in relation to gods, the deceased, or royalty, and thus this motif places Bata in the realm of gods and kings.

The description of the beauty and fertility of the cattle as a result of Bata's care recalls the biblical narrative of Jacob enjoying a similar success with Laban's flocks in Genesis 30:29 and 31:30,[24] and carries the inference of special, perhaps divine, powers—at least powers blessed by the gods. In fact, Brunner stated: "Bata is clearly a divinity in the d'Orbiney (2,1), who cares for the fertility of his herds."[25]

The emphasis on Bata's extraordinary powers as shepherd immediately relates him to the ideology of kingship, because from the Middle Kingdom on, the king was perceived as the shepherd par excellence. It was the king's responsibility to care for the *ʿwt nt nṯr*, "the cattle of the god," a phrase used in the "Instruction for Merikare" to describe the people.[26] This document, generally related to the First Intermediate Period, outlined the god's concern for his people, showing how the king was responsible for enacting the god's wishes regarding them.[27] The same kind of phrase appears in the Westcar Papyrus in Djedi's response to the king's request to have a man cut into pieces so the magician could demonstrate his powers of restoration:

> *mk n wḏ.tw irt mnt iry*
> *n tꜣ ʿwt špst* (West. 8,17)
> Behold, it is forbidden to do the like
> to the noble small cattle.

Generally, however, the kings of the Middle Kingdom took seriously their responsibilities as the divinely appointed shepherd of the people. For example, in the Berlin Leather Roll, 1,6,[28] Sesostris I says:

> *rdi.n.f wi r mniw tꜣ pn*
> *rḫ.n.f sꜣq<.i> n.f sw*
> he (Harakhti[29]) made me shepherd of this land,
> for he knew <I> would pull it together for him.

Later, the fifth hymn of Sesostris III[30] describes the king as:

> *mniw.n rḫ snfy* (3,14)
> our shepherd who knows how to give breath.

In the New Kingdom, the shepherd nature of the king, who was now perceived as elected to his position by the god,[31] was emphasized by his frequent depiction with the crook and the flail, symbols of the shepherd, and his epithets *rs-tp,*"watchful," and *qni,* "strong," words commonly used to describe shepherds.[32] For instance, Tuthmosis I was the *nr Kmt,* "shepherd (protector) of Egypt" (*Urk.* IV, 268, 16), and Hatshepsut was

> *sḫʿt.n Imn ḏs.f ḥr nst.f*
> *m iwnw šmʿw*
> *stp<t>.n.f r mniw Kmt*
> *r nryt pʿt rḫyt* (*Urk.* IV, 361,16–362,1)

the one whom Amun himself placed on his throne
in Thebes,
whom he chose for shepherd of Egypt
to protect the patricians and the common folk.

Amenhotep II reports:

rdi.n.f wi r mniw tꜣ pn (*Urk.* IV,1327,1)
he (Amun) made me shepherd of the land,

while an inscription from Karnak describes Amenhotep III as:

mniw nfr
rs-tp n ḥr nbw (*Urk.* IV,1723,19)
the good shepherd,
the watcher of everyone.

Similarly, Ramesses II is eulogized as:

nṯr nfr
Rʿ n tꜣ
Tm ʿnḫ n Kmt
mniw nfr n rḫyt
wbn.f ʿnḫ ib.sn[33]
good god,
sun god of the land,
living Atum of Egypt,
good shepherd of the people;
when he appears, their heart lives.

The descriptions provided by the opening of this narrative thus relate Bata to the attributes of the royal ideology, setting the scene for all subsequent events. Certainly the audience would be well aware of these implications in their understanding of the tale to come.

Attempted Seduction

The attempted seduction of Bata by Anubis's wife is the first major event of the tale and the one for which it is best known,[34] largely because of its Biblical parallel in Genesis 39:6–18.[35] It is what gets the story moving, breaking the initial idyllic situation. The seduction episode begins with Bata's encounter with Anubis's wife as her hair was being done, when he returned to the house for seed. Hair was considered to be a sexual lure in ancient Egypt, and the elaborate coiffure or well-cared-for wig was made part of the toilette of a woman "who expects to make love,"[36] as is attested by a Beni Hasan depiction of a woman with a "great wig" who is involved in intercourse.[37] In fact, an elaborate hairdo served as the hallmark for Hathor, the goddess of love, who bore the epithet *ḥnskyt,* "the one with the braided hair."[38] Further attestation of hair as sexually attractive occurs in the love songs,[39] as might be expected, and also in the mortuary literature. Spell 154 of the Coffin Texts speaks of a woman with braided hair, *st-ḥmt ḥnsktt,* who serves as a trap[40] for a dangerous demon. This imagery recalls the love poems in which the beloved's hair is perceived as a lure.[41] Thus, the dressing of hair serves as a logical introduction to an episode that involves a seduction attempt.[42] Furthermore, when the events are recounted to Anubis by his wife in the evening, not only the words exchanged but also the facts of the hair are altered in the retelling: where initially someone else was attending the wife's hair, in the later version Bata is said to have told her to *wnḫw p3y.ṯ nbd* (d'Orb. 5,2), "loosen (or put on) your hair or wig,"[43] depending on the translator's interpretation of the verb. Later in the tale, the odor of a lock of hair served as the lure of Bata's wife for the king.

Anubis's wife was attracted to Bata because of his sexual strength, *pḥty,* and his physical strength, *ṯnr,* an attraction made clear in her response to his load of sacks, three of emmer and two of barley:

wn pḥty ꜥ3 m.k
ḫr twi ḥr ptr
  n3y.k tnr (sic) *m mnt* (d'Orb. 3,5–6)
Great strength is in you;
Behold I see
  your great strength every day.

The narrator of the tale then notes:

iw ib.st [r] rḫ.f
  m rḫ n ꜥḥ3wty (d'Orb. 3,6)
she desired to know him
  as to know a young man.

and so she proposed:

> *my iry.n n.n wnwt sḏr.wn* (d'Orb. 3,7)
> Come, let us spend an hour lying together,

even trying to tempt him with the promise of new clothes. Bata's angry rebuff frightened her and led to his downfall because, in her fear, she reversed the incident in relating it to Anubis. This fear derived from the well-known consequences of adultery, the best-known example of which occurs in the second tale of the Westcar Papyrus, dating from the late Middle Kingdom, and tells of the adulterous activity of the wife of Webaoner with a townsman. Enamored of the tradesman, the woman had sent him a chest of clothes (West. 2,1), after which he had returned with the wife's servant and, having determined the availability of a lake house, said to her:

> *mtn ir.n ꜣt im.s* (West. 2,6)[44]
> Come, let us spend a while in it.

The parallels to the d'Orbiney are obvious, even though the words in the Westcar are spoken by the man. The end result differs in the Westcar, however, for the adultery is carried out, and both the man and the woman pay with their lives.[45] Other punishments for adultery cited in various nonliterary texts from the New Kingdom include being cursed, deported, and mutilated.[46] Thus, it is clear that the reversal by Anubis's wife was a defensive act. She was out to save her skin in a society that had looked on behavior such as hers with disfavor for over a thousand years.[47]

The wife's attempt at seduction recalls an apparent seduction attempt that appears in pBerlin 3024, the "Story of the Herdsman."[48] This tale, which lacks a beginning and an end and probably dates from the twelfth dynasty,[49] tells of a shepherd to whom appears a fearful woman (line 3), either part animal and part human[50] or a woman with strange coloration,[51] who is later referred to as a goddess (line 23). Her appearance disturbs the shepherd to the extent that he plans to leave his otherwise secure pasture area on the day following this encounter. Before he departs, however, the woman reappears, naked and with mussed hair. At this point the story breaks off, leaving its exact theme unclear, although one might surmise that it was attempted seduction from the fact that the shepherd says he will not do what she said (line 6). It was this statement which Hermann cited for his conclusion that the goddess had attempted to seduce the shepherd,[52] a conclusion which her second appearance (naked and with mussed hair) seems to confirm. Hermann also stated that the goddess was "obviously Hathor herself,"[53] and certainly the seductive behavior of the goddess in this case resembles that of Hathor in other contexts.[54] Goedicke also has concluded that the goddess, who takes the initiative in inviting the man to a tête-à-tête,[55] is Hathor. He derived his opinion from the epithets used of the female in the tale, *wsr.t* (line 21) and *nb.t t3wy* (line 22), and her double-natured appearance of animal and enchantress, each characteristic of Hathor.[56]

It is doubtful, however, that the attempted seduction in the "Story of the Herdsman" and that of the d'Orbiney are related to each other.[57] The one tells of the encounter of a man with a goddess,[58] while the other is a meeting of in-laws of the same corporeal nature. In addition, the "Story of the Herdsman" presents elaborate descriptions of the goddess who is attempting to seduce the shepherd, but the d'Orbiney speaks only of the attractiveness of Bata, saying virtually nothing of the wife. The latter even lacks a name, a noteworthy feature considering the explicit and meaningful names borne by the brothers. Nevertheless, it is quite possible that Anubis's wife represents a form of Hathor, considering the emphasis on her hair, a significant feature of the goddess, and on her seductive behavior, recalling Hathor's behavior towards the sulking Pre in the "Contendings of Horus and Seth." Furthermore, one also finds that Hathor, Mistress of Gebelein, and Anubis, Lord of the Dawning Land, are closely connected during the reign of Merneptah,[59] a particularly significant fact given the date of the d'Orbiney as late in his reign.

Reactions of the Brothers

Bata's immediate reaction to the attempted seduction was one of great anger, as was that of Anubis at his wife's report. Each brother

ḥr ḫprw mi ꜣbw šmꜥt (d'Orb. 3,8; 5,4–5)
became like an Upper Egyptian leopard.

The panther or leopard skin, *bꜣ šmꜥ* [60] or *ꜣbwy/ꜣbw šmꜥ*, [61] was characteristically worn both by the crown prince and by the *sm*-priest,[62] the latter originally the eldest son,[63] the new Horus, who attended his deceased father the king for his final mortuary rites. Wolfhart Westendorf relates this garb to the old leopard goddess *Mfdt,* who was probably an Upper Egyptian leopard and who functioned as the royal protector warding off and annihilating the king's enemies. She symbolized his latent power as she accompanied and protected him.[64] Thus, when the brothers are so described, each may be seen in relation to the kingship, anticipating the end of the tale, when each in turn becomes king. In addition, Anubis's wrath and his pursuit of Bata, spear in hand, evokes the negative aspect of his mortuary nature.

In his flight before his brother's wrath, Bata successfully petitioned the sun god Pre-Harakhty for aid. The expression of this type of personal piety was a common theme during the New Kingdom, as is attested by numerous ostraca from the early eighteenth dynasty[65] and by stelae from the Amarna and Ramesside periods.[66] It is also found in many prayers and hymns dating to the same periods.[67] Pre's response to Bata, the placing of a river filled with crocodiles between the two brothers, not only protected the hero but also presented the Egyptian audience with the mixed imagery of the crocodile, not unlike the mixed imagery of Anubis. Generally for the Egyptian, the crocodile belonged to the evil of this world.[68] This sense is clearly illustrated in the following phrase from the "Admonitions of Ipuwer":

iw ms msḥw [. . .] n iṯtt.n.sn
šm n.sn rmṯ ḏs iry[69] (Adm. 2,12)
Lo, the crocodiles [gorge] on their catch,
for men go to them of their own accord,

and when the crocodile acted as the instrument of death in the adultery episode from the Westcar Papyrus. The crocodile was also a menace in the mortuary world, where it was viewed as a threat to the unjustified sinner.[70] In fact, chapters 31 and 32 of the Book of the Dead are spells for driving off the threatening crocodile.

In the mythical world, the crocodile was perceived mostly as an enemy, especially when seen as a son or companion of Seth,[71] and it also represented the lower hemisphere as the reptile of the Underworld. In this guise, it swallowed the sun each evening and gave it forth each morning, and thus it was an incorporation of darkness.[72] From this behavior, however, it also gained a positive aspect, which it likewise had when Horus, in the form of a crocodile, collected Osiris's parts.[73] In the "Tale of Two Brothers," it is the dangerous side which predominates, but in the danger there is benefit as well: the crocodile-infested water prevents Bata from being killed by his brother.

Bata Confronts Anubis

Bata's words to Anubis from across the river reflect traditional Egyptian values, and his question to his brother illustrates judicial procedure:

> *iḫ pꜣy.k iyt m-sꜣ.i*
> *r ḫdbw m grg*
> *iw nn sḏm.k r.i ḥr mdt* (d'Orb. 7,4)
> What is your coming after me
> to kill (me) wrongfully,
> not having listened to me on the matter?

Théodoridès states that *m grg,* "wrongfully," the antonym of *m mꜣꜥt,* "in truth," implies the right to defense, with the sense that a different judgement would have ensued had he been heard. It places the passage in a climate of justice, of judging, *wpi,* between *p ꜣ mꜣꜥty,* "the innocent" and *pꜣ ꜥḏꜣ,* "the guilty,"[74] which is what was indicated by Bata's words to his brother the previous evening:

> *wnn pꜣ itn ḥr wbn*
> *iw.i ḥr wpwt ḥnꜥk m-bꜣḥf*
> *mtw.f ḥr dit p ꜣ ꜥḏ ꜣ n pꜣ mꜣꜥt* (d'Orb. 6,9–7,1)
> When the sun rises,
> I will contest with you before him,
> he will give the guilty to the just.

These words also reflect the position of the sun god Re as Lord of Justice,[75] which can likewise be seen in Spell 75 of the Coffin Texts:

> *nb m3ʿt*
> *ẖtm ʿw3w* (*CT* I, 352*d*)
> Lord of Justice,
> who locks up the robber.

Finally, as Bata states, Anubis's behavior contradicts the Egyptian teachings about relationships between people. For instance, Merikare warns a person:

> *s3w.ti ḥr ẖsf m nf* (Merikare, line 48)
> Beware of punishing wrongfully,

and Amenemope counsels:

> *sḏr ḥ3t mdt* (Amenemope V, 13)
> Sleep a night before speaking.

In a similar vein, Ptahhotep says:

> *im.k wḥm mski n mdt*
> *n sḏm.k sw* (Ptah. 350–351=11,5)
> Do not repeat slander,
> and do not listen to it;

and Any advises:

> *s3w.t tw r spy snkt*
> *r mdt bn sw* (Any, V,5)
> Guard against the crime of fraud,
> against words that are not true.

These teachings, especially those from the New Kingdom,[76] assure the listener that the person who is guilty of wrongdoing will reap his reward by being punished by the god or by natural justice.[77]

After stating his case against Anubis's impulsive behavior, Bata tells Anubis what actually happened, saying he could not have behaved as he was accused of doing because both his brother and his brother's wife acted as virtual parents in relation to him. Specifically, in the "Instruction of Any," the hearer is enjoined to support and care for his mother as she did for him as an infant.[78]

The Separation of the Brothers

The parting of the brothers, Bata to the Valley of the Pine and Anubis to his home to tend his cattle, was marked by Bata's self-emasculation and his contract with his brother. The first appears as part of an oath before Pre:

wn.in.f ḥr ʿrqw.f n Pꜣ-Rʿ-Ḥr-ꜣḫty m ḏd
ir pꜣy.k <iyt> r ẖdbw(.i) m grg
iw.k ẖry pꜣy.k niwi
ẖry st-r n kꜣt tꜣḥwt (d'Orb. 7,7–8)
Then he swore before Pre-Harakhty,
"As for your <coming> to kill me wrongly
with your spear
on the word of a filthy whore,"

after which Bata severed his phallus.[79] Then he set up a contract with his brother, the major motif through which previous scholars have related this tale to other two brothers tales.[80] In this situation, Bata's charge to his brother carries the implication of the latter's indebtedness:

istw ir sḫꜣy.k wʿ n bin
istw bw irw.k sḫꜣy wʿ n nfr
m-r-pw wʿ n nkt iw iry.i sw n.k (d'Orb. 8,2)
"If, on the one hand, you recall something evil,
will you not, on the other, recall some good
or something I have done for you?"

Bata then explains that he is going to cut out his heart and place it on a tree; if the tree is cut, he will die and his heart must be rescued to revive him. This is the task he gives to Anubis, and he explains that the latter will know that the proper time has arrived when he is given a jug of foaming beer (d'Orb. 8,6).

Upon their separation, Anubis returned:

. . . r pꜣy.f pr
iw dt.f wꜣḥ<.ti> ḥr ḏꜣḏꜣ.f
iw.f wrḥw n iwdnt (d'Orb. 8,7)

. . . to his house,
with his hand on his head
and (his body) smeared with dirt.

This demeanor was the typical sign of mourning and sorrow used to express proper lamentation.[81] In fact, the narrator later states explicitly

iw.f ḥms m gꜣs
n pꜣy.f sn šri (d'Orb. 8,8)
he (Anubis) sat in mourning
for his younger brother.

It is possible to interpret Anubis's act in two different ways: it is either an extreme reaction by Anubis to his separation from his brother and the circumstances under which it occurred, or it serves as a sign that he perceived Bata to be dead. Assmann suggests the latter, basing his idea precisely on Anubis's mourning posture.[82]

Excursus I

The Papyrus d'Orbiney and Genesis 39[1]

There are many parallels from the ancient world for the theme of attempted seduction, and the example from the d'Orbiney is one of the earliest, if not the earliest. Its inclusion as the Potiphar's wife motif, K2111, in Stith Thompson's motif index, attests to its widespread presence in traditional narrative generally, not just in that of the ancient Near East. Thompson describes the structure of the motif very simply: "woman makes vain overtures to a man and then accuses him of attempting to force her,"[2] but the examples from Genesis and the d'Orbiney as well as most of those from the classical world and other ancient Near Eastern contexts show that the motif is more complex than this description suggests. At the very least, one must add that the man is unjustly punished for his alleged attempt to seduce the woman, for I know of no example of the motif which lacks this third part. When this part is included, the motif may also act as a tale type, that is a tale in itself, for there exist some examples of it as an independent narrative.[3]

According to Delbert Hillers's study of many of the earliest examples,[4] the theme or pattern of attempted seduction commonly consists of the following characteristics: the approach is generally sexual; the male is nearly always younger than the woman; the male is a hunter, or at least portrayed as very masculine; and the male resists, resulting in his downfall and death. Only in the nature of the death do the tales lack uniformity.[5] In addition to the Egyptian example from the d'Orbiney, Hillers derived his pattern from the tales of Aqhat, Adonis, Attis, Kombabos and Stratonice, Eshmun and Astronoe, and the sixth tablet of the *Epic of Gilgamesh*.[6] In his study, Redford includes other parallels, such as the stories of Bellerophon and Hippolytus.[7] In all cases the young male suffers some kind of death from his spurning of the woman's advances.

The continued scholarly interest in the parallel between the attempted seduction of Bata from the Papyrus d'Orbiney and of Joseph in Genesis 39 suggests the value of a new examination in the context of the present study. Expanding on Hillers's pattern and making use of a recent article by J. Robin King,[8] I propose using the following pattern to examine these two narratives. In this way new ideas about structure, purpose, and result may serve to present the tales in a slightly different way.

In a schematic form, the revised pattern takes the following shape:[9]

1. a male, usually young and without exception virile, coexists with an older female who is in a position of authority;
2. the female, attracted by the male, attempts to seduce him or offer him marriage;
3. the male refuses for reasons appropriate to his culture and place;
4. the female falsely accuses him of attempting to seduce her;
5. severe punishment is inflicted to the male, usually administered by another male in a position of authority;
6. exile, analogous to death, results;
7. an exilic challenge is issued;
8. an exilic battle takes place;
9. a victorious outcome effects a return from exile to reconciliation;
10. upon return, the male assumes a different, often higher, status from that in which he was when exiled;
11. the community benefits.

This pattern, like any narrative pattern, functions only as a guide; it is a tool for analysis. As such it will appear in various forms, sometimes with parts missing and/or with significant variations on the presentation of the different parts.

It is important to observe that in its overall presentation, the Potiphar's wife episode constitutes the first part of a rite of passage, the separation, according to the classic tripartite formulation observed by Arnold van Gennep[10] and elaborated by Victor Turner.[11] Such a rite of passage, the effect of which is to move an individual from one social status to another within the community, consists of separation, transition, and incorporation. In the pattern above, parts one through five represent the separation, six through eight the transition, and nine through eleven the incorporation.

Beginning with the episode from which the motif takes its name, even though chronologically its appearance in writing makes it later than the d'Orbiney, one notes that the actual Potiphar's wife episode in Genesis 39 is one chapter in a longer narrative treating Joseph (Genesis 37–50), itself part of an even longer narrative about the Israelite patriarchs (Genesis 12–50). Some scholars consider it to be a later addition to this overall tale, probably having had an independent existence apart from the patriarchal saga,[12] while others take the view that it fits nicely into the whole.[13] In this chapter, Joseph, already exiled to Egypt because of the jealousy of his older half brothers, has been bought by Potiphar, an Egyptian official. In time, Potiphar gave Joseph full responsibility for running his household, in the exercise of which the Israelite had full run of the house. Potiphar's wife thus had ample opportunity to see him and, finding him attractive [1],[14] made multiple efforts to get him to sleep with her [2]. Joseph repeatedly denied her, stating that to sleep with her would be wicked and a sin against God [3]. One day, however, during one of these attempts, she managed to grasp his garment, which he left behind in her hand as he fled. She then called the servants and claimed that he had attempted to seduce her [4]. On hearing his wife's tale, Potiphar had Joseph arrested and thrown into prison [5], effectively removing him from his position of status [6].[15]

The following chapters of Genesis relate that Joseph, who had had an earlier reputation for the successful interpretation of dreams (Gen. 40), subsequently used this talent to interpret correctly [8] two of the king's dreams [7]. They foretold a severe and lengthy famine, and Joseph advised the king to choose an able administrator to plan against it (Gen. 41:33–36). It was Joseph, freed from prison [9], whom the king eventually chose to fill the job [10], and from this position, the Israelite, graced by the presence of God, acted as the salvation for his own family [11] when the famine-affected Israelites sought grain in Egypt (Gen. 41:37–46:7).[16]

Clearly, this narrative relates a rite of passage: Joseph was separated from his secure, comfortable position in the Egyptian official's household by a powerful woman and sentenced to prison. His imprisonment is analogous to death: he was removed from the land of the living, from normal existence, such as occurs in an initiatory rite of passage.[17] In the continuation of the biblical narrative, Joseph was eventually released from jail and placed in a position of responsibility over the whole land, thus completing the initiatory rite of passage by means of which an individual is moved from one stratum of society to another.

Set in this fuller context, one can see that the apparently negative effect of the wife's accusation actually resulted in the positive elevation of Joseph into a position to help his own family, the descendants of Abraham, and thus ensured the continuation of the Israelite people. In addition, the episode, when set within the patriarchal stories, served as continued evidence to the Israelites that they were the chosen people of God.

While there is no question that Semitic peoples, including Israelites, lived in Egypt during the second millennium B.C.E. and that occasionally famines, sometimes lengthy, occurred, the actual historicity of the episode cannot be proved or disproved. Most significantly there is no attestation of Joseph or Potiphar in Egyptian sources, although the name *P3-di-p3-Rꜥ* is known from the late period.[18] Nevertheless, such an episode could have occurred, and the Israelites understood that it did, its features most likely being transmitted orally before they were included within the Genesis narrative and written down.

In the Egyptian tale, the actions of a vindictive and scared woman also effected the move of a young man from his safe and secure situation into a death and then a rebirth at a higher stratum of society. Briefly summarizing the tale in the context of the suggested pattern, Bata, "a beautiful young man" (d'Orb. 1,3) [1], so attracted his sister-in-law with his sexual and physical strength that she invited him to sleep with her [2]. Bata became very angry, telling her that she and her husband were like parents to him [3]. She was fearful at the vehemence of his response and distrustful as well, and turned the incident around to her advantage in relating it to her husband Anubis [4]. The latter then sought to kill Bata [5] but was unsuccessful. After explaining the situation to Anubis, Bata emasculated himself and went to the Valley of the Pine in Syria [6]. After more betrayals by his divinely formed wife [7] and various types of renewal [8], Bata was reborn from his wife [9] as crown prince [10] and eventually succeeded to the throne of Egypt [11].

Like the biblical narrative, the Egyptian tale presents a rite of passage with regard to its hero. The young shepherd, separated from his comfortable life through the destructive act of an older, authoritative female figure, goes through a series of deaths, to be reborn into a higher stratum of society. It is a story of the earthly succession of kingship.

One cannot escape the parallels of the Egyptian and Hebrew expressions of the motif: both men are young and very attractive; both live in a household with an older woman and her husband; both are approached sexually by the older woman; both refuse the woman on moral grounds; both are falsely accused by her; both are separated from the household into exile/death; and both eventually return from their exile/death to rule over much more than had been theirs previously.

Finally, like the Hebrew tale, the Egyptian tale points far beyond what is apparent, but an examination of its reflexes shows how very different a purpose it served in its cultural and religious/ideological context from that of the Genesis narrative. While the latter tells of humans and human behavior and extols the actions of the one God who acts for his people in history, the former relates the actions of gods, albeit gods living on earth like humans. Furthermore, the gods involved, Bata and Anubis, relate clearly and directly to the mortuary realm and to kingship. Anubis was the mortuary god par excellence in ancient Egypt, the deity responsible for the successful transition of the deceased to the next world, most especially the king, while Bata, in his *Bt* form, also shows clear otherworldly connections dating at least as far back as the late Old Kingdom. Moreover, in the d'Orbiney, he shows distinct similarities to Osiris, the King of the Otherworld, in his loss of his phallus, eaten by a fish, followed by his death, rebirth, and accession to the throne. In both narratives, a woman is central to the transformation needed for the succession to the kingship, but the light in which she appears depends on which narrative dominates. In the traditional Osiris narrative,[19] the death of the hero—Osiris—occurs at the hands of a male, his brother Seth, and the revivification takes place by means of the ministrations of a female, his sister-wife Isis, who conceives the new king Horus by him. Two males, Osiris and his son Horus, and one female are involved, and the female appears in a wholly positive light. In contrast, in the d'Orbiney, Bata's death is effected through the actions of a female, not a male, while his rebirth to eventual kingship occurs normally by means of a female. Only Bata and his wife are involved, and he becomes his own child.[20] Thus in this ancient example of the Potiphar's wife motif, one finds that the female figure is presented ambivalently, in both an obviously positive role as well as a clearly negative one.[21]

It is possible that the Egyptian narrative contains reflexes of an actual historical situation. There exists debate among scholars over who succeeded Merneptah in the last years of the nineteenth dynasty when the tale was written down.[22] This modern confusion may itself point to a contemporary confusion over who was the next legitimate king, and it is possible that this tale could have served as a kind of legitimation by focusing on one particular aspect of succession: the transformation of the hero into the king through the wife-mother figure.

In the end, both Genesis 39 and the Papyrus d'Orbiney appear to be dominated by evil women, as in each the male finds himself in a typical no-win or "Catch-22" situation: he will be destroyed if he accepts the proposition and he will be destroyed if he does not accept it. He risks virtual death no matter what his choice, and the powerful female puts him in this position. In many respects, her actions closely resemble those of the evil stepmother of so many folktales. Yet when each of these ancient episodes is followed to its conclusion, the male returns in a transformed state to a new position in a new stratum of society. Each thus forms the first part of a typical tripartite rite of passage. In each example, the narrative relates to the beliefs and ideologies of its culture, and each also touches in some way on its culture's history. One can see that the apparently destructive female in fact effects long-term positive results which affect not only her male target but also his people. Clearly, the Potiphar's wife motif encompasses more substance than is at first apparent[23] and is not simply a folktale motif, at least in these early examples.

4
The Phallus, the Valley, and the Heart

When Bata severed his phallus, went to the Valley of the *ʿš,* and cut out his heart, he separated himself from life as he had known it, removing himself to the Otherworld. When each of these acts is considered separately, each has implications that suggest Bata underwent a kind of death, and all three together emphasize that Bata had indeed entered the Otherworld by the time he settled in the Valley.

Bata's Phallus

The tale's narrator described Bata's self-emasculation as follows:

iw.f ḥr in wʿ n sfd g(ꜣ)sy
iw.f ḥr šʿd ḥnw.f
iw.f ḥr ḫꜣʿ.f r pꜣ ʿmw
iw pꜣ nʿdw(!) ḥr m.f
iw.f ḥr gnn
iw.f ḥr ḫprw ẖsy sw (d'Orb. 7,8–8,1)
He (Bata) brought a reed knife,
and he cut off his phallus
and threw it into the water,
(where) the *nʿr* fish swallowed it,
and he was weak
and became faint.

A number of Egyptologists have stated that Bata's emasculation probably expressed the physical affirmation of his innocence, but they have done little more than to draw a parallel between the swallowing of the phallus by the *nʿr* fish and the loss of Osiris's phallus to fish. For example, as early as 1868 Georg Ebers wrote, "Now Bata related the actual course of events and cut off his phallus, probably to confirm the truth of his words."[1] Similarly, over a century later, J. Gwyn Griffiths wrote that Bata's "mutilation is self-inflicted in order to suggest his innocence,"[2] an idea also expressed by Delbert Hillers and Donald Redford. In fact, Redford views the motif as being an extreme means of proving innocence,[3] while Hillers discusses the theme as one which "springs from man's experience of woman as attractive, yet threatening to his sexuality and his life,"[4] thus venturing into the realm of the psychological. Gerald Kadish also considers Bata's act to be a statement of his innocence, adding, "it is clearly labeled an extraordinary action. It is intended as a literary device."[5] Others, like Maspero, emphasizing the loss of the phallus to the fish, used this part of the tale to relate it to the legend of Osiris.

The implications of emasculation were certainly known to the Egyptians of Ramesside Egypt. They knew that the phallus had semen in it,[6] and that the semen was ejected from it[7] by means of coitus[8] or masturbation.[9] Further, in discussing Egyptian medical practice, Hermann Grapow asserted that they knew what the loss of the testicles meant, noting that the testicles and the phallus were always depicted with the phallus in an erect position.[10] The medical texts also show that by at least 1550 BCE, the Egyptians believed the testicles were the repository of semen, which originated in the heart:

> *iw mty [m ib]*[11] *n ẖrwy.f*
> *nt sn dd mtwt* (Eb. 100,7)
> two vessels are [from the heart]
> to the testicles which give semen.

It is thus clear that for the Ramesside Egyptian, Bata's self-emasculation represented the loss of seminal delivery and the means of coitus,[12] and thus the power to procreate.[13]

In one sense, Bata's act moved him from the man's world to

that of women, and later in the narrative, he tells his divinely formed wife:

> *pꜣ wn tw.i* <*m*> *st-ḥmt mi qd.t* (d'Orb. 10,2)
> I am a woman <like> you.

Nevertheless, although calling himself a woman, Bata never refers to himself as a eunuch; indeed, there is no conclusive proof of the existence of eunuchs in ancient Egypt.[14] Not only is there no certain way of proving that a person was a eunuch in Egyptian representations, but unambiguous terminology is lacking as well.[15] Even Seth's loss of his testicles to Horus never caused him to be represented or referred to unambiguously as a eunuch,[16] although there was a tradition that he was a homosexual.[17]

There is no question, however, that eunuchs were present in other parts of the ancient Near East. In the Graeco-Roman period, for example, Lucian reports a case of self-castration.[18] During this late period, there was cultic self-castration as well, generally occurring within the context of a festival and having a significance more related to the subsequent devotional life than to the actual act.[19] Both the time and the circumstances preclude any relationship to Bata's emasculation, which must be considered in the light of older, native Egyptian sources, namely those telling about the phallus of Osiris.

Osiris's Phallus

The parallel of Bata's loss of his phallus with that of Osiris's loss of his is one that has been commonly remarked,[20] but the tradition about the loss of Osiris's phallus is far from being uniform. There is a clear tradition of Osiris's continuing procreative power, along with a less clear tradition concerning his severed phallus, and finally a very subdued, yet persistent tradition of a lost or swallowed phallus. The Papyrus d'Orbiney may be a part of this last tradition.

The strongest tradition is that of Osiris's continued possession of his phallus so that he was able to engender Horus/Harpokrates posthumously. The best-known document attesting this act is Chapter 19 of Plutarch's *De Iside et Osiride,* but there are rich Egyptian sources as well. For instance, *Pyr.* § 632*a–d* (and almost identically, *Pyr.* §§1635*b*–1636*b*) reports:

ii n.k snt.k ꜣst
ḥꜥꜥ.t n mrwt.k
d.n.k s tp ḥms.k
pr mtwt.k im.s
spd.t m Spdt
Ḥr spd pr im.k
m Ḥr imy Spdt
Your sister Isis comes to you,
rejoicing at love of you.
You place her upon your phallus,
and your semen comes forth into her,
she being ready as Sothis,
and Horus-Sopdu comes forth from you
as Horus who is in Sothis.

Spell 148 of the Coffin Texts states that Isis wakes up with the semen of her brother Osiris within her, and in Spell 94, the deceased states:

ir.n <.i> Wsir m rḏw n iwf.f
mtwt pr.t m ḥnn.f (*CT* II, 68*b–c*; 71*b–c*)
<I> remade Osiris with the efflux of his flesh
from the semen which issued from his phallus.

From the New Kingdom, the "Hymn to Osiris"[21] includes an extended section on the conception and infancy of Horus:

ꜣst ꜣḫt . . .
. . .
sṯst nnw n wrḏ-ib
ḫnpt mw.f ir.t iwꜥw
šd.t nḫn m wꜥꜥw
n rḫ bw.f im
bs.t sw
ꜥ.f nḫt m-ẖnw wsḫt Gb
Psḏt ḥr rs
ii.wy Wsir sꜣ Ḥr
mn ib mꜣꜥ ḫrw
sꜣ ꜣst iwꜥ Wsir
(Louvre C 286, ll. 14,16–17)

Powerful Isis . . .
. . .
(it is) she who raised the inertness of the weary-hearted
and received his seed, bearing the heir,
and who nursed the young one in solitude,
his place being unknown;
(it is) she who introduced him,
when his arm was strong, into the hall of Geb,
and the Ennead was joyful,
"Welcome, Horus, son of Osiris,
firm of heart, justified,
son of Isis and heir of Osiris."

In another example, in a prayer to Osiris dating from the time of Ramesses IX, the god is referred to as:

sꜥḥḥ ꜣw mṯꜣ[22]
the mummy, extended of phallus,

while the title of Spell 576 from the Coffin Texts, "Copulation by a Man in the Realm of the Dead," suggests that in the deceased's identification with Osiris the phallus remained intact so that copulation should and would occur. And finally, from the later period come various depictions of the mummified Osiris with an erect phallus.[23]

Simultaneously, there also existed a tradition of the severed phallus of Osiris. J. Gwyn Griffiths has suggested that it may be an intrusive element from the Greek, perhaps reflecting the severing of Chronos's phallus reported in Hesiod.[24] There are, however, three references in the Pyramid Texts that appear to contradict this suggestion. The texts in question, *Pyr.* §§ 805*c,* 1018*c,* and 1684*c,* mention Osiris's *dmꜣwt,* (*dmꜣt* in § 805*c*), which Kurt Sethe[25] and, more recently, R. O. Faulkner[26] have translated as "amputated/dismembered parts," from *dmꜣ,* "to cut off." The first and second citations occur within the context of resurrection texts, while the third forms part of Horus's reconstitution of his father. Although none of these references specifies the phallus in particular, one assumes that it was one of the mentioned parts,[27] especially since by the twentieth dynasty, there existed a tradition of the preservation of the phallus. Dating from that time, pChester Beatty VIII relates the locations of the relics of Osiris, specifically including that of the phallus, which was to be found at Herakleopolis.[28] In later times, other documents variously report it at other locations, such as Mendes in the Delta,[29] Hebenu in the seventh Upper Egyptian nome, and Bechem in the seventeenth Upper Egyptian nome.[30]

The tradition of the loss of a special part of the corpse can be found as early as the Coffin Texts, most expressly in Spell 155:

> *iw rḫ.kwi ḥḏt ḫnt ḫꜣt*[31] *m ʿ Inp*
> *ḫꜣwy pw n kꜣpꜣp wrmty.f* (*CT* II, 300*b*–302*a*)
> I know what was lacking from the corpse in the hand of Anubis
> (in) the night of covering his testicles(?).[32]

Again the word for phallus does not appear explicitly, a fact which one might explain in terms of the traditional Egyptian reluctance to specify certain dangerous things, in this case the lack of a phallus in the Otherworld. A variation on the theme is found in Spell 36 of the Coffin Texts:

> *kf n.f bꜣgw.i*
> *di mꜣn.f sqrw.i*
> *i.in Wsir* (*CT* I, 141*g*–142*b*)
> "Uncover for him my injured privy parts,[33]
> let him see my wounds."
> thus says Osiris,

in which *bꜣgw* and, in parallelism with it, *sqrw* give the same sense as *dmꜣwt* from the Pyramid Texts. There can be no real question of a significant injury to the genitalia, especially the phallus, since that is what persists in the tradition.[34]

It is striking to note the persistence of this tradition despite the fact that in the process of mummification, all body parts except the viscera were generally preserved intact. Among the very rare exceptions are the royal mummies of Ramesses II, whose external genitalia were removed,[35] and of Merneptah, whose scrotum was severed, probably "either after death or . . . within a short time of death."[36] The reasons for these removals are unknown[37] and are most uncharacteristic, since the other royal mummies known from the eighteenth and nineteenth dynasties show no such treatment.

Although tradition does not specify until late that it was

specifically the phallus that the fish swallowed, early tradition clearly attests to a swallowed part:

> *n ʿm.n RN pn ʿt m Wsir* (*Pyr.* §1450*d*)
> This king did not swallow the member of Osiris.

While the word *ʿt,* "member," does not necessarily designate the phallus, again the persistence of the tradition that it was swallowed suggests that in this case *ʿt* designates the phallus. This phrase follows another in which the king asserts that he does not swallow the eye of Horus, both phrases forming a kind of negative confession in order to gain entrance to the Otherworld.[38]

The *nʿr* Fish

The swallowing of Bata's phallus by the *nʿr* fish would have carried a whole series of associations for the ancient Egyptian. The most striking of these would have been Bata's similarity to Osiris in that the phallus of each was swallowed by fish, the *nʿr* in the case of Bata, the oxyrhynchos, lepidotus, and phagros in the case of Osiris. The *nʿr,* or wels, fish, actually written *nʿdw*[39] in the Papyrus d'Orbiney, corrected by Gardiner to *nʿrw,*[40] is one with a long history in ancient Egypt. It was a member of the family of fish known as *Siluridae,*[41] and the appellation *nʿr* applies to two genera[42] of this family, the *Clarias* and the *Heterobranchus.* The former is characterized by a single dorsal fin, while the latter has a bipartite dorsal fin. Both are able to live out of water for varying periods of time because they both possess a rudimentary lung. Both also have whisker-like appendages on their heads. Further, each genus is composed of two species, each commonly confused with the other, thus making it possible to see that *nʿr* may actually designate any of four species of fish. Of the two genera, however, only the *Clarias* was commonly found along the entire Nile from the Delta to its upper reaches. The *Heterobranchus* appeared rarely in these areas, and when it did, it was usually in the uppermost, i.e., the southern, sections of the Nile, for its spawning areas were the lakes of Abyssinia and the interior of Africa.[43] Nevertheless, both types are attested to in the early history of Egypt: the *Clarias* is depicted in numerous reliefs in Old Kingdom tombs,[44] and both the *Clarias* and the *Heterobranchus* appear in various writings of Narmer's name.[45] Gaillard shared two amusing notes about the *nʿr:* when it is out of water, it can emit a sound that sounds rather like a cat in heat, and it will jump for food.[46]

The longstanding Egyptological interest in the *nʿr* derives not only from what the fish did in the d'Orbiney but also from its use in Narmer's name, its presence in the "Shepherd Song," and its portrayals in the Underworld Books. Each of the various ideas concerning why it was used in the early king's name comes from the assumption that the fish possessed some characteristic the king wished to have for himself. Godron has suggested the name was theophoric and meant "Beloved of *nʿr*, *nʿr* being a protective divinity.[47] His evidence that the *nʿr* functioned in a protective fashion came from Jean Capart's publication of a picture painted on a skin, possibly from Nagada, showing two wels-headed figures linked by a rope[48] as well as an apparently protective *nʿr* fish appearing on an ivory piece from Hierakonpolis, published by Georg Möller.[49]

However, New Kingdom examples of the *nʿr,* or wels, figures tend to suggest they have a relationship to the course of the sun.[50] An example from the upper register of the Eighth Hour of the Amduat shows a wels-headed figure labelled *iffy,* an appellation that Erik Hornung suggests served as an alternative name for the *nʿr.*[51] Another example, from the upper register of Third Division of the Book of Caverns, depicts seven wels-headed figures standing under a serpent over which is the sun disk.[52] And finally, two (four) of them are shown holding a rope along which the god Aker is rolling a ball symbolizing the sun disk, in three nearly identical scenes found in the tomb of Ramesses IV and also on the royal coffin of Ramesses III and the nonroyal coffin of *Ns-sw-Tfnt* (twenty-sixth dynasty).[53]

Another suggestion is that the *nʿr* served as a symbol of fertility and was used in Narmer's name for this reason. Although generally the *tilapia* or *int* fish was considered the most explicit symbol of fertility among fish in Egypt,[54] I. Gamer-Wallert reports that in an unpublished work, H. Ganslmayr shows that the wels does symbolize fertility in some African cultures.[55]

Perhaps its fertility accounts for its portrayal as part of an offering scene, possibly a Sed-fest, on the Hierakonpolis tablet belonging to Djer.[56] It is clear from the depictions in the Underworld Books and on the coffins of the New Kingdom, however, that even if a tradition of fertility was linked to the *nꜥr* fish in the Early Dynastic and Old Kingdom periods,[57] that tradition was lost before the New Kingdom.

Still another approach describes the fish as vicious or raging, and Wolfgang Helck has suggested that Narmer adopted this name in order to gain the vicious powers of the fish,[58] which the Hierakonpolis tablet depicting the *nꜥr* with a club appears to show.[59] There is a question, however, whether the *nꜥr* was truly a vicious or raging fish,[60] for recently Gamer-Wallert has shown that other fish common in ancient Egypt exhibited the trait of viciousness far in excess of that of the wels. She suggests that, had Narmer wished to opt for viciousness, he would have been better advised to choose from the so-called robber fish: the *Nilbarsch* or *Hydrocyon forskalli.*[61] The latter, whose Egyptian name is unknown, was depicted in a tomb of the First Intermediate period[62] and "nicknamed by the ancients 'greedy' or 'eater',"[63] while the *Nilbarsch,* or *Lates niloticus,* was called *ꜥḥꜣ,* "fighter," by the ancient Egyptians, who thus expressed their perception of it as a fighting fish.[64]

The few texts in which the *nꜥr* is mentioned are as inconclusive about its nature as are the depictions. In the Old Kingdom "Shepherd Song," the *nꜥr* is one of two fish with which *Bt* converses while in the water, an act which conveys the idea that *Bt* is in the mortuary realm. The same idea is conveyed by the explicit reference in the song to *Bt n Imntt,* "*Bt* of/in the West," i.e., the Otherworld. Kaplony has suggested that in the song, the shepherd *Bꜣti* is admonishing the wels—at times the helper, at other times the enemy, of Osiris—to seek the limbs of Osiris, doing them no ill,[65] thus connecting the fish with the mortuary world.

A New Kingdom example giving the sense of the mortuary realm appears in an example from the Dreambook found in pChester Beatty III, dating from the time of Merneptah:[66]

ḥr wnmw nꜥr wgs.f
ḎW: iṯt.t(w).f in msḥ (pChester Beatty III, 7,8)

(If a man see himself in a dream,)
eating a *nʿr* fish that has been split open,
BAD: it means he will be seized by a crocodile.

Together these texts convey the idea of death, and the seizing or swallowing action gives some credence to Altenmüller's idea that the *nʿr* is the fish designated as the *phagros* of Osiris.[67] Because the word *phagros* means eater,[68] and since the wels is an eater, he reasons that *phagros* is the Greek name for the wels.[69] However, d'Arcy Thompson has shown that the Greeks called other fish besides the wels *phagros,*[70] thus leaving it unclear if one can truly equate the wels with it.

In the end, it is clear that during the New Kingdom, the *nʿr* carried mythic associations that joined it with the mortuary realm. These relations, which date at least as early as the late Old Kingdom, incorporate the predatory nature of the fish, and by the New Kingdom place the fish in specific relation to the night journey of the sun. And so the *nʿr* appears to act ambiguously: it swallows or destroys in the mortuary realm, but it also aids in rebirth, as in the solar journey.

The Effect of Bata's Self-Emasculation

The effect of Bata's self-mutilation was that he "was weak and became feeble." From the physiological viewpoint this is not surprising, for he severed an organ which has many blood vessels, and thus he would have suffered the loss of much blood, perhaps even death, as a result, since no apparent measures were taken to staunch the flow.[71] The text, however, does not report his death but merely describes his condition. The words used, *gnn,* "weak," and *ẖsi,* "weak, feeble,"[72] recall that it was common for the Egyptians to refer to their deceased as the "weary of heart," *wrḏ-ib,* or "weary," *bꜣg*. For instance, *Pyr.* § 2118*a* says the "king will not be weary-hearted (*wrḏ-ib*)," the Coffin Texts frequently refer to Osiris as *wrḏ-ib,*[73] and pChester Beatty VIII reads:[74]

dd tꜣw n wrḏw-ib (pChester Beatty VIII rect. 1, 2)
Breath[75] is given to the weary one (Osiris).

Another text using *wrḏ-ib* is the "Hymn to Osiris" on Louvre Stela C 286,[76] which reads:

sṯst nnw n wrḏ-ib
ḫnpt mw.f (line 16)
she who (i.e., Isis) raised the inertness of the weary one (i.e., Osiris)
and who received his fluid (i.e., semen).

An example of *b3g* in reference to the deceased occurs in Spell 335 of the Coffin Texts:

nḥm.k wi m-ʿ nṯr pw
. . .
snḏ n.f imyw b3gw (*CT* IV, 319*e*–320*d*)
Save me from that god
. . .
whom the ones among the weary ones fear.

This accumulation of terms meaning "weak" and "weary" in reference to Osiris or, more generally, to the deceased, suggests that the use of similar terms relative to Bata places him in a state analogous to death. Although no known uses of either *gnn* or *ḫsi* precisely support this idea,[77] the sense conveyed by the words, along with the likely physical result of the act, makes such a conclusion plausible, especially when coupled with anthropological evidence regarding genital marking (e.g., circumcision) in initiatory rites of passage.[78] In fact, I. Jesi states that Bata's severing of his phallus easily links him to the chastity ritually imposed on the initiate in primitive society,[79] and the death that results is a living death.[80] Considering that Bata's act immediately precedes his departure for life in the valley of *ʿš,* a location outside Egypt and therefore carrying the implication of a living death,[81] and further that a living death is characteristic of the transition segment of a rite of passage and marks the movement of an individual from one status in a society to another, Jesi's interpretation is very significant.

With a slightly different emphasis, H. te Velde drew an analogy between the self-castration of Attis, who "did not suffer death in the usual way," and Bata, who likewise "does not die in a normal way but is continually reborn, until he reached the highest possible status by Egyptian norms, that of king."[82]

One concludes, therefore, that Bata's severing of his phallus marked his move from the ordinary world of the living into a transitional state, a life in exile, or what one might describe as a living death.[83]

The Valley of the ʿš and Its Significance

The valley of the ʿš to which Bata went when he parted from his brother is a place whose location has long been disputed. Ideas about where it is have varied widely over the years. In 1882 Maspero thought it probable that it was "a mystical name of the Other World,"[84] an idea supported by Philippe Virey during the following two decades.[85] Maspero, however, altered his view fairly quickly, and in 1889, at the time of the second edition of *Les Contes populaires,* he stated that the valley corresponded to the funerary valley that Amun visited annually in order to pay homage to his parents, a valley on the bank of the Nile where the river descended from heaven to the real world.[86] In 1931, Vikentiev suggested that it lay in the Faiyum,[87] while in 1933 Gardiner located it in Lebanon.[88] Gardiner's location, later affirmed by Vikentiev, but for different reasons,[89] was based on the Kadesh Battle Inscription of Ramesses II, which reads:

> *ist ḥm.f m-ḥr Rʿ-imn-mr-mss*
> *pꜣ dmit nty m tꜣ in<t> pꜣ ʿš*[90]
> His majesty was in Ramessemeramun,
> the town which is in the valley of the ʿš

after he passed the fortress of Tjel and just before reaching the hills of Kadesh.[91]

The Syrian location has been confirmed many times over in different ways during the last half century. It is interesting to note, however, that in all the discussions about it, only Emile Chassinat observed the presence of internal textual evidence of the d'Orbiney itself which showed that it lay outside Egypt.[92] In the pertinent passage, the narrator relates that, after spending three years searching for Bata's heart:

> *iw ḥꜣty.f iꜣbw iyt r Kmt* (d'Orb. 13,5)
> his (Anubis's) heart wished to return to Egypt.

Two other passages in addition to that noted by Chassinat also make it clear that the valley of the ʿš lay outside Egypt. In the first, the scribes tell the king:

ḫr sw m nḏ-ḥr.k <*m*> *kt ḫꜣst* (d'Orb. 11,5)
therefore it (the hair) is your greeting <from> another land.

The second relates that:

wn.in tꜣ st-ḥmt ḥr iyt
r Kmt ir-m.s (d'Orb. 12,1–2)
the woman (Bata's wife) came
to Egypt with her.

Wolfgang Helck has suggested more precisely that the valley lay between Lebanon and Antilebanon,[93] thus in central Syria in the area of Amki (el-Biqa),[94] inland of Byblos and Sidon.[95] It is an area that was considered a dependency of Egypt during the New Kingdom, as attested in seven Amarna letters.[96]

The texts and records that refer to the products of the *ꜥš*-tree and their origin attest to its location in Syria and further report that the *ꜥš*-tree of Syria was highly valued in Egypt. In particular, its resin was used for mummification, while its wood was employed for temple doors, the sacred bark of Amun, masts for boats, and temple pylons.[97] Helck has also noted that coniferous woods, among which is the *ꜥš,* were used for coffins,[98] and that the late Ramesside *Daily Book* indicates the presence of large amounts of *ꜥš*-wood in the land.[99]

Specific examples of Egyptian texts citing *ꜥš*-wood come from all periods of history. For instance, on the Palermo Stone, dating to the fifth dynasty, it is said that in the fourth dynasty in the time of Snofru, forty ships filled with *ꜥš*-wood were brought.[100] In the late seventeenth dynasty, on his Second Stela, Kamose reports:[101]

n wꜣḥn.i pḫ ḫr bꜣw 300
n ꜥš wꜣḏ
mḥ w m . . .
inw nb nfr n Rṯnw (lines 13–15)
I did not leave a plank of the 300 galleys
of new *ꜥš*-wood
which were filled with . . .
all good products of the *Rṯnw,*

and in the eighteenth dynasty Hatshepsut relates:

in.n.sn n.i stpw Ngꜣw
m ꜥš, wꜥn, mrw (*Urk.* IV, 373, 3–4)

They (the Asiatics) brought me the choicest
(products) of Syria
including *ʿš, wʿn,* and *mrw*-trees/wood.

Her inscription is one of several citing *Ngꜣw,* Syria, as the point of origin of the *ʿš*-tree, a place-name mentioned as early as the Pyramid Texts.[102] Her coregent and successor Tuthmosis III also cites *Ngꜣw* as his source of *ʿš*-wood,[103] and he mentions that he had *ʿš*-trees felled for the ships which he used on the Euphrates.[104]

Mortuary and literary sources likewise provide evidence of the use of products from the *ʿš*-tree. A Pyramid Text gives a spell which ends with *ḥꜣtt ʿš-mrḥt,* "first quality *ʿš*-oil,"[105] a text which forms part of the ritual of the "Opening of the Mouth."[106] The Coffin Texts place the deceased in a position of commanding or piloting:

m smʿ n mḥ 40
srd n ʿš n Kbn (*CT* I, 267*f*–268*a*)
with a forty cubit pole
grown of *ʿš*-wood of Byblos.

The "Admonitions of Ipuwer," purportedly from the time of troubles after the Old Kingdom, also discusses *ʿš*-tree products in the context of lament:

n ms ẖd.tw r [Kb]n min
pw-ti irt.n r ʿš n sʿḥw.n
qrs.tw wʿb m inw.sn
sdwḫ.tw [šps]w m sfṯ iry
r-mn-m Kftyw (Ipuwer 3,6–8)
None indeed sail north to [Bybl]os today.
What shall we do for *ʿš*-trees for our mummies?
The pure (free) are buried with the produce;
the nobles are embalmed with oil therefrom
as far (away) as Crete.[107]

Over the years, the identification of the *ʿš*-tree has been disputed. In his last edition of *Les Contes populaires,* as well as in the English translation, Maspero discussed the different suggestions for the type of tree: acacia, cedar, pine, cypress. He noted that Victor Loret had suggested the pine, though he himself did not agree, preferring the acacia.[108] In fact, soon after Maspero's English edition appeared, Loret published a cogent discussion arguing that the *ʿš*-tree represented either the *Abies cilicia* or the *Pinus Pinea,*[109] an argument that scholars still consider valid.[110] Nevertheless, when Helck discussed the issue, he felt it useful to make explicit that the *ʿš*-tree is not the cedar, as it is still sometimes translated,[111] but is the pine:[112]

1. *mrw*-wood[113] is red-brown while *ʿš*-wood is light yellow,
2. *ʿš*-wood is from a resinous tree, while cedar has little resin,
3. *ʿš*-wood is used for temple masts, so it must be high and slender.

Despite the relative certainty about the actual location of the valley and the identification of the tree, modern scholars have tended to believe that in the tale, the Valley of the Pine represents an "over-there-and-far-away" motif. Helck suggested that the territory might have had "value as a scene of folktale events" for the ancient Egyptians,[114] while K. A. Kitchen noted that Syria frequently provided "a 'romantic' background or setting"[115] for Egyptian tales.[116] Both scholars appear to view the tale as a Märchen or fairy tale. Altenmüller, emphasizing the mythological elements of the story, considers the valley to be the Otherworld, stating, "Bata no longer lives in fertile land but in the waste in which the necropolis also lies." Among the points he marshalls for his argument are the facts that the area is a source of funerary materials, that Bata does not have his heart in his body, and that Bata and his wife each leave the area "only with outside help."[117]

In addition, Bata's presence in the valley, outside Egyptian environs, places him in the mainstream of Egyptian literary exiles such as Sinuhe and the writer of the "Tale of Woe." A major concern of the subjects in each of these works is that of not receiving a proper burial because they were living outside Egypt. The idea is that life away from Egypt represents a living death according to Egyptian standards. The concept is stated most explicitly in the last line of the Stela of Exiles, where it is said that living outside of Egypt constitutes:

> *sm3 rmṯ ʿnḫw* (line 23)[118]
> killing living people.

This sense of exile derives from a strongly Egyptocentric idea of existence. John Baines has put it succinctly in discussing Sinuhe's exile:

> Flight from Egypt and Egyptian values is difficult to accomplish and intensely painful. An Egyptian may well succeed in another type of life abroad, but his success is hollow, because the great triumph there is nothing to a position of modest esteem in Egypt. Egyptian values supplant others. The king is the centre of Egyptian values.[119]

Thus Bata's existence in the valley must be considered as one of an exile with all its attendant implications, a life in the Otherworld, death to his old life.

Bata's Heart and Egyptian Beliefs about the Heart

The removal of Bata's heart has been discussed by many commentators, especially since the idea appears to be contrary to Egyptian thought. In his study of the heart, Alexandre Piankoff considered this instance to represent a "special case,"[120] while Helmut Brunner described it as "a fairy tale-like trait,"[121] and Blumenthal observed that its removal is a common folk- and fairy tale motif.[122] However, a close look at the Egyptian ideas about the heart, especially with regard to mortuary practices, shows that one can understand the removal of Bata's heart in the context of ancient Egyptian tradition.

For the Egyptian, the heart was essential, both physically and spiritually. Physically, it was absolutely central in the body, the place from which the twenty-two body vessels led to all the body parts, the place through which air passed on the way from the nose to the anus,[123] while spiritually, it was the seat of reason, thought, reflection,[124] love,[125] and even memory.[126] Further, it acted as the alter ego, the companion, as is shown by the tale of the "Shipwrecked Sailor":[127]

> *ir.n.i hrw 3wʿ.kwi*
> *ib.i m snw.i* (Len. 1115, lines 41–42)[128]
> I spent three days alone
> (with) my heart being my (only) companion.

Its loss meant death or the loss of reason, resulting in senseless acts.[129]

The heart was considered equally essential after death, as can be observed in mortuary practices: it was not removed from the body, but was generally left there, as Diodorus Siculus reported.[130] This fact has been confirmed repeatedly in the studies of mummies done in the twentieth century CE,[131] although Brunner observed, without citation, that in the third millennium BCE, the heart was removed and placed in canopic jars along with the other viscera.[132]

The mortuary texts emphasize the importance of the heart's being with its owner after death, both by the expression of fear of its removal[133] and by the affirmation of its restoration or presence. For instance, in a Middle Kingdom spell, the deceased states:

> *n snt.tw ib-ḥ3ty.i* (*CT* III, 296*h*)
> my heart will not be cut out (of my body).

and the titles of Spells 387 and 388 of the Coffin Texts are, "NOT TO SEIZE THE HEART OF A MAN IN THE NECROPOLIS." The Book of the Dead likewise contains chapters for not taking a man's heart.[134] In addition, there is a Coffin Text which asks:

> *in ii.n.k r iṯ ḥ3ty pn n N* (*CT* V, 54*c*)
> have you come to take this heart of N?

Spell 335 of the Coffin Texts, which appears later as Chapter 17 of the Book of the Dead, requests protection from the seizer of hearts:

> *nḥm.k wi m-ʿ ṯnṯr pw*
> . . .
> *ʿm šwywt*
> *ẖnp ḥ3tyw* (*CT* IV, 312*b*–314*c*)
> Save me from that god
> . . .
> who swallows shades
> and seizes hearts.

A great number of texts from all periods are concerned with the return of the heart to the body and with reassembling the entire body, many with a special mention of the heart.[135] A fine example from the Pyramid Texts appears in two virtually identical utterances:

> *ẖnm.s kw*
> *ḫw.s gꜣw.k*
> *d.s n.k tp.k*
> *iʿb.s n.k qsw.k*
> *dmḏ.s n.k ʿt/ʿwt.k*
> *int.s n.k ib.k m ẖt.k* (*Pyr.* § 828*a–c* = § 835*a–c*)
> She (the protective goddess) will protect you;
> she will prevent you from lack;
> she will give you your head;
> she will reassemble your bones;
> she will join your "severed member";
> and she will bring you your heart from your body.[136]

This restoration of the heart is reiterated time and again in the Pyramid Texts,[137] as well as in the Coffin Texts[138] and in the Book of the Dead.[139] Of particular interest is its presence within the daily ritual of the cult of Amon-Re in which the priest greets the god and says:

> *in.n <.i> n.k ib.k m ẖt.k*
> *r dit ḥr st.f*[140]
> <I> have brought you your heart from your body
> to put in its place.

In addition, a passage from the Pyramid Texts affirms the presence of the heart in the body:

> *ib.k n.k Wsir . . .*
> *ib n RN n.f ḏs.f . . .* (*Pyr.* § 364*a–b*)
> (As) your heart is yours Osiris . . .
> so the king's own heart belongs to him . . . ,

and

> *ib.k n.k n ḏt.k* (*Pyr.* § 1921*e*)
> your own heart belongs to you.

The constant repetition of this theme can suggest that the heart was removed from the deceased, at least in early times as Sethe and Brunner have said.[141] While one can argue tha the returning of the heart was simply the return following its weighing, the texts do not show this theme explicitly until the New Kingdom. Furthermore, that such a thing—or something analogous—must have been the case, despite Diodorus and the modern studies of mummies,[142] can also be deduced from the ubiquitous presence of the heart scarab with the mummy.[143] These heart scarabs were already present under Den, the fourth king of the first dynasty,[144] and their explicit function was to act as substitute hearts:[145]

> *ir.n n.f it.i ib.f*
> *ky šd(y)*[146] *n.f*
> *ẖ3k.f ir pr.f r.f ir pt* (*Pyr.* § 1162*a–b*)
> my father has (re)made his heart,
> (for) the other has been cut out for him
> since it objected to his going to the heaven.[147]

Their continued use is attested by a version of Chapter 30 of the Book of the Dead, which instructs the speaker to say the spell over a scarab and[148]

> *rdit m-ẖnw ib n s*
> put (it) in place of the heart of a man.[149]

The heart scarab also may have served as a substitute heart for the man who had an uneasy conscience, especially to be used for his confrontation with the tribunal in the Otherworld.[150] The vignette which often accompanies the text of the "Negative Confession," Chapter 125 of the Book of the Dead, shows a balance, on one side of which is placed the heart of the deceased and on the other side of which is placed the feather of *M3ʿt*.[151] The same is the case for the vignette for Chapter 30B[152] and the Fifth Hour of the Book of Gates.[153] In addition, Chapters 30A and 30B are concerned with not allowing the heart to oppose the deceased in the Otherworld.

Together, the mortuary texts and the heart scarab, whether as a substitute heart because the deceased's own heart "objected to his going to heaven" or because the owner was concerned about facing the tribunal, suggest that the heart could be separated from the corpse following death and make it clear that the Egyptians worried about such an event.

The issue may be a reflection of the ancient practice of exposure[154] in which unmummified corpses were left in the desert on the western boundaries of the cultivated lands.[155] There they attracted canidae and other predatory animals and birds that would devour the fleshy parts of the corpse, including the heart, leaving the bones scattered. The many texts that mention a collecting or joining of the bones, as well as a bringing of the heart of the deceased,[156] support such an idea. In practice, the corpse would have been put out, followed later by a gathering of the remains (i.e., the bones) and the bringing of a manufactured heart to ensure a good afterlife.

From the reality of the separation of the heart in the Egyptian mortuary tradition, it follows that resuscitation by replacing the heart falls well within Egyptian tradition and represents more than simply Thompson's motif E 30, "resuscitation by replacing heart."[157] Thus Bata's eventual revival is described as follows:

> *iw.f ḥr in wʿ n gꜣy n mw qb*
> *iw.f ḥr hꜣʿ.f r.f*
>
> . . .
>
> *iw Inpw pꜣy.f sn ʿꜣ*
> *ḥr iṯꜣ pꜣ gꜣy n mw qb*
> *nty ḥꜣty n pꜣy.f sn šri im.f*
> *iw.f <ḥr dit> swr.f sw*
> *iw ḥꜣty.f ʿḫʿ r st.f*
> *iw.f ḥr ḫpr mi wnn.f* (d'Orb. 13,8–9;14,2–3)
> and he (Anubis) brought a bowl of cool water,
> and he placed it (the heart) in it,
>
> . . .
>
> and Anubis, his older brother,
> took the bowl of cool water
> in which was the heart of his younger brother,
> and he caused him to drink it,
> and his heart stood in its place,
> and he became as he had been.

In this episode Anubis acts in the role of refresher and revivifier that follows from his designation as *ḫnty sḥ nṯr*. A text from the pyramids that particularly shows this revivification reads as follows:[158]

qbḥ.s n.k ib.k m ẖt.k
m pr it.s[159] *Inpw* (*Pyr.* §1995*b*)
she refreshes your heart in/from your body for you
in the house of her father, Anubis.

In the Book of the Dead, Chapter 173, it is Horus rather than Anubis, in the interchangeability of their mortuary role, who acts in this way:

hꜣ Wsir
ink sꜣ. k Ḥr
ii.n.i
in.n<.i> n.k qbḥw m ꜣbw
qbḥ ib.k ẖr.f[160]
Oh, Osiris,
I am your son Horus;
I have come,
and <I> have brought cool water from
Elephantine for you,
that your heart may be refreshed
through it.

And later, at Edfu, in a section of the Sed-fest which closely resembles the mortuary cult, the actor is the Horus king:[161]

in.i n.k wḏ
m ḥʿw nṯr
swr.k m.sn
sqbḥ ib.k
ḥtp.k
I bring to you a jug
with the god's parts (i.e., the Nile)[162]
that you may drink from them
and your heart may be refreshed
and you may be peaceful.

Thus it is clear that all acts related to the heart in the d'Orbiney fall well within Egyptian tradition.

Bata's Heart on the Tree

Like the motif of resuscitation by replacing the heart, the motif of the heart on the tree, with the owner's life dependent on the tree remaining intact, is a common folk motif.[163] Blumenthal has suggested that in the d'Orbiney, this motif may incorporate the indigenous Egyptian concept of the god on the flower,[164] for in the d'Orbiney, the heart was placed precisely

> *ḥr ḏ3ḏ3 n t3 ḥrr p3 ʿš* (d'Orb. 8,4)
> upon the top of the blossom of the pine.

According to a recent work of Hermann Schlögl, the motif of the god on the flower has purification-regenerative connections and eventually assumes solar implications as well.[165] This scholar has shown that Nefertum, in association with the *sššn/sšn,* "lotus bloom," served as a symbol of regeneration in both the Pyramid Texts and the Coffin Texts, and further that the *sšn,* "lotus bloom," is related to the lotus sea, the area of purification and regeneration to which the deceased, accompanied by the sun god, goes to be purified.[166] In the eighteenth dynasty, the name of the king and the lotus bloom are found joined as an amulet in the form of an *ʿnḫ* sign,[167] which brings "to expression the concept of rebirth."[168] By the nineteenth dynasty, the sun god was joined with the lotus bloom as the creator born every morning in the cup of the blossom, and the deceased king, in his identification with the sun, participated in this rebirth.[169] Therefore, Bata's heart on the flower of the tree incorporates an ancient symbol of rebirth and regeneration and relates him as well to the later concept of the deceased king and solar rebirth. The latter presages his accession to kingship.

It is important to emphasize, however, that Bata's fate was dependent on the fate of the tree. In his discussion of Bata and the *ʿš*-tree, Edmund Hermsen recalls that in "a very old, general idea of mankind the life of a man was linked with a tree or a plant in the sense of a parallelism of life power. Whatever happened to the tree—that happened to the man."[170] Thus the *ʿš*-tree served as Bata's life tree, and his life depended on it. In this idea one can see an analogy to Osiris's dependence on a tree for his continued existence, as demonstrated by the beginning of Pyramid Spell 574:

> *inḏ-ḥr.ṯ nht ḫnmt nṯr* (Pyr. § 1485*a*)
> Greetings tree/sycamore, which encloses the god.

Thus to find Bata's continued existence bound to a tree fits clearly into Egyptian beliefs and, incidentally, relates him the more strongly to Osiris.

The Secret of the Heart

Another sense of the heart is evident when Bata was so enamored of his divinely created wife that

> *wn.in.f ḥr wpwt n.s*
> *ḥ3ty.f m qi.f nbt* (d'Orb. 10,3–4)
> he opened[171] his entire heart to her.

In essence, he revealed the secret that he held within his "heart," the key to his existence: his heart lay on the tree, the felling of which would end his life. A commonly cited biblical parallel appears in the story of Samson and Delilah, in which Samson reveals to Delilah the secret of his strength.[172] The revelations of these men made them vulnerable to the women involved, and, as Brunner notes, the "heart" means the innermost secret in both instances.[173] Certainly in the case of Bata, it has to involve this type of metaphor, for his actual heart is not even in his body, and it is this knowledge that he reveals.

At first glance, the conception scene from the birth ritual at Deir el-Bahri[174] in which Amun

> *sw rdi ib.f r.s*
> gave his heart to her (Ahmes)

appears to be similar to that which is found in the d'Orbiney. Certainly D. Müller viewed it this way.[175] Amun's act, however, results in the conception of Hatshepsut, quite in line with the medical understanding that the semen of the male, by which the woman was impregnated, emanated from the heart, as seen above. This interpretation is confirmed by the "Hymn to Min" from the thirteenth dynasty:

> *nk.n.f sy*
> *di.n.f ib<.f> r.s*
> *imw.f r imw.s*
> *n nwr.f*[176]
> he copulated with her,
> and he gave <his> heart to her,

his loins to her loins
without ceasing.

In a similar way, a passage from the Coffin Texts says:

iw ib <.*f*> *n ḥmt ẖr.f*
r ṯnw nk.f (*CT* VI, 191*m–n*)
<his> heart comes to the woman under him
whenever he copulates.[177]

Perhaps the similarity of the d'Orbiney expression to that from Deir el-Bahri is deliberate and is intended to disclose the irony of Bata's position. He opens his heart to his wife—the appropriate act of a husband to a wife—yet he is doubly impotent: he lacks the heart which gives the semen and the phallus to deliver it. Instead, he gives his secret to her, and thereby literally places his life in her hands. The whole reminds one of the ancient Egyptian enjoyment of paronomasia, of which this is a fine example.[178]

A comparison of all these passages suggests that the word *ḥ3ty* was used to speak of the spiritual, reasoning heart and *ib* was used to refer to the physical heart, the organ itself. This suggestion contradicts the conclusion Piankoff reached when he tried to distinguish between the two words,[179] and in fact, Ebers 103,2–3 uses *ḥ3ty* rather than *ib* to designate the heart as the source of semen.[180] It thus appears that a clear consistency in the use of the two words does not exist.

Finally, the fact that the physical shape of the heart resembles the shape of a pine cone has been mentioned by various scholars. Brunner noted that its color and size are also similar to the color and size of the pine cone.[181] Helck has further suggested, unfortunately without discussion, that the link of the heart with the fir/pine tree is a motif of Syrian origin.[182] Curiously, however, when the heart was actually found, it was described as *i3rrt,* a bunch of grapes (d'Orb. 13, 1), for which one can suggest no explanation except that the shape of the heart, perhaps even the color, may have been perceived as similar to a cluster of grapes, certainly a fruit more familiar to the Egyptian than the pine cone.[183]

Excursus II
Osiris in Byblos

More than eighty years ago Sethe drew an analogy between Osiris in Byblos with the tree and Bata with the "cedar,"[1] while more recently Emile Chassinat compared Osiris's loss of his genitals and his stay on the Phoenician coast with Bata's castration and stay in the valley.[2] Both scholars certainly wrote with Plutarch's *De Iside et Osiride* in mind, and probably Lucian's *De Dea Syria* as well. In the early second century CE, these Greek writers each wrote about Osiris in Byblos, showing that at that time there existed some kind of tradition concerning Osiris's arrival and presence in Byblos, thus providing evidence that the god had a Roman, possibly a Hellenistic, cult there.[3] In *De Iside et Osiride* 15, Plutarch reported the arrival of Osiris in a coffin on the Byblian coast, about which grew up some type of tree, and in *De Dea Syria* 7, Lucian tells how the head of Osiris came from Egypt to Byblos each year.

Sethe's analogy between Bata and Osiris was based on the *ερεικη* tree of Plutarch, which he felt showed the misunderstanding of another word for a tree of the same or similar type as the *ʿš*.[4] The *ερεικη* is really a heath tree, a tree of the scrub variety, not the type of tree that would be used as a temple pillar.[5] Chassinat proposed that Plutarch transcribed the local Semitic name as **ερεινη*, without giving the Greek translation, and that later copyists replaced it with *ερεικη*, which was graphically similar and more familiar to them. He noted that sometimes the Hebrew *ʾōren* is translated as "pine,"[6] and that the tree seen with Osiris's coffin in the bas-relief at Dendera reminded him of the "needles" of the pine.[7] Although this speculative thinking arose partly from his trying to relate the *ʿš* of the d'Orbiney to the *ερεικη* of Plutarch, it also derived from the anomaly that Osiris's coffin was incorporated by the scrubby *ερεικη* and then used for a temple pylon.

The real questions are whether Plutarch's report rests on earlier Egyptian sources and whether Osiris can be found at Byblos in prehellenistic times. Griffiths has stated categorically that in early myth there is no trace of Osiris in Byblos,[8] and he argues that Brunner's attempt[9] to see Osiris in Byblos in Chapter 125 of the Book of the Dead is ill-founded since there are no precise references to Byblos in the passage in question.[10] He agrees, therefore, when Herrmann questions whether the tradition of Osiris at Byblos is any older than the Osiris-Adonis worship there,[11] since Herrmann states that it is impossible to determine whether Osiris was ever independent of the worship of Adonis at Byblos.[12] Nevertheless, Griffiths does report that some statuary found in excavations at Byblos has provided evidence of a Byblite cult of Osiris in the New Kingdom.[13] One must make a distinction, however, between his cult and his myth: Osiris can be worshipped in places with which he has no mythical relationship.

Although the question of whether Osiris had a mythical connection with Byblos and its environs cannot be answered definitively, there are Egyptian texts which appear to suggest that some aspects of Plutarch's report had ancient precedents. The possibility thus arises that other aspects may be valid as well. For instance, a resurrection text from the pyramids implies that the sea is to be Osiris's home:

> *šsp.k n.k dpwy.k ipw*
> *wʿ n wʿn snw n sḏd*
> *ḏꜣ.k š n pr.k wꜣḏ-wr* (*Pyr.* §§1751*b*–1752*a*)
> take these, your two oars,
> the one of *wʿn*-wood, the other of *sḏd*-wood,
> and ferry across the waterway to your house, the sea.

Certainly this text, like Plutarch's, conveys the sense that Osiris spent time traveling on the sea. Further, there is the long tradition of drowning, which eventually became a divine death because of Osiris's fate.[14] The Pyramid Texts testify to this mode of his death:

> *rdi.n Ḥr*
> *ip n.k msw.f*
> *ḏr bw mḥ.n.k im* (*Pyr.* § 766*d*[15])
> Horus has caused
> his children to muster for you
> in the place where you drowned,

and a twentieth-dynasty magical text reads:[16]

di.f mḥ.f ḥr mw
ḏ3t [ḥ]ʿwt.f nbt pšt
he caused him to drown in water,
the coffin and all his separated members,

which further confirms the drowning, in this case in the coffin. Thus, the text is even more like Plutarch. In addition, two later, well-known reports, the Memphite Theology on the Shabaka Stone, most likely from the twenty-fifth dynasty,[17] and the Metternich Stela of the thirtieth dynasty,[18] also support the tradition.

In a similar way, an Osirian relationship with trees appears in Egyptian tradition. For instance, the planting of trees in burial precincts was a common practice in Egypt. For Griffiths, this is the probable origin of the association between Osiris and trees,[19] but one might argue that it was precisely Osiris's association with trees that led to their being planted within these areas. One Pyramid Text appears to testify to just such a relationship:

inḏ-ḥr.ṯ nht ẖnmt nṯr
ʿḥʿt nṯrw niwtyw ḥr.s
fst ḏrw.s
is ʿẖt imt.s
m3ʿt p3swt (*Pyr.* §1485*a–b*)
Greetings tree/sycamore, which encloses the god,
under which the gods of the lower heaven stand,
whose ends are burnt,
whose insides are cooked,
and which sends forth pains of death.

In his commentary on the passage, Sethe related this tree to the one which stands over Osiris's grave, a truly primeval, holy tree, which protected Osiris, even as Nut, the goddess of the sycamore, protected the deceased.[20] Elsewhere, Chassinat has suggested that the Djed pillar that is depicted on the inside or outside of many New Kingdom coffins symbolized Osiris's enclosure in the tree.[21] Chassinat also noted Lefébure's citation of the late Latin author Firmicus Maternus, who reported the custom of taking pine, extracting material from it, and using it to fashion an image of Osiris for an Osirian feast.[22]

In addition, there are at least two Egyptian texts that relate Osiris specifically to the pine: the Papyrus Louvre 3148 and the Embalming Ritual. The Papyrus Louvre 3148, dating from the twenty-sixth dynasty, speaks of it as follows:[23]

i Wsir N
iw n.k ʿš pr m Wsir
O, Osiris N,
the pine which goes out from Osiris comes to you.

The Embalming Ritual contains a similar strophe, which Jean-Claude Goyon has translated as follows: "The *ʿš*-pine comes forth for you from Osiris; it will save you from the hand of your enemies."[24] The date of the papyri containing this last text is the early part of the first century CE,[25] but the similarity between it and the twenty-sixth-dynasty papyrus is undeniable.

Certainly, then, Osiris's link with the Syrian tree predates Plutarch, suggesting that his report may ultimately derive from Egyptian tradition and that Sethe and Chassinat may be correct in their analysis of the tree in Plutarch. Perhaps it is merely that wood for coffins and resin for mummification came from the pine and the Byblian environs, and are thus associated with Osiris, the deceased par excellence. The water journey, too, could arise from the deceased's trip across the river to the necropolis on the west bank. Nevertheless, it does not seem easy to dismiss an Osirian connection with Byblos, even though no text states it explicitly.

Finally, I would like to observe that Osiris's presence in Byblos was as a deceased deity. Analogously, Bata was an exile and thus also dead, in the Otherworld like Osiris.

5
Life in the Valley

Bata as Hunter

The solitariness of the hunting routine into which Bata settled once he was in the valley recalls predynastic times.[1] Although on the most basic level he must have hunted to sustain himself, for those of the New Kingdom such hunting could evoke both royal sport and the mortuary realm. At this time, hunting, and especially hunting by an individual, was almost exclusively the sport and activity of the king. It formed part of the royal dogma,[2] and success in the hunt allowed the hunter to appear as a hero, like certain gods who hunted, such as Horus, Onuris, and Shu.[3] Thus, hunting served as a point of identification of the king with these gods, and in his solitary hunting, Bata gains a similar identification.

The location of the hunting activity in the wasteland gives rise to its other association, that with the mortuary realm.[4] Several references in the Pyramid Texts speak of *Nwt.k-nw,* who, according to Sethe, may be an opponent of the deceased. Alternatively, the term may designate a place where death takes place, that is, the wasteland, or even death itself.[5] In *Pyr.* §851*b,* there is reference to:

> *ir.t n Nwt.k-nw r.k*
> what *Nwt.k-nw* did against you (the deceased),

while *Pyr.* §1905*c* reads:

n rdi.n ṯw n Nwt.k-nw
I have not given you to *Nwt.k-nw.*

Pyr. § 350*a,* the earlier version of §1905*c,* reads:

n rdi.n.f sw n Wsir
he[6] will not give him to Osiris,

making an equation of *Nwt.k-nw* and Osiris and conveying a sense of danger to the deceased. Sethe continues by suggesting that if *-nw* is not a demonstrative but rather signifies the hunter, then the whole reads, "of your hunter's hunting area." On the other hand, following a discussion on the position of the determinative, he concludes it is also possible to read the name as a fixed expression, "that is your *nw.t.*" As explanation, he states that *nw.t* is the place where game succumbs and where man, "the one who is thought of as hunter," also succumbs through death.[7] Seen in this light, it is hard to escape the sense that in Bata the hunter we have to do with a mortuary area, the Otherworld.

It is important to note, however, that *nw* is not the word used for Bata's hunting and to see also that the texts connected with the mortuary aspect of hunting are very old relative to the d'Orbiney. Thus it may not be too much to say that to the New Kingdom listeners/readers the royal side of the solitary hunter was probably of higher import than the mortuary aspect. When the notion of the royal hunter is set alongside the connotations of the king as shepherd par excellence, one easily sees a description of Bata as eminently fitted for kingship. Symbolically, the vision of the activities of hunting and herding in one person represented the original unification of Egypt, the joining of the pastoral and hunting inhabitants of the Nile valley.[8] It was this unification that the accession of each king celebrated.[9] Thus, one can see Bata as having the needed attributes for the throne to which he finally succeeds.

In a final note on Bata the hunter, it should be observed that the description of his hunting activity after he received his wife makes him look rather like a priest:

iw wrš.f ḥr bḥs iꜣwt n ḫꜣst
ḥr in wꜣḥ m-bꜣḥst (d'Orb. 9,9–10,1)

and he spent the day hunting small game
and bringing (it) to place before her.

Since the narrative relates that the fluid of every god was in his wife, that is, she was divine, he appears to be making daily offerings to a deity. This ritual activity was the sole prerogative of the king, the *one* priest, the intermediary between mankind and the gods,[10] though in fact he delegated it to appointed priests. One can understand Bata's act of placing his kill before his wife, a divinity, as similar to the act of the king in his cultic role. It is also possible, however, to interpret this activity as a simple sign of husbandly devotion.

Bata, Bull of the Ennead

After Bata had spent a while in the valley and had built himself a house, ostensibly because he wished to set up a household, he encountered the Ennead,[11] which was "out walking, administering the land" (d'Orb. 9,2–3).[12] This meeting instigated the subsequent events of the tale, beginning with their greeting him as:

kꜣ n tꜣ psḏt (d'Orb. 9,4)
"Bull of the Ennead."

Although in normal usage the word *kꜣ* designates the "lord," the "master," or any prestigious member of a society or group,[13] clearly Bata was not a member of the Ennead, and thus, he could not be its "master" or "lord." According to Sethe, he was rather its "friend" or "favorite."[14] On the other hand, Brunner considered the greeting to be an "honorary title,"[15] while H. Jacobsohn suggests that the address presages Bata's future.[16] In reality, the title occurs in mortuary texts from all periods in reference to the deceased, who is newborn of the Ennead that addresses him.[17] For example, *Pyr.* § 717*a* reads:

RN pw kꜣ psḏt
this king is Bull of the Ennead.

Similar and slightly varying readings can be found in numerous Coffin Texts,[18] most especially *CT* III, 169*a:*

> *ink kꜣ psḏt*
> I am Bull of the Ennead.

Chapter 110 of the Book of the Dead[19] also states a comparable idea:

> *[ink] nṯr pn, kꜣ nb nṯrw*
> [I am] this god, bull, lord of the gods.

Thus the Ennead's greeting adds to the evidence already shown, which places Bata in the mortuary realm. The apparently odd address of the Ennead is then not odd at all, but simply appropriate, since he was actually in the mortuary realm, the Otherworld.

Bata's Wife

When Bata met the Ennead,

> *iw ḥꜣty.sn mr n.f r iqr sp sn* (d'Orb. 9,5–6)
> their heart was exceedingly pained because of him,

and so Pre commanded Khnum:

> *iḫ qd.k wꜥ n st-ḥmt n Bi-ti*
> *tm.f ḥms wꜥ* (d'Orb. 9,6)
> Now, make a wife for Bata
> that he not live alone.[20]

Accordingly,

> *wn.in Ḫnmw ḥr irt n.f iry-ḥmsw*
> *iw.st nfr<.ti> m ḥꜥwt.st*
> *r st-ḥmt nbt*
> *nty m pꜣ tꜣ ḏr.f*
> *iw <mw n> ntr nb in.st* (d'Orb. 9,7–8)
> Then Khnum made a female companion for him,
> and she was more beautiful in body
> than any woman
> who was in the whole land,
> for the fluid of every god was in her,

thus acting in the role he took in the birth scenes of the king, which are portrayed at Deir el-Bahri and at Luxor.[21] As the finale of this creation, also acting in their traditional role, the Seven Hathors,[22] the determiners of fate, decreed:

> *i.irt.st mt dmt* (d'Orb. 9,9)
> of/by the knife she will die.

The wife of Bata therefore incorporates the traits of divine origin, supreme beauty, and an ominous end, each of which functions significantly in the rest of the tale.

The one thing Bata's wife lacks is a name. In the course of the tale, in addition to the references to her as *st-ḥmt* (d'Orb. 9,6), "wife," and *iry-ḥmsw* (d'Orb. 9,7), "female companion," cited above, she is called *tꜣ ꜥḏdw* (d'Orb. 10,5), "the young woman," *wꜥ šriw n Pꜣ-Rꜥ-Ḥr-ꜣḫty* (d'Orb. 11,5), "a daughter of Pre-Harakhty," *špst ꜥꜣt* (d'Orb. 12,3), "great noble lady," *tꜣ špst* (d'Orb. 15,8; 16,1; 17,5; 17,9; 18,4), "noblewoman," *nsw-ḥmt tꜣ špst* (d'Orb. 18,4), "the royal wife, the noblewoman," and, finally, *tꜣy.f ḥmt* (d'Orb. 17,6; 19,5), "his (Bata's) wife." None of these is a proper name.[23] In fact, it is probable that she is deliberately anonymous.[24] Nevertheless, as early as 1912, Sethe suggested that perhaps the Papyrus d'Orbiney reflects a legend of fetching Hathor from afar, from her cult home in Byblos, in a fashion similar to the way the return of Tefnut-Hathor, the sun-eye, reflects the return of Hathor from Nubia.[25] He observed that among the various tales of her return, the Onuris legend reports that Shu designates Tefnut as the *iry-ḥms nfr,* which recalls *iry-ḥmsw* as a designation for Bata's wife (d'Orb. 9,7). He stated that the term, which he translated "life's companion," does not belong to the "common linguistic heritage,"[26] implying that its use in the d'Orbiney sets the tale apart from a common tale.

Other aspects of the tales about Hathor's return provide striking parallels to the Papyrus d'Orbiney. In the tale of the return of the sun-eye from Nubia, Thoth needed to use attention, gifts, stories, and other entertainments to succeed in his mission,[27] just as the woman in the d'Orbiney used jewelry to entice the young woman to return with her to Egypt (d'Orb. 12,1–2). The rejoicing at the return of the sun-eye likewise reminds one of the jubilation accorded the arrival of Bata's wife in Egypt.[28] Its parallel is present in the Onuris legend as well.[29]

The story of the "Destruction of Mankind," which is found in the tombs of Seti I, Ramesses II, and Ramesses III[30] and is thus contemporary with the Papyrus d'Orbiney, shows another side of Hathor for which a parallel also exists in the tale about Bata's wife. There, Hathor's insatiable lust for mankind's destruction corresponds to the repeated and persistent attempts by Bata's wife to destroy him. In the end, both women were thwarted, a denouement which further emphasizes the similarity of the two deities.

Correspondences between the two also occur outside myth and legend. Hathor, definitely an Egyptian deity, had enjoyed long-standing connections with the *tꜣ-nṯr,* "the god's lands," a term designating those lands lying outside the Egyptian domain:[31] Punt,[32] the Sinai,[33] and of course Byblos. No later than the time of the Coffin Texts, she was known in Egypt as *nbt-Kbn,* "mistress of Byblos,"[34] although whether or not she filled this role during the Old Kingdom, when there was much commerce between Byblos and Egypt, is uncertain.[35] During the New Kingdom, Tuthmosis III had a temple built for her in Byblos.[36] In addition, a hieratic papyrus from Kahun describes Hathor of Byblos as the protector goddess of Egypt.[37] Thus, the similarity of the physical location makes further identification of the two possible.

Their respective beauty also connects the two deities. The narrator describes Bata's wife as "more beautiful of body than any woman in the whole land" (d'Orb. 9,7–8). Correspondingly, Spells 483 and 484 of the Coffin Texts speak of the beauty of Hathor, and in *Pyr.* §1208*b, CT* V, 15*c,* and *CT* VI, 162*q,* she is designated *nfrt,* "the beautiful one." Both females were desirable as well. In the "Contendings of Horus and Seth," Hathor uses seductive behavior and presumably her innate beauty to delight her sulking father, Pre,[38] while Bata's wife, also a daughter of Pre (d'Orb. 11,5), was desired by her husband (d'Orb. 9,9) and was loved by the king (d'Orb. 12,2). Again there appears good reason to see in Bata's wife a reflex or form of Hathor.

The presence of Bata's wife in the Valley of the Pine, an Otherworld location, is analogous to the understanding of

Hathor as a mortuary deity, one of the Souls of the West, the deceased.[39] She was friends with the deceased,[40] and received offerings as goddess of the necropolis.[41] She also had a cult home in the western hills of Thebes, where she was called *nbt mšrw,*[42] "Mistress of the Western Mountain" or "Mistress of the Evening," depending on how *mšrw* is interpreted.[43] At Giza and Memphis, she was called *Ḥwt-Ḥr nb.t smywt,* "Hathor, mistress of the desert."[44] She is further related to the mortuary realm by means of texts which tell that she cared for Osiris[45] and which refer to a female deceased as a Hathor.[46] Like Hathor, Bata's wife received offerings—Bata placed his day's kill before her (d'Orb. 10,1)—and finally she was associated with Bata in his exile, his living death.

One can see another parallel between Hathor and Bata's wife in their relations to the king. Each was mother-wife to the king, for Bata's wife became his mother, and he eventually became king. This role, apparent in the etymology of her name, *Ḥwt-Ḥr,* "house of Horus,"[47] was a traditional and well-known one for Hathor[48] and is particularly basic to her character.[49] While symbolically one might construe the "house" as her womb, more likely it refers to the vault of heaven in which the falcon god Horus flew. Certainly Hathor was the original mother of Horus.[50] In the Pyramid Texts, the deceased king is asked:

> *ṯwt RN nṯr smsw s3 Ḥwt-Ḥr* (*Pyr.* 466*a*)
> Are you the king, the god, the eldest, the son of Hathor?

Further emphasis on her royal relationship lies in her title *nbt t3wy,* "Mistress of the Two Lands,"[51] a title which parallels that of the king, *nb t3wy,* "Lord of the Two Lands." Her closeness is also emphasized in four fourth-dynasty sculpted triads in which the king appears with a Hathor-coiffed female and the personification of one of the nomes.[52] In addition, the close relation of the king with Hathor is seen in the cultic use of the sistrum, for the king was the only male who could use it, and he was allowed to do so because she was his divine mother.[53]

Hathor's position as wife of the king can be derived from her relationship with the queen. Initially, during the Old Kingdom, various daughters of the kings, as well as other female royal relatives, were among the priestesses of Hathor,[54] and under Mentuhotep II, the main royal wife was a *ḥmt-nṯr Ḥwt-Ḥr,* "priestess of Hathor."[55] By the end of the Middle Kingdom, the queen was perceived as the embodiment of Hathor and was designated by the relevant epithets in Sinuhe: *pt.k,* "your heaven,"[56] *nb.t r ḏr,* "Mistress of All,"[57] and *nb.t pt,* "Mistress of Heaven."[58] The queen also bore the title *nbt tꜣ,* "Mistress of the Land,"[59] similar to the designation of Hathor as *nbt tꜣwy.* Her identification with Hathor was further strengthened by her role as mother of the king, a role giving her a higher rank than that held by the wife of the king.[60] Not only did she physically bear the king, recalling the etymology of Hathor's name, but she also played a special role in his legitimation.[61] Bata's wife resembles Hathor on both counts, being not merely the king's wife, as she became when she went to Egypt, but also bearing the king.

Although Bata's wife can be identified very closely with Hathor, it is well to ask if there are not other goddesses with whom she can be identified, but in fact her foreign origin effectively eliminates Egyptian goddesses other than Hathor. Even Isis, who does appear outside Egypt, provides no real parallel, for her strength in foreign lands dates to Graeco-Roman times.[62] It is possible to suppose that some of the foreign goddesses from Syria-Palestine, especially those who came to Egypt at some point, might be identified with her. Among these are Astarte, Anat, and Qudšu, who appear mostly in royal inscriptions.[63] Noninscriptional references include that of Astarte in the story of the sea in the Astarte Papyrus[64] and that of Astarte and Anat in their designation as the daughters of Pre in the "Contendings of Horus and Seth."[65] Elsewhere they are absent, however, and one must conclude that they do not contribute significantly to the understanding of Bata's wife.

Although she lacked foreign connections, it is quite possible that Bata's wife was seen by the nineteenth-dynasty audience as related to Isis, for differences between Isis and Hathor were much less clearly delineated then than earlier.[66] Both were designated *nb.t tꜣwy,*[67] and both were depicted with the headdress of the sundisk between cow's horns. Isis, whose name has been taken to designate the personification of the throne or to mean that she is the incorporation of the throne,[68] is the mother of Horus by means of a mythical pregnancy, like that of Bata's wife.[69] Her role as mother of the king likewise recalls the wife. Finally, in the Kamutef concept,[70] in which the old Horus procreated the new Horus, the mother and wife is Isis.[71] Despite this possibility, however, the foreign locale and the tale's concern with the hair, as well as the fact that she actually became queen, suggest that Bata's wife most likely was understood by the tale's audience as a form of Hathor.

P3 Ym

Because Bata knew his wife was in danger from the sea,[72] his first words to her were a warning:

> *m ir pr r-bwn-r*
> *tm p3 ym iṯ3.ṯ* (d'Orb. 10,1–2)
> Do not go out
> lest the sea seize you.[73]

The picture here is of a personified, active, if not predatory, sea, which stands in contrast to its more usual Egyptian descriptions. Normally, the term *p3 ym* served to designate bodies of water referred to previously by the term *w3ḏ-wr,* "the great green."[74] As a loan word from Northwest Semitic **yammu, p3 ym* denoted any sizable body of water, such as large rivers, basins, and the sea,[75] and in New Kingdom Egypt, it designated not just the Nile and the Mediterranean with their associated fresh and salt waters but the Faiyum as well.[76]

The only possible Egyptian parallel to an active, predatory sea appears in the Astarte Papyrus, where the sea demands ever-increasing tribute from the gods.[77] Helck believes that neither of these examples is Egyptian in tenor, mostly because of his opinion that the Astarte Papyrus is basically not Egyptian.[78] Although one may argue with this last idea, the Egyptians appear to have derived their concept of a divinized sea from their Semitic neighbors. Certainly Lefebvre felt so,[79] as did Brunner-Traut, who wrote, "The motif of the woman-robbing sea in the Asarte papyrus was unthinkable without the influence of a Syro-Palestinian mythical material."[80] In fact, Egyptian sources show only a few instances in which waters appear in personified form. For example, Nun, "the primordial ocean . . . the amorphous mass,"[81] appears paired with Naunet in the Hermopolitan Ogdoad, shows a close relationship with Ptah, is occasionally identified with Amun as the primordial creator,[82] and is called on by Re in the "Destruction of Mankind." The *wꜣḏ-wr* is attested to in personified form only once: in the tomb of Sahure at Abusir,[83] and *pꜣ ym* is personified only in the Astarte and d'Orbiney papyri. The Nile god Hapi is frequently personified as a god of fertility and the beneficent flood, also appearing alongside Nun as god of the primordial waters.[84] In no case, however, does one encounter him as a predatory deity of the sort encountered in the narrative.

Although the sea behaves similarly in the d'Orbiney and the Astarte Papyrus, the incident in the d'Orbiney is not a variation derived from the Astarte Papyrus. Very briefly, the Astarte Papyrus, which dates from the time of Haremhab and exists in badly damaged condition, tells of ever-increasing demands on the gods by *pꜣ ym*. At the point when *pꜣ ym* sees Astarte, the daughter of Ptah, her attractiveness incites him to demand her in addition to his other tribute. It has been deduced, despite the badly damaged ending, that eventually *pꜣ ym* is overcome by Seth, most likely by means of his voice.[85] In comparison, *pꜣ ym* in the d'Orbiney makes only one demand: Bata's wife, who in this case is not the heroine but the antagonist. Furthermore, while Seth quells the sea in the Astarte Papyrus, Bata states he is incapable of doing so:

> *ḫr nn iw.i <r> rḫ nḥm.ṯ m-di.f*
> *pr-wn tw.i <m> st-ḥmt mi qd.ṯ* (d'Orb. 10, 2)
> I am not able to rescue you from it
> because I am a woman like you,

referring to "his general incapability to be able to preserve the young woman before 'the greed of the sea'."[86] It is clear that in this situation, Bata could not be considered as a form of Seth.

6
Royal Egypt

Bata's Wife Goes to Egypt

When, in typical folk-narrative style,[1] Bata's wife did go out despite the warning, the sea behaved not just as a predator, taking a lock of hair,[2] but also, and perhaps more significantly, as a messenger. The sea provided the means whereby the king gained knowledge of the woman's existence, rather than seeking the woman for its own ends, as in the Astarte Papyrus, and it is the king, not the sea, who is the ultimate abductor. He was attracted by the scent of the hair[3] that had permeated his washed clothes, provoking the search for its source.[4] When the scent was found to come from a lock of hair, its identification by the sages as belonging to a daughter of Pre-Harakhty, presumably by the odor, is typically Egyptian, for Egyptian gods were distinguished by a special smell. A Pyramid Text states:

> *sṯ.f sṯ nṯr* (*Pyr.* §1241*a*)
> his odor is the odor of a god,

and in the birth scene at Deir el Bahri, when Amun visited Queen Ahmes for the procreation of Hatshepsut:

> *rs.n.s ẖr sṯi nṯr* (*Urk.* IV, 219, 13)
> she (Ahmes) awoke because of the odor of the god.

This special odor, the chief trait that distinguishes gods from people, emanated from all gods.[5] *De Iside et Osiride,* Chapter 15, reports that the presence of Isis in Byblos became known to the Queen of Byblos through the same means. The queen's maidservants carried the divine odor on their skin, arousing in her a longing for Isis's hair and skin, very like the king's longing for Bata's wife.[6]

The wife's loss of a lock of hair to the sea strengthens her identification as a form or reflex of Hathor. A magical text from P. Ramesseum XI refers to a tress of hair lost by Hathor. The mythological reference is obscure, but in the text, fragmented as it is, the reference stands in parallel form to the loss by Horus of his eye, by Seth of his testicles, and by Thoth of his shoulder.[7] In fact, apparently on this loss alone, Posener draws a comparison between Bata's wife and Hathor.[8] Going even further than Posener did and using the two hair motifs, H. 1213.1 and T 11.4.1, Love through Sight of Hair of Unknown Woman, one must note that the wife's hair, or rather more precisely its odor, and the king's reaction to it recall the part hair plays in Egyptian love songs. When one also remembers that Hathor is frequently the deity invoked in these songs as the goddess of love,[9] it is truly difficult to escape the sense that Bata's wife is indeed a form of Hathor.

The sages called the hair *nḏ-ḥr,* a "greeting" or "gift" from another land (d'Orb 11,5), which was interpreted by Sethe as booty or tribute from another land, similar to hunting booty.[10] His emphasis evokes the frequent tomb paintings from the New Kingdom that depict foreign booty, goods, and prisoners being presented to the king.[11] In addition, its source in another land, specifically the Asian area, reminds one of the enigmatic reference to the tresses of an Asiatic woman, *nbḏt Sṯt ḥmt,* in Chapter 172 of the Book of the Dead.[12] It is tempting to see some common tradition underlying this reference, but it is not possible to prove.

Without explanation, the sages tell the king to send envoys, *wpwt,*[13] all over to search for her, but

ḫr ir pꜣ wpwt nty
  iw.f r tꜣ int pꜣ ꜥš
imi šmt rmṯ qnw ḥnꜥ<.f> r int.s (d'Orb. 11, 6–7)

As for the messenger who
goes to the Valley of the Pine,
have many people go with <him> to bring her back.

The need for "many people" to go with the messenger to the Valley of the Pine suggests a prescience reminiscent of Bata's warning to his wife about the sea. In fact, this kind of foreknowledge is quite typical of traditional folk tales. One might even see it as an emphasis on Bata's successful resistance to this first mission, a resistance which is striking when it is compared with the words to his wife that he was a woman like her and could not rescue her from the sea. Several plausible explanations exist to account for this anomaly. It is possible to see the sea episode on a cosmological level in which Bata is unable to combat the sea, lacking the cosmic force of Seth, but he can resist the men. It is also possible to view his fighting as a hearkening back to his statement that he would fight whoever felled the tree on which was placed his cutout heart (d'Orb. 8,5–6), although this is not precisely the situation, since the soldiers were after his wife. The third and most likely possibility derives from the need to depict his fighting prowess in anticipation of his assumption of kingship later in the tale, for kingship ideology demanded that the king be a successful warrior.[14] Illustrative of this ideology is Ramesses II's Kadesh Battle Inscriptions that describe how the king, virtually single-handed, defeated his foes.[15] Another example appears on a gold coffer of Tutankhamon where the young king, still a boy, is depicted overcoming his enemies.[16]

To all appearances, the success of the second mission to get the young woman is due ostensibly to the presence of the woman with jewelry, but part of it may also arise from the possession of the lock of hair itself by the king, that is, by force of sympathetic magic.[17] Although I know of no similar situation in ancient Egypt to confirm this idea, the concept is amply attested to in ancient and modern cultures throughout the world.[18]

When Bata's wife arrived in Egypt, she was received with great joy and excitement, and

wn.in ḥm.f ʿws ḥr mrwt st r iqr sp sn
iw.tw[19] *ḥr thn*[20]*.st r špst ʿ3t* (d'Orb. 12,2–3)

the king loved her exceedingly
and appointed her as Great Noble Lady.

L. Manniche has stated that the title *špst* was rare during the New Kingdom, noting that Isinofret, the wife or daughter of Merneptah, was the one woman so designated during the Ramesside Period.[21] The title was also carried by Kiya, "the 'other' wife of Akhenaton."[22] Because one of the references to Kiya calls her *tꜣ špst* <*n*> *Nhrn,* "the noble lady of Nahrin," and because there are several other references which recall practices of the Amarna period,[23] Manniche has suggested that at this point, the story may represent an allegorical rendering of the arrival of Akhenaton's Mittanian wife.[24] Despite the fact that Kiya was not the only royal wife or mistress of Asiatic origin during the New Kingdom,[25] Manniche's argument is an attractive one. Nevertheless, the fact that in at least one instance the wife of Merneptah and mother of Seti II (the crown prince under whose aegis the d'Orbiney was written) carries the epithet *špst* inclines one to relate its use to a time closer than over a century previous, as would be the situation in deriving it from Kiya. In any case, the title serves to lend to the tale the possibility of historical reflexes.

Bata's Death and Anubis's Search

The king's inquiry to Bata's wife about her husband led to the betrayal of Bata's secret and resulted in his death. In a sense, Bata was the cause of his own downfall because he shared the secret of his life with his wife. Indeed, Egyptian wisdom literature counsels against doing just what he did:

imi.k wṯs *ib.k n pꜣ s ḏrḏri*
r rdit gm.tw.f r.k
. . .
whn tꜣ pr rmṯ ḥr ns.f (Any 7, 7–9)
Do not reveal your heart to a stranger
in order that it may be used against you
. . .
The land and house of a man may be ruined because of his tongue.

Thus when the soldiers came a third time, Bata did not fight them but fell dead as they

šʿd tꜣ ḥrr nty ḥꜣty n Bi-ti ḥr.st (d'Orb. 12,6–7)
cut the blossom on which was Bata's heart.

Jacobsohn views this death as Bata's real death, after which he cannot be killed again. He considers it to be the result of Bata's inability to satisfy his wife sexually, because of his lack of a phallus and of a heart, the latter being the source of creative power.[26] On the other hand, one may view it as the main turning point of Bata's transition from one existence to another in his rite of passage from shepherd-farmer to king. It is the climax of his separation from his previous existence, representing his death to his old position.

In the traditional folk narrative, a similar symbolic death virtually always takes place as the hero moves from his lowly position as shepherd or youngest son to success, marriage, and rulership. From a purely Egyptian viewpoint, in Egyptian mortuary practice, a significant period of time elapsed between the death of an individual and his or her reawakening in the next world, accomplished by means of the "Opening of the Mouth" ritual. During that time (seventy-two days according to Herodotus) much was done to the corpse, and it is not difficult to see an analogy to events between Bata's loss of his phallus and heart and the preparations of the deceased for his or her next life.[27] In fact, the cutting of the tree with Bata's heart on its blossom makes possible Bata's resuscitation to his new life. In other words, in this narrative one may see several stages on the journey between the departure from the ordinary world in death and the eventual and successful arrival in the Otherworld.

On another plane, Bata's murder is necessary in order to make his wife's life with the Pharaoh legitimate, for, as seen above, adultery was condemned. It also is possible to see his murder as a continuum and fulfillment of the previous adultery scene in which the explicit attempt to kill Bata by Anubis's adulterous wife was unsuccessful. It likewise parallels the pattern of an unsuccessful attempt followed by a successful one to remove Bata's wife to Egypt.

When Anubis received the signal of Bata's death, it was not simply the foaming beer, as arranged (d'Orb. 8,6), but included sour wine as well (d'Orb. 12,9–10). Both beer and wine were drinks common in the everyday life of Egypt, and each was one of the elements of the offering ritual, especially beer. Because the traditional beer-holding jug was one of the types of vessels employed for the revitalizing waters in mortuary, royal, and divine purification rituals,[28] it is possible that the beer anticipates Bata's future revival by Anubis. It is also possible to see an association of unnatural foaming and sour smells with putrefaction of a corpse; such signs would be an appropriate indicator of death. In addition, various Pyramid Texts dealt with the efflux of Osiris, the liquids of putrefaction, and refreshment of the deceased.[29] That Anubis, the mortuary god, receives these indicators is most appropriate, even apart from the fact that he is Bata's brother. Thus, the symbolism of the foaming beer and sour wine contributes to the emphasis on Bata's death.

One finds Bata's death emphasized again in the description of Anubis's arrival at Bata's house, where:

> *iw.f ḥr gm pꜣy.f sn šri*
> *sḏr ḥr pꜣy.f ḥꜥt(i)*
> *iw.f mt* (d'Orb. 13,2–3)
> he found his young brother
> lying dead upon his bed.

This image calls to mind the many portrayals in New Kingdom tombs and papyri of Anubis standing over the deceased as he or she is laid out on the lion bed in the tent of purification, the *sḥ-nṯr*.[30] The house that Bata had built and furnished for himself now serves as the place in which he is laid out and revived. It functions truly as the *sḥ-nṯr* in which Anubis will perform his life-renewing role.

Anubis's search for and finding of Bata's heart, an integral part of Egyptian mortuary beliefs,[31] recalls Isis's search for Osiris in *De Iside et Osiride* 18. An example of her search that is more contemporaneous with the d'Orbiney comes from the eighteenth-dynasty "Hymn to Osiris," Louvre C 286:[32]

> *ꜣst ꜣḫt nḏ.t sn.s*
> *ḥḥ.t sw iwtt bꜣgg.s*
> *pẖr.t tꜣ pn m ḥꜣyt*
> *n ḫn.n.s n gm.tw sw* (lines 14–15)

mighty Isis who protected her brother,
who sought him without tiring,
who traversed this land in mourning,
not stopping until she found him.

It is easy to see an identification of the act of Isis with that of Anubis in their respective searches and ultimate successes. The search thus provides another example of identification between Osiris and Bata.

After Anubis had found Bata's heart and had followed his brother's instructions concerning its treatment, Bata became as he had been:

wn.in wʿ qni wʿ im.sn (d'Orb. 14,3–4)
then, the one embraced the other.

Both Frankfort[33] and Brunner-Traut[34] view the embrace as a way to impart life, and in support Frankfort cites the following text:

hꜣ Wsir RN
Ḥr nw m-ẖnw ʿwy.k
inḏ.f ṯw
ꜣḫ n.f ʿn ḥr.k
m rn.k n ꜣḫt prrt Rʿ im.k
sbḫ n.k ʿwy.k ḥꜣ.f ḥꜣ.f (*Pyr.* § 636*a–c*)[35]
Oh, Osiris King,
this is Horus in your embrace;
he protects you.
It is well with him again with you
in your name of "the horizon from which Re goes forth."
Clasp your arms around him, about him.[36]

This description evokes the tomb scenes in which the god is depicted embracing or reaching to the king, often with the *ankh* sign in his or her hand, thereby imparting to the king new life.[37] One must understand that in this act, Anubis confirms Bata's new life and suggests his future role as king.

Bata as Bull: Life and Death

After Anubis, acting in his traditional mortuary role, had revived Bata, Bata said:

ptr iw.i <*r*> *ḫprw m wꜥ n kꜣ ꜥꜣ*
iw.f m inw nbt nfr
iw nn rḫ.tw pꜣy.f sḫrw (d'Orb. 14,5)
See I <will> become a great bull
of every beautiful color,
whose nature is unknown.

His appearance as this bull the next morning recalls the daily rebirth of the sun as the calf-to-be-bull, the ultimate symbol of revival. Here one meets Bata as bull for a second time, but this time it is with connotations for life rather than for the mortuary realm. The living bull carried implications of power and fertility in relation to the royal ideology, and the many predynastic and early dynastic materials depicting bulls in attitudes of power[38] attest to their historic veneration by the Egyptians. In fact, by the eighteenth dynasty, kings had begun to assume the designation "strong bull" at the beginning of their titulary, portraying themselves as bulls, a practice continued with a vengeance through the end of the Ramesside period.[39]

The importance of bulls as a symbol of the fertility[40] necessary for an agrarian people is evident in the presence of the bull, most particularly a bull with special markings, as an integral part of harvest festivals. In these celebrations, bulls were led on a course over the fields to assure fertility of the fields and the herds.[41] The special markings took different forms, depending on the locality in question. Each of the known sacred bulls had its own special markings: Apis was black with a white triangle, a crescent moon, and an eagle on his body;[42] Mnevis was all black with a line of coarse hair running the length of his body and tail;[43] and Mont was a white bull with a black head.[44] None of these descriptions quite fits Bata as bull despite the earlier references to him as Apis.[45] Erman points to the unknown aspect of the Bata-bull,[46] which, Griffiths suggests, highlights the significance of his coloring.[47] The result is to set Bata as bull apart from any known bull while at the same time incorporating in him the power and fecundity inherent in the bull as symbol and relating him to royalty.

The welcome accorded Bata on his arrival in Egypt in the

form of this magnificent bull recalls both that given to his wife on her arrival and the rejoicing that accompanied the discovery of a new Apis[48] and, most probably, that of other special bulls as well. It was the first of three celebrations for him, each affirming the special nature of his existence and his particular form at the time.

Each of the first two festivals on his account and the one given his wife on her arrival in Egypt presaged her unsuccessful attempts to destroy him. This destructive behavior results in her fated death by the knife (d'Orb. 9, 9), but the role in which she is depicted is not unusual as far as women in ancient Egyptian history and literature are concerned.[49] There is the documented harem conspiracy dating to the time of Ramesses III,[50] while an apparent female conspiracy against the king is seen in the "Instruction of King Amenemhet I for his son Sesostris I."[51] In addition, the flight of Sinuhe seems to have been caused by the death of Amenemhet I at the hands of the harem,[52] and the "Destruction of Mankind"[53] relates Hathor's lethal behavior.

The power of Bata's wife to act repeatedly against him derives from the information he continually revealed to her, namely that he was still alive. She accomplished each of her attempts in the same way: She and the king were sitting, *ḥr irt hrw nfr* (d'Orb. 16,2), "spending a holiday," a phrase that carries a double connotation, one from daily life and the other related to death and the afterlife.[54] She placed the king under an oath to act according to her wish, a wish she revealed to him only after he took the oath (d'Orb. 16,3–4, 17,9–10). He was then constrained to carry out his word despite his personal unhappiness, for such was the nature of the oath.[55] In this, there is a certain resemblance to the passing of a punishment on oneself, as Seth did in the "Contendings of Horus and Seth," although otherwise there is no apparent parallel.[56]

The excuse used by Bata's wife for killing the bull was her desire for his liver. An animal's or bird's liver has been considered to have magical properties in all times,[57] especially an ability to effect cures; the Egyptian medical texts themselves attest to this concept.[58] The bull was also a common offering in the mortuary and temple cults of all periods,[59] and so it is significant that Bata as bull became an actual offering, even as the slaughter of a bull formed a regular part of the "Ritual of the Opening of the Mouth."[60]

Eberhard Otto suggests that the standard for the eleventh Lower Egyptian nome depicting a bull with a knife represents the possibility of an old bull cult. In the late period, this nome was proscribed in the belief that it was here that Osiris was killed,[61] and Otto thinks this belief represents a mixing of the death of Osiris and a myth of a slain bull god, perhaps represented by the reading of the standard: *ḥsbw,* "the slaughtered one." Whether and how to relate these ideas and facts to the slaughter of Bata in his bull form in this nome is questionable, especially since Bata is connected with Upper Egypt. The presence, however, of a reference to *K3 nb S3k3,* "Bull, Lord of Saka," on the Leyden V,1 stela[62] and Bata, Lord of Saka, in his bull form suggests to Otto the vestige of a bull cult in Upper Egypt and, by implication, similar practices.[63]

Bata as Persea

The procreative power exhibited in the blood that fell from the neck of the slaughtered Bata-bull, producing two *šwb*-trees, perseas, belies his previous impotence. It also recalls the power of the drops of blood from the phallus of Re that became Hu and Sia in Chapter 17 of the Book of the Dead.[64] In addition, the offering the king made to the trees evokes the practice of worshipping the embodiment of divinities in trees,[65] Hathor especially.[66] The significance of the trees extends further, however, and originates both from their natural proclivities and from their mythical significance.

The persea, or *šwb*-tree, is not counted among the holy trees of Egypt.[67] Instead, it derives its meaning from its association with the inundation. Derchain, relating it to Heliopolis, has shown that the ripened fruits of this tree fall precisely at the inception of the flood.[68] Because of this fact, the *šwb*-tree is related naturally to the funerary symbolism of rebirth, announcing a return to life, even as does the flood.[69] Although in the Papyrus d'Orbiney it is not the fruits that fall, but the trees themselves,[70] the same symbolism can be supposed to be present, especially since the felling (which initially represents

Bata's death) results in his rebirth as crown prince. At the same time, it recalls the earlier feeling of the pine, which also resulted in death followed by revival.

Another tree identified as the persea is the *išd,*[71] although neither the *Wörterbuch* nor the *Concise Dictionary* defines it as such, the one calling it a "holy tree"[72] and the other simply "a tree."[73] In the *Lexikon* article on the *išd,* Kákosy writes "(Persea?)."[74] In contrast to the *šwb*-tree, the *išd* is most definitely a holy tree.[75] It was associated with Heliopolis and known especially for its relation to the king, for on its leaves was written the name of the king.[76] It was also familiar for its association with the Osiris grave in the later New Kingdom,[77] and in the Coffin Texts and the Book of the Dead, it was split by the Great Cat, Re, on the night of the annihilation of the enemies of the Lord of the Universe.[78] In addition, *išd*-bouquets were placed about for the deceased,[79] and it is well known that two *išd*-trees flanked the representation of the eastern horizon in the Temple of Dendera, attesting to its cosmic association with the sun.[80] Two of them also marked the entrance to the mortuary temple of Hatshepsut at Deir el-Bahri.[81]

Although both the *šwb*- and the *išd*-trees have been identified and interpreted as the persea, and both were related to Heliopolis, whether they were related to each other is open to question. Indeed two notable scholars disagree on the classification. Moftah states the *išd*-tree is the *Mimusop Schimperi Hochst,* while Keimer says that the *Mimusop Schimperi Hochst* is the *šwb*-tree.[82] In the Papyrus d'Orbiney, it appears the two carry a similar or identical symbolism and perhaps an association, for the pairing of the trees on either side of the palace gate through which the king appeared recalls the *išd*-tree, while correspondingly, the felling of the trees represents the sense of renewal and new life shown by the falling fruit of the *šwb.* The fact that felling a holy tree was proscribed[83] could explain why this tree is the *šwb*-tree rather than the *išd*-tree. This is to speculate that the persea is equally the *išd*- and the *šwb*-tree, the one under its holy, cosmic guise and the other with more secular, agricultural, renewal connotations. Moftah also feels that *šwb* is a general designation of the *išd*-tree, itself the ancient name of the tree and one which appears in religious literature to designate a holy tree.[84]

The same procreative power that Bata showed on being slaughtered in his bull form appears again in his tree form when his wife becomes pregnant by swallowing the splinter of the felled tree, and it again directly contradicts his earlier emasculated state. Her conception via the mouth recalls Seth swallowing Horus's semen in the "Contendings of Horus and Seth."[85] It also recalls the solar motif of Nut swallowing the sun each evening and giving birth to it each morning, an analogy initially proposed by Maspero.[86] This motif forms a major part of the solar mythology in which the extinguished sun, like the dead body, joined Osiris, becoming Osiris, encountering the dangers of the Underworld, and then being reborn the following morning.[87] The *Book of Day* and the *Book of Night,* examples of which appear on the ceilings of corridors C, D, and E and in Sarcophagus Hall I in the tomb of Ramesses VI,[88] depict this idea. In them Nut is shown with the sun entering her mouth, passing through her elongated body,[89] which stretches from horizon to horizon, and being born from between her legs.[90] Similar depictions of this distinctive activity of Nut[91] appear in the Osirion of Abydos (Seti I), the tomb of Ramesses IV, and two demotic papyri as well as variant forms elsewhere.[92] The swallowing portion is expressed in an address to Nut found in the Pyramid Texts:

RN pw mtwt nṯr
  imwt.ṯ[93] *Nwt*
šsp n.ṯ sw RN pn
  mr šsp.ṯ s3 nṯr (*Pyr.* §1417*a–b*)
The king is the semen of the god
  which is in you, O Nut;
receive this king
  as you would the son of a god.

The Pyramid Texts also tell of the birth of Re from Nut:

ḥms.k r.k ḥr ḫndw pw n Rʿ
  wḏ.k mdw n nṯrw
n ṯwt is Rʿ pr m Nwt
  mss.t Rʿ hrw nb
ms RN pn hrw nb mi Rʿ (*Pyr.* §§1688*a–c*)
Sit upon the throne of Re
  and command the gods,

for indeed you are Re who comes forth from Nut
who bears Re daily,
and you are born daily like Re.

Kamutef

When Nut is perceived as the cow goddess who bears the sun, the calf, which grows to become a bull that then impregnates her to be reborn,[94] one encounters the cosmological expression of *Kꜣ-mwt.f,* Kamutef, "Bull of his mother." The following texts from the pyramids give an early presentation of the idea:

RN pw dmḏ mwt.f smꜣ.t wr.t
mwt nt RN smꜣ.t
ḥmst tpt ḏw smy tpt ḏw sḥsḥ (*Pyr.* §§388*c*–389*a*)
The king joined his mother, the great wild cow;
the mother of the king is the wild cow
who dwells on the mountain of pasture and the mountain of the *sḥsḥ*-bird.
[iw.n] RN pn ḥr.k Rʿ
bḥs n nbw msw pt
ḥꜣḏ n nbw qmꜣw Ḥsꜣt (*Pyr.* §1029*a–c*)
This king [has come] to you, Re,
a calf of gold, born of heaven,
a fatted calf[95] of gold which Hesat created.

Later, *Kꜣ-mwt.f* appears specifically in the Coffin Texts:

iw ʿnḫ ḫr.k
nb imntt
sꜣ Ḥr-ꜣḫty
kꜣ-mwt.f Nwt (*CT* I, 237*b*)
You will have life,
Lord of the West,
Son of Harakhty,
Bull of his mother, Nut.

In recent years, Kamutef has been the major concept informing scholars in their studies of the Papyrus d'Orbiney, especially Jacobsohn.[96] In fact, Griffiths thinks this idea is more significant in relation to Bata than the view that he is an Osirian character.[97] The essence of the concept is that the future king is procreated by the god, united in form with the present king,[98] who himself was thus conceived. Going to the queen, a woman "more beautiful than any woman in the land,"[99] the god begets his son and the heir. In the next generation, the same act will occur again, so that the son becomes the father united with the god to procreate a new son.[100] Thus the divine king, the one who is the incarnation of the god,[101] is responsible for the divine renewal over the generations, and he unites the divine and earthly realm, joining "the divine as something over-worldly and beyond time with the world of appearances."[102] As Jacobsohn explains it, Kamutef functions as the "binding member" of the father-son succession.[103]

According to Assmann, in the concept of Kamutef the immaterial and the timeless are bound to the present, which progresses into the future,[104] standing as a complement to, and probably older than, the concept of Horus kingship.[105] The latter emphasizes the son as successor to the father,[106] and the two together, Horus and Kamutef, provide continuity to kingship. In addition, Kamutef relates the king to the picture of Osiris, of which Otto says, "In it is met the patriarchal-nomadic concept of sovereignty (father-son succession) with the farmer-vegetative concept of life (immortality in the plant resurrection)."[107]

The New Kingdom, especially the nineteenth and twentieth dynasties, was the period which saw the floruit of the concept of Kamutef. Its expressions are recognizable in the cult actions and renderings of the cultic texts and offering rituals of the time.[108] It is thus most appropriate to see the d'Orbiney as a literary expression of this important idea. In fact, in some ways the narrative of Bata explains the Kamutef concept much more clearly than is possible through any abstract discussion, perhaps providing a reason for its existence in the first place. The divinely formed woman becomes the *nsw ḥmt* (d'Orb. 18,4), "royal wife," and Bata, in the form of a splinter, impregnates her, making her his wife.[109] It is just at this point that he achieves the act of procreation which characterizes Kamutef and which he was unable to accomplish with his wife in his castrated, heartless form in the Valley of the Pine.

When he is born as the crown prince, he brings to full cycle the idea of Kamutef: he is his own father/he is his own son, that is, an aspect of the father,[110] his reincarnation,[111] by means of the queen, and insofar as his wife is identified with Hathor, the mother of kings, Bata is even further fitted for the role of king.[112] It is notable that the crown prince, whom the audience *knows* is Bata because of the preceding episodes, is never called Bata by name. Presumably this apparent omission allows the heir to carry his own name, consonant with historical reality. One might also see it as an affirmation that in Bata the audience is hearing about the god Bydis mentioned in Manetho,[113] as Lauth, Gardiner, and Helck have suggested.[114]

The moon and its phases represent another expression of Kamutef,[115] for the ancient Egyptians perceived the lunar cycle, with its waxing and waning, as different stages of fertility and growth, thus aptly fitting the Kamutef concept.[116] According to Jacobsohn, this Kamutef "is one who renews himself monthly as 'Bull of the Ennead'."[117] Indeed, the repeated and regular self-renewal of the moon[118] represented the essence of the Kamutef idea, earning it the epithet "Bull of the Ennead"[119] that was derived from its new-moon form.[120] With this sense in mind, Jacobsohn suggested that the Ennead's address to Bata as "Bull of the Ennead" was a prophecy, foretelling his eventual fulfillment of all the facets of Kamutef and his becoming king.[121]

Bata's Birth

Bata's actual birth as heir comprises the final component needed to fit him for kingship. The words and phrases employed in describing the events surrounding his birth place him clearly within the royal succession:

ḫr ir m-ḫt hrw qnw ḥr-sꜣ nn
wn.in.st ḥr msyt wꜥ n sꜣ-ṯꜣy
    iw.tw ḥr šmt r ḏd n ḥm.f ꜥws
        msy.tw n.k wꜥ n sꜣ-ṯꜣy
wn.in.tw ḥr int.f
    iw.tw ḥr dit n.f mnꜥt ḫnmw
    iw.tw ḥr nhm <n.f> m pꜣ tꜣ ḏr.f
    iw.tw ḥms ḥr irt hrw nfr

iw.tw ḥr ẖpr m rnn.f
iw ḥm.f ꜥws ḥr mrwt.f r iqr iqr
m tꜣ wnwt
iw.tw ḥr thn.f sꜣ nsw n Kꜣš
ẖr ir m-ẖt hrw qnw ḥr-sꜣ nn
wn.in ḥm.f ꜥws ḥr dit.f
r r-pꜥt n pꜣ tꜣ ḏr<.f> (d'Orb. 18,6–19,2)
Now many days after this,
she gave birth to a son,
and his majesty was told,
"A son is born to you."
He was brought
and he was given a *mnꜥt*-nurse and *ẖnmw*
-nurses,
and there was shouting <for him> in the whole land,
and he (the king) sat for a feast day
and *ẖpr m rnn.f*
and his majesty loved him very much
from that moment
and he was appointed "Royal Son of Kush."
Now, many days after this,
his majesty made him
prince in the whole land.

My particular concerns focus on the use of *ẖpr m rnn.f* (d'Orb. 18,10), the two types of nurses (d'Orb. 18,8), the title "Royal Son of Kush" (d'Orb. 19,1), and Bata's appointment as *r-pꜥt n pꜣ tꜣ ḏr<.f>* (d'Orb. 19,1). The first, second, and fourth items associate Bata with the position of crown prince and heir, while the third, the one that looks most as if it had a strong connection with the kingship, proves to be otherwise.

The issues involved in *ẖpr m rnn.f* involve its grammatical sense and form, its meaning, and its connotations. When Maspero last treated the passage, he read, "they began to be in his name."[122] Although he did not question the meaning of *rnn* itself, he did evidence some hesitation over the significance of the phrase. As possible interpretations, he suggested that it signified either the custom of other children being given the prince's name, or the beginning of the achievement of his personality on the reception of his name.[123]

When Gardiner approached the same passage, he chose to

emend the text with the determinative of the "man with hand to mouth" (A2) so it could be read "to begin to be in jubilation." He suggested that the *f* in the hieratic copy might be due to a misreading by the copyist, resulting in a faulty transcription.[124]

Grammatically, the phrase forms part of a series of consecutive narrative forms, in which *ḫpr* is the active verb. In this case it appears to give verbal force to *rnn* when one views the word *rnn* as an infinitive. Although Erman notes that *ḫpr* is not commonly used as a helping verb in Late Egyptian, when it is so used, "it signifies originally that a condition enters in, an action begins."[125] He does not, however, include this passage among his examples, some of which are drawn from the d'Orbiney; in fact, he shows only one passage in which *ḫpr m* is used. This he does in a note to his discussion in which he observes that *ḫpr m* is used with the infinitive of verbs of going, signifying the beginning of going.[126] In its use with *rnn,* it thus might carry a sense of movement, which coincides well with the various definitions given to the word since the mid-1930s. Specifically, the *Wörterbuch* defines it as "to bring up," especially the king, by goddesses.[127] Faulkner defines it as "to caress, to nurse,"[128] a meaning that Lichtheim[129] and Brunner-Traut[130] have extended to mean "to hold, to take on the lap." The idea of nurturing implies movement in the sense of growth, and hence one might use *ḫpr m* to introduce its inception.

On the other hand, it is also possible to consider *rnn* as a participle, and then the phrase *m rnn* would be the predicate, with the meaning that the king became an embracer, one who takes on the lap. In this case, *ḫpr* carries its customary meaning "to become."

When Brunner-Traut discussed the phrase, she commented that the king's gesture in the story represents part of his act of recognition of the child, which is followed by his official appointment as crown prince.[131] The fullest expression of this act can be found in Scene XI of the birth cycle of Hatshepsut at Deir el-Bahri,[132] a scene depicting Amun as taking the newborn on his lap,[133] with an accompanying text that reads:

sn.s
ḥpt.s

rnn.s
mr.n.f s<t> r ḫt nb (*Urk.* IV, 229, 3–6)
she is kissed,
she is embraced,
she is taken on the lap,[134]
for he loved her more than anything.

At Luxor, the text for the same scene can be read as an imperative, in this case a command of Hathor, as well as the indicative, a statement by Amun. Brunner considers each alternative possible:[135]

rrn sw
mr.n sw r[136]
Take him on the lap/I take him on the lap,
for I (Hathor or Amun) have loved him more (than anything).

One should note the parallels between the phrasing in the d'Orbiney and the recognition scenes of Hatshepsut and Amenhotep III. In each case the line containing the verb *rnn* is followed in the next line by the verb *mri,* to love, itself followed by the superlative. At the very least, the scribe of the d'Orbiney intended to draw a parallel between the recognition of the crown prince—for that is who Bata is—and the recognition of the newborn kings at Deir el Bahri and at Karnak.[137]

Emphasizing the long history of the use of *rnn* as part of the recognition of the king in Egyptian is its presence in the Pyramid Texts:

ḥʿw.f m ḥsf.k
di.f ʿw.f ir.k
isn.f ṯw
rnn.f ṯw (*Pyr.* § 656*a–b*)
he rejoices in meeting you,
and he places his hands on you;
he kisses you,
and he takes you on his lap.

The next clause reads:

wd.f ṯw ḫnt ʿḫw
iḫmw-skw (*Pyr.* § 656*c*)
he places you at the head of the spirits,
the indestructible stars,

which attests to the antiquity of the relation between *rnn* and the following appointment as king, in this case in the Otherworld. Brunner observed, "In the secular sphere one does not meet the word (*rnn*), only in the royal and divine world."[138] Thus one sees that its use is bound up with the legitimation of kingship, and it is used in this way in the d'Orbiney, just as it is in the texts concerning the legitimation of Haremhab (*Urk.* IV, 2113,11), which come from the historical realm.[139]

Bata's care was entrusted to two kinds of nurses, a *mnʿt*-nurse and the *ẖnmw*-nurses. In general, according to Brunner, the *mnʿt*-nurse, *mnʿ* when male, was responsible for the upbringing of the infant child, and performed the *rnn,* "caressing," or *šd,* "suckling."[140] *Rnn* is also juxtaposed with *ẖnm* in the eleventh hour (Hornung's twelfth of the Book of Gates in relation to the emergence of the sun in the east as follows:[141]

94.	*wnn.sn m sẖrw pn* *ntsn ẖnm*[142] *Rʿ* *ḫpr msw.f m tꜣ*	94.	They are these planners; it is they who embrace Re and cause his birth to occur in the land
95.	*wnn.sn m sẖrw pn* *ntsn rnn Rʿ* *sʿꜣ rnw ḫprw.f nb*	95.	They are these planners; it is they who caress Re and make great the names of all his forms.

According to Barguet's study, the *sẖrw,* the planners, are the divinities, the ancient kings and queens, who preside at the sun's birth and who thus transmit their royal power through their acts, *rnn* and *ẖnm,* relative to the sun.[143] Thus I surmise that in the use of *ẖnmw*-nurses, as well as in the *rnn* act, Bata receives further royal legitimation, here in special association with the solar rebirth.

The third element of interest in the d'Orbiney birth passage was Bata's appointment to be *sꜣ nsw n Kꜣš,* "Royal Son of Kush" (d'Orb. 19,1). On investigation, this title does not carry the mark of royal acceptance that the name implies. Brunner found that it is not part of the ancient birth cycle,[144] and therefore it does not relate to the legitimation of the king. Instead, it turns out to be an administrative title[145] given to overseers of the southern countries, the viceroys of Kush, during the eighteenth to twentieth dynasties. It is possible that the first two titleholders, *Tti* and *Ḏḥwti,* who acted under Kamose and Ahmose respectively, may have been true king's sons, but subsequent administrators lacked royal lineage.[146] In light of these facts, the inclusion of the appointment of Bata to this position is curious. Perhaps it reflects the two "real" royal sons in this position, but since their "reality" is not wholly certain, such an idea cannot be confirmed. It may be that the narrator wanted to root some of the story in the historical-political reality of the day, but again, such an idea is merely speculative. In the end, the question must remain open.

In contrast, *r-pꜥt,* Bata's final title, is clearly related to royalty. It is attested from the time of the first dynasty,[147] and although it was not always reserved solely for the crown prince, by the time of the New Kingdom the crown prince alone used it. According to Helck, Haremhab assumed the title to assist in the legitimation of his accession to the throne.[148] Gardiner suggested that when the title is used in conjunction with *sꜣ-nsw* to designate the crown prince, it evokes an air of ancient descent and law of inheritance.[149] In addition, a certain divine legitimation occurs when it occurs as *r-pꜥt* on the throne of Geb, as it does in an Abydos inscription of Ramesses II. Here the king says:

> *iw.i bs.kwi <m sꜣ> smsw.*
> *m r-pꜥt <ḥr> nst Gb*[150]
> I was installed <as the> eldest son
> and heir <upon> the throne of Geb.

Helck's study of this last variant shows that in all times, *r-pꜥt* is an epithet bestowed by the king alone.[151] The crown prince so identified is also a son of Geb, the royal son and heir in association with the myth of Geb, Horus, and Chons, and is the leader of men.[152] Indeed Geb himself is called *r-pꜥt,*[153] "leader of the inhabitants of the earth."[154] The bestowal of the title on Bata grants him further legitimation for his later assumption of kingship.

With his birth as crown prince, the audience finally reaches the last in Bata's series of transformations. Although his series of changes from human to bull, to tree, and, finally, to heir have provoked great interest among the folklorists and Egyptologists for their folklore parallels,[155] such a sequence actually falls well within Egyptian beliefs. In the "Contendings of Horus and Seth," Isis transformed herself into an old woman,[156] then into a young girl,[157] and finally into a kite that flew away.[158] In the same tale, Horus and Seth changed themselves into hippopotamuses.[159] The mortuary texts, too, speak extensively of transformation, and various Coffin Texts are titled as transformation spells, such as Spell 147—"Becoming a Falcon"; Spell 148—"Taking Shape as a Falcon"; Spell 208—"To be the Scribe of Hathor and to become the Bull of On"; and Spell 287—"Becoming a Goose."[160] Such transformations are very much a part of entering and living in the Otherworld, as Bata did when he went to and lived in the Valley of the Pine, an existence that persisted through his return to Egypt until he was reborn of his wife.

Another aspect of these transformations recalls very clearly the common folk-narrative pattern of the hero's unrecognized return. Perhaps the best-known example occurs when Odysseus returns in disguised form to his wife and retainers, in which form he tests and is tested and is then recognized (*Ody.* Bks. 14–21, 23). Similarly, in his altered form, Bata returns and is tested in the sense of his resilient life while at the same time testing his wife, confirming her perfidy. The return of the folk-narrative hero in disguise most commonly follows a long period of absence,[161] a feature Bata also shares. In a sense, the disguise can represent or foretell the change in the hero himself, as is true with Bata, who, having gone through his disguises, each significant to royalty, becomes king.

Accession

The ending of the tale is terse but not insignificant. After Bata acceded to the kingship, he called his officials to inform them of his wife's actions:

> *wn.in.tw in n.f t3y.f ḥmt*
> *iw.f ḥr wpwt ḥnʿ st m-b3ḥ.sn* (d'Orb. 19,5)
> his wife was brought to him
> and he judged her in their presence.

In this act, Bata finally avenged himself as he said he would, both relative to the calumnious acts of Anubis's wife (d'Orb.

8, 5–6) and to the betrayals by his own wife (d'Orb. 14,6–7). Bata's act of judging also, and very importantly, affirms his kingship, in that the king functioned as the ultimate judge in ancient Egypt. Once he had satisfied himself in this way, he appointed his brother *r-pʿt* and ruled for thirty years, at which point he died and Anubis took his place.

7
Conclusion: An Egyptian Tale

The "Tale of Two Brothers" relates a unified story of how a shepherd became king in true fairy- or folktale fashion, but it does so with an ancient Egyptian twist: the dramatis personae are gods, as demanded by the ideology which characterizes ancient Egyptian kingship. That the style and many of the incidents resemble those of typical folktales shows that at the very least, the types of ideas in foundation materials for the modern world of folk narrative also entertained the people of ancient Egypt.[1] Nevertheless, no modern terminology adequately describes this tale;[2] unfortunately the ancient Egyptians provided no terminology either, although they did for some other types of literature.[3] Indeed, one would like to know what the ancient Egyptians themselves called such works, a need clearly delineated by Edmund Meltzer when he wrote that there exists a "necessity for isolating and appreciating the categories recognized and utilized by ancient Egyptian culture rather than imposing our own."[4]

For the modern world, however, there is no question that de Rougé's excitement over the fairy-tale nature of the "Tale of Two Brothers" in the Papyrus d'Orbiney was soundly based. The tale's narrator employs many formulaic expressions,[5] repeats many passages, and describes the situations and events tersely, all of which are stylistic features of the typical fairy tale.[6] In common with the fairy tale, the hero of the d'Orbiney leaves home[7] after establishing a visual sign to bind him with his now-separated brother.[8] The Egyptian tale has the usual folktale timelessness, emphasized by encompassing well over a lifetime for Bata, extending to his rebirth, after which Anubis, his older brother, assumes the throne. Furthermore, the fact that the king sends for the young woman on the advice of his sages, with the qualification that many soldiers go; the finding of Bata's heart at the last possible moment; and the viability of the hero when his heart exists outside his body are all characteristics of folk- and fairy tales.[9] Finally, the motifs of the d'Orbiney are drawn from the religious, mythical,[10] and political life outside the tale itself, as is done in traditional tales.[11]

Not surprisingly, given its antiquity and cultural-temporal demands, the fairy-tale classification of the d'Orbiney breaks down on many points. Because Anubis and Bata are gods, the d'Orbiney fails to distinguish between the beings of this world and those of the other world, a distinction present in traditional folktales.[12] Within the traditional folktale, objects usually have no depth and are not a part of daily life,[13] whereas in the d'Orbiney objects, like Anubis's spear, are regularly used. The sign which binds the brothers to each other is not an object but is a drink and is atypical.[14] Furthermore, when mutilations occur in folktales, they are not visualized, nor do they obviously affect the hero or heroine,[15] but the opposite is found in the Egyptian tale, in which Bata becomes weak and feeble when he severs his phallus and in which he recalls the previous mutilation when he later tells his wife that he is a woman like her. Normally the expression of emotion is rare in the folktale,[16] but in the d'Orbiney both Bata and Anubis are described as being angry (*qnd*), Anubis's wife is said to be frightened (*snḏ*), and Bata and the king are each very much attracted to the divinely created young woman, the former desiring (*ꜣb*) her very much and the latter loving (*mr*) her very much. In addition, the emotional response of fear and perhaps betrayal rather than the usual folktale challenge or quest provoked Bata's leaving,[17] and Anubis demonstrably mourns his brother's separation and death. Furthermore, although the hero of a folktale normally does not work miracles, but instead receives magic objects,[18] in the d'Orbiney Bata receives no magic objects, but rather transforms himself "miraculously" three times. Finally, the punishment or revenge in a folk- or fairy tale is rarely carried out by the hero himself,[19] while in the d'Orbiney, both Anubis and Bata are responsible for punishing their respective wives.

The Papyrus d'Orbiney is not unique among ancient Egyptian works in exhibiting folktale motifs,[20] but it is the only one known which truly shows the type of transition or rite of passage of the hero that typifies the traditional folktale.[21] Characteristically in these tales, a young man in impoverished circumstances leaves his home life, travels to a foreign land, and returns married and/or as king, or at a minimum, wealthy and prosperous. For the d'Orbiney, as for the modern folktale, the basic structure runs A^1–B–A^2, where A^1 represents the home situation, B represents departure to and life in a foreign land, another world in some real way, and A^2 represents return to the homeland in an altered state.

It was in apparent consideration of this structure that Assmann proposed that the d'Orbiney may reflect an initiation ritual, despite the recognized lack of knowledge about such a rite from ancient Egypt. He outlined his thought as follows:[22]

1. the intentional leaving of the original life;
2. departure and passage of tests;
3. death and resurrection;
4. unrecognized return;[23]
5. identification in the form of a proof;
6. the transfiguration and reintegration in the form of accession and wedding.

He also suggested a division of the tale into three books fitting into a broader initiation scheme of

1. separation,
2. journey to the Otherworld,
3. unrecognized return.

There is clearly no question that the tale presents a rite of passage, but its events and symbols point less to a general initiation (that is, the maturation of a youth to an adult) than to a rite of passage to kingship, i.e., accession.[24] In this identification lies the answer to the thorny problem of why clearly identifiable gods function as the main characters in a tale so strongly resembling modern folktales: the Egyptian king, a divine king, must originate from the world of the divine. The birth narratives from the New Kingdom attest to this need. Thus it would be most inappropriate for the main characters to be normal human beings, and none of them is, despite their frequent very human behavior.

Bata, the central figure, is unquestionably a god, as the orthography of his name shows. It also appears most probable that he is the New Kingdom expression of *Bt,* an Old Kingdom deity who seems to have certain mortuary traits. In addition, Bata's analogies to Osiris place him in the proper line for the kingship he eventually assumes: the Osiris he was, procreated the Horus king he became. The details of the narrative portray in him all the attributes characteristic of a New Kingdom ruler:

1. strong, both sexually and physically;
2. a superior shepherd to whom his cattle spoke, helping him to help them and aiding and warning him;
3. a solitary hunter;
4. a priest who brings offerings to a goddess;
5. angry like a leopard, a royal animal;
6. losing his phallus to the fish, as did Osiris;
7. related to the solar mythology, specifically the rebirth of the sun, through his heart on the flower;
8. living in the mortuary realm;
9. Bull of the Ennead;
10. the husband of a divinely-created wife;
11. a successful warrior;
12. rescued from the mortuary realm by Anubis, the royal mortuary god;
13. resuscitated and revived by Anubis, the royal mortuary god;
14. revival takes place in a *sḥ-nṯr,* i.e., his house in the Valley of the Pine;
15. having his heart brought back to his body and being revived in the same fashion as Osiris;
16. a bull of every color and unknown, in essence, a royal symbol;
17. two persea (*šwb*) trees which are related to solar rebirth;
18. Kamutef;
19. recognition and loving by the king as his offspring;
20. having nurses of the type that raised princes, especially heirs;

21. *r-p'ʿt,* i.e., crown prince and heir;
22. acceding to the throne;
23. ruling for the requisite thirty years; and
24. dying after that time in the fashion of kings.

This Bata is also very much the New Kingdom Bata, for despite assertions to the contrary, it is clear that he is not the Bata of the Ptolemaic Papyrus Jumilhac. In the latter, Bata is equated with Seth, but the Ptolemaic equation of Bata with Seth is with a Seth who was hated,[25] differing radically from the Seth of the Ramesside period, who was highly venerated.[26] Furthermore, a comparison of the tales from the Jumilhac and the d'Orbiney shows a great divergence from one to the other.

The characteristics which Anubis brings to the tale are those related to his function as a mortuary deity, especially in his relationship to the king. The mixed role he plays as mortuary functionary—both dangerous and beneficial—is that which he plays with respect to his brother. In particular, one notes the special relationship deriving from the concept that the king lived again after death and Anubis, the regenerator-revivifier, was responsible for the king's new life. In other words, he was a king-maker. In fact, the Egyptian narrator enjoyed a bit of paronomasia in that in the mortuary realm Anubis (*Inpw*) regenerated the new-born king (*inpw*), who became the crown prince in the real world (*inpw*),[27] and Anubis himself (*Inpw*) eventually became the crown prince (*inpw*).

Although both wives are anonymous, there is good reason to think that each represented one or more forms of Hathor. The traits of Bata's wife are so delineated as to leave little question that she embodies different aspects of Hathor. The wife's destructive behavior, her sexual attractiveness, her divine lineage, her coming from afar, and finally, her dual relationship of wife and mother of the king support this contention. Anubis's wife does not incorporate as many of Hathor's traits, but nonetheless she too appears to embody traits of the goddess. The concern with her hair, her seductiveness, and her destructiveness align her with Hathor, an alignment which is strengthened when one knows that Hathor, Mistress of Gebelein, had long been associated with Anubis, Lord of the Dawning Land. To view both wives as Hathorian supports the old contention that Bata's wife is a reincarnation of Anubis's wife—one of the unifying themes of the narrative.

The tale also incorporates many features reflecting the milieu of ancient Egypt that are not necessarily specific to the royal ideology, including:

1. life in rural Egypt with its economic activities;
2. household practices and relationships;
3. hair, its coiffure, and odor as distinctive attractions in sexual and love relations;
4. adultery as a reprehensible offense, warranting severe punishment;
5. the impropriety of acting in anger;
6. explicit parallels to Egyptian juridical terminology;
7. mourning behavior;
8. beliefs and practices concerning the heart as the spiritual and physical center of the person both in this world and in the Otherworld;
9. the revelation of inmost secrets as dangerous, even fatal;
10. the wasteland and hunting areas as the mortuary realm;
11. the relationship of the *ʿš*-tree to the mortuary realm;
12. the sea as a messenger;
13. the persea (*šwb*) tree as a portent of new life; and
14. the position of *sꜣ nsw n Kꜣš* as honored but not necessarily royal.

Although it is speculative to try to relate the tale as a whole to a historical situation, it is possible that the narrative was composed in response to disturbances within the royal household and the royal succession. In all times of Egyptian history, there was a real reluctance, if not a true taboo, to speak straightforwardly of difficulties within the royal sphere. When they were expressed at all, they appear delineated in fictional, mythical, or allegorical terms, as in Sinuhe, the "Contendings of Horus and Seth," and the Westcar Papyrus.

The reflection of royal ideology and Ramesside Egypt in the "Tale of Two Brothers" indicates contemporary, Ramesside composition by the scribe or his employer,[28] although many motifs and episodes derive from earlier materials. The subtleties and nuances of the tale, both royal and nonroyal in nature, suggest that it was directed to a sophisticated audience, thus precluding the thought that the tale was written down from one in oral circulation among the general populace. Certainly it was the creation of a gifted and imaginative tale-teller who was able to interweave into his story a great number of divergent aspects of Egyptian culture.

Appendix: Selections from the Papyrus Jumilhac[1]

IV: Anubis vs. Seth-Bata (III,12–25)

Now after that, as night (III,13) approached, Seth knew that Anubis had gone out. He transformed himself (III,14) into Anubis so the guards would not be able to recognize him. (III,15) Then he entered, and he stole the *ḫt-m-ḫftyw* (III,16) of the body of the god. He crossed the river, carrying them, and went to the west. Anubis became aware immediately; (III,17) he followed after him with the gods of his entourage and (III,18) overtook him. Seth disguised himself by assuming the appearance of a bull. Anubis, (III,19) however, bound him by his arms and his legs and cut off his phallus and testicles. (III,20) He placed upon his back the things which he had taken. Then Anubis imprisoned him (III,21) in a place of punishment and returned the things which he had stolen to their place.

He is called (III,22) Bata in Saka because of it. The place where he was imprisoned is called Saka (III,23) until this day. Because of this, there has been a stable for cattle in this land. On account of that, the *wr-irw* are sent (III,24) to Saka to this day after completing it (the rites) in the *wʿbt*.

II: Anubis and His Allies Against Seth and His Companions (I,x + 4–II,20)

(x+3) *Ḏsr-tp* (x+4) observed *Dm-ib* when the latter came at dusk. He (*Dm-ib*) (x+5) succeeded in avoiding him (*Ḏsr-tp*) and arrived in the crypt. (x+6) Then *Imꜣḫw-m-ʿnḫ* marched at the head of the gods who were watching over Osiris; he (x+7) found *Dm-ib* and cut off his head so that he was anointed (x+8) with his [blood].

[Seth came] in search of him after transforming himself into Anubis. (x+9) Then he fled before him, after stealing [the things, namely the *ḫftyw* of the divine body(?)]. (x+10) Next he fled carrying what he had taken, but Horus [and Anubis] ran [after] him, (x+11) and they overtook him on this mountain. Then Thoth [pronounced] (x+12) his charms against him [again, causing him to fall to earth before them, and Anubis bound him] (x+13) by the arms and the legs, and he was placed as a seat under Osiris. Then Isis sank (x+14) her teeth into his (Seth's) back, and Thoth pronounced his charms against him. (x+15) Then Re said, "This seat is assigned to the 'Tired One.' How well regenerated he is! How beautiful he is! Let Seth be placed under him (x+16) as a seat. It is just, because of the hurt which he has done to all the parts of Osiris." (x+17) Then Isdes made an inquiry about Seth on account of the evil which he had done, but he (Seth) fled into the desert, into the wadi which is to the east of *Ḥwt-rḏw.* They were found (II,1) fallen into the mountain, their sacks of leather being under them. He (Isdes) dispatched (II,2) them without exception, and he saw the humors under them, and Horus carried them (II,3) flying to the receptacle of the humors of the body of this august god, and they were interred in this Gebel (II,4) in the crypt(?) which is there, a serpent called *Ḥmt-mi-db/ibḥ* being placed at . . . the entry(?) (II,5) in order to guard them.

But Seth succeeded in avoiding them and transformed himself into the (II,6) panther of this nome. Anubis, however, seized him, and Thoth (II,7) read his magic formulas against him again. Therefore he (Seth) fell to the ground before them; Anubis bound him (II,8) by the arms and the legs, and he (Seth) was consumed in flame from head to foot in (II,9) all his body, to the east of the august room. The smell of his fat, having reached (II,10) the sky, spread out in this magnificent place, and Re (II,11) and the gods regarded it (this odor) as agreeable. Then Anubis split(?) the skin of Seth, (II,12) snatching his skin (from him) and put his (Seth's) skin over him(self). After that he entered the *wʿbt* of Osiris in order to make libations (II,13) to his father, saying, "Seth is there." The *wʿb*-priest of this god has been called *stm* on account of that. (II,14) And he (Anubis) stamped his mark on him (Seth) with red iron (which remains) until this day. The *stm* priest wears a (II,15) panther skin on account of this until today. Then the friends of Seth (II,16) came to seek him. Very numerous, they were found on this mountain which is (II,17) to the south of *Dwn-ʿwy*. It was then that Anubis, going against them by night, made (II,18) a great massacre among them; with one blow, he severed their heads, (II,19) and his name (Seth's) was no longer ever loved(?) there. Their blood spread (II,20) over this mountain; this is why they had in *Dwn-ʿwy* the mineral called *šsꜣyt* until this day.

XXIX: Saka (XX,1–22)

(XX,1) As for the *Inpwt* nome, also called Saka: it was Seth who had caused his messenger named *Dm-ib* (XX,2), the great chief of his companions, to come with his knife in his hands to inspect (XX,3) Osiris on his litter, while *Ḏsr-tp* was watching (XX,4) over him. He (*Dm-ib*) succeeded, nevertheless, in avoiding him, and he arrived (XX,5) behind the leaves of the door. Then he entered the embalming room. *Imꜣḫw-m-ʿnḫ* (XX,6) went to the great Ennead, having cut off the head of *Dm-ib*, so that he was (XX,7) spattered with his blood. Seth searched for him after transforming himself (XX,8) into Anubis, and he knocked over the cult-objects of Osiris. Thoth spoke (XX,9) to him with his incantations, and he fell to the ground, not knowing his body or (XX,10) the place which he was in. He was tied by his legs and arms and placed (XX,11) under Osiris. Then Isis transformed herself into Anubis and she seized (XX,12) Seth, sinking her teeth into his back; he fell under her, and (XX,13) he said to her, "Why have you come from(?) the lake against this innocent dog?" Thus his name became (XX,14) *Inpw*.

As for this image, it is Seth. As for this justified one(?) who is upon his back, (XX,15) it is Osiris. As for Saka, it is Seth, having this god upon his back.

He came into this town (XX,16) after transforming himself

into a bull. Anubis has bound him by his arms and (XX,17) legs and cut his phallus and testicles, and he has placed him as a seat under Osiris, this god being upon (XX,18) his back.

He (=Seth) is called Saka (on account of this). As for Bata, he is Seth. A thing was made/done for him which he holds in abomination (XX,19): he had a treasure which he had acquired himself. Anubis enclosed him and imprisoned him (XX,20) in this place. It was because of this that a stable for cattle came to be in this land. His (Bata's) abomination (was that) a man be allowed (XX,21) in his presence having had intercourse the same day.

Iȝkby is the name of its *wʿb*-priest. (XX,22) Young willow (is the name of the sacred tree). Lake of the willow is the name of the lake of its god. *Stȝ-pw* is the name of its sacred mound.

III: Intervention of Isis (II,21–III,12)

(II,21) Seth reassembled his allies, but Isis marched against them. (II,22) She hid herself in this Gebel which is the south of *Dwn-ʿwy* after transforming herself into her mother Sekhmet. She sent a flame out against them all, causing them to be burned and (II,24) devoured by her flame. (Therefore) she is called Hathor, Mistress of the Two Braziers. (II,25) She built a place there from which she could observe what the Wicked One and his allies prepared. It was called (II,26) "the House of the Mistress of the Two Braziers," and the *wʿb*-priest of this goddess is called *Wr-wnm* (=the great one who devours).

When Seth (III,1) saw Isis in this place, he transformed himself into a bull in order to run after her, but she disguised herself by assuming the appearance of a dog with a knife at the end of its tail. Next she (III,3) began to run before him, and Seth was not able to overtake her. Then he scattered his seed (III,4) on the ground, and this goddess said, "It is an abomination to have scattered (your seed), O Bull." His seed sprouted (III,5) on the Gebel into plants which are called *bdd-kȝw*. (III,6) Then this goddess entered this mountain and settled herself there(?): it is called (III,7) *Ḥwt-qʿḥt*. After that she went northward, and after transforming herself into a snake, she went into this(?) mountain which is in the north of this nome in order to (III,8) watch over the allies of Seth when they would arrive at the beginning of night. She is called Hathor, Mistress of Geheset. (III,9) This goddess saw the allies of Seth when they arrived from the Oxyrhynchite nome, and as they crossed the land to reach the eastern Gebel. (III,10) Then they were all stung, and she made her venom (III,11) penetrate their flesh so well that they perished immediately, all together; their blood (III,12) was spread out on this mountain, and that is why there is *prš* at Geheset.

IX: Sethian Aspects of Anubis (VI,17–VII,1)

(VI,17) To know the names (of the forms) of Anubis into which Seth is equally transformed.

As for Anubis, (VI,18) master of Henu of (or in) Saka, he is Seth after his entry into the noble room. Isis came (VI,19) against him in order to cut him up after he had entered. But Seth said to her, "Why therefore have you come when (VI,20) you have not seen what I have done?" Thus it was that the name of Anubis, master of Shestit existed.

As for Anubis, master of (VI,21) *Tꜣ-ḥḏ* which is to the south of Thebes, it is Seth.

As for Anubis, the "guide of the Two Lands" (*ssmw tꜣwy*) in Memphis, it is (VII,1) Seth.

As for Anubis, master of Inet, it is Seth and he is there with Nut.

XII: Legends Relative to These Toponymns (VIII,7–12)

(VIII,7) As for *Tꜣ-ḏsr,* (VIII,8) Seth has done there through hatred of Osiris: he cut up (VIII,9) all the members of his enemy, but Anubis, having gone to seek them in the towns (VIII,10) and in the nomes, returned with them into the district of *Dwn-ʿwy/Ḥr-dy,* and they were reunited in the Imiut and placed in the (VIII,11) *sḥn-ṯr* in the nature of *ḏsr-wr* of such a kind that no other god could see them. It is called *Tꜣ-ḏsr* because of (VIII,12) that.

Vignette XX

1st Vignette
Bull lifting his front feet as if he were represented at a gallop. In fact he can no longer run, for Anubis has bound closely its hind legs and holds in his slightly advanced hand the end of the cord. Anubis is represented in a classic manner: head of a dog, tripartite wig, short loin cloth, partially pleated, and with a false tail hooked to his girdle. On the back of the bull, a mummy is seen which, according to the text, is that of Osiris (Jum. XX,15), the bull himself being a personification of Bata, Master of Saka, that is to say Seth. The vignette makes allusion to a legend (Jum. III,15ff) which explains, or at least which wishes to explain, the name of the village of Saka.

(The accompanying hieroglyphic text reads):

> *Bṯ nb S3-k3, rsw n Dwn-ʿwy*
> Bata, Lord of Saka, south of *Dwn-ʿwy*

2nd Vignette
Ram-headed, asexual god seated on a rectangular socle, the legs raised and widely separated. The god, who wears a tripartite wig, is entirely nude; he has let his arms fall in separating them sensibly from his body, which ought to be a sign of feebleness. The hands are open and the head is turned to the right.

(The accompanying Demotic text reads):

> *ky ḏmʿ ḥr msḥ*
> Another chapter on the crocodile.

Abbreviations

ABAW — Abhandlungen der Bayerischen Akademie der Wissenschaften
ADAIK — Abhandlungen des Deutschen Archäologischen Instituts, Kairo
AB — Anchor Bible
AE — Adolf Erman, trans. A. Blackman, *The Ancient Egyptians*
AECT — R. O. Faulkner, *The Ancient Egyptian Coffin Texts,* 3 vols.
AEL — Miriam Lichtheim, *Ancient Egyptian Literature,* 3 vols.
AEPT — R. O. Faulkner, *The Ancient Egyptian Pyramid Texts*
Äg.Ab. — Ägyptische Abhandlungen
Äg. For. — Ägyptische Forschungen
Aeg.Hel — Aegyptiaca Helvetica
ÄHG — Jan Assmann, *Ägyptische Hymnen und Gebete*
AfO — Archiv für Orientforschung
AKM — Abhandlungen für die Kunde des Morgenlandes
*ANET*³ — James B. Pritchard, ed., *Ancient Near Eastern Texts relating to the Old Testament,* 3d ed.
An.Or. — Analecta Orientalia
AOAT — Alter Orient und Altes Testament
APAW — Abhandlungen der Preußischen Akademie der Wissenschaften
ASAÉ — Annales du Service des Antiquités de l'Égypte
ASAW — Abhandlungen der Sächsischen Akademie der Wissenschaften zu Leipzig
BAe — Bibliotheca Aegyptiaca
BD — *Book of the Dead*
BdÉ — Bibliothèque d'Étude
BÉ — Bibliothèque Égyptologique

BIFAO	Bulletin de l'Institut français d'Archéologie orientale
BiOr	Bibliotheca Orientalis
BMMA	Bulletin of the Metropolitan Museum of Art
CAD	*Chicago Assyrian Dictionary*
CAH[3]	*Cambridge Ancient History,* 3d ed.
CD	R. O. Faulkner, *The Concise Dictionary of Middle Egyptian*
CdÉ	Chronique d'Égypte
CT	A. de Buck, *The Coffin Texts*
DAWW	Denkschriften der Kaiserlichen Akademie der Wissenschaften in Wien, Phil.-hist. Kl.
EA	J. Knudtzon, ed., *Die El-Amarna-Tafeln*
Edfu I	Marquis de Rochemonteix, *Le Temple d'Edfou* I, MMAF 10
EM I	*Enzyklopädie des Märchens,* Vol. I
EPRO	Études préliminaires aux religions orientales dans l'empire romain
FFC	Folklore Fellows Communications
FIFAO	Fouilles de l'Institut français d'Archéologie orientale du Caire
GMAÄ	H. Grapow, et al., *Grundriß der Medizin der alten Ägypter*
GOF	Göttinger Orientforschungen
HO[2]	Handbuch der Orientalistik, 2d ed.
IÄF	Peter Kaplony, *Inschriften des ägyptischen Frühzeits*
JARCE	Journal of the American Research Center in Egypt
JBL	Journal of Biblical Literature
JEA	Journal of Egyptian Archaeology
JEOL	Jaarbericht van het Vooraziatisch-Egyptisch Genootschap (Gezelschap) "Ex Oriente Lux"
JNES	Journal of Near Eastern Studies
JSS	Journal of Semitic Studies
JSSEA	Society for the Study of Egyptian Antiquities, Journal
LÄ	*Lexikon der Ägyptologie*
LES	*Alan H. Gardiner, Late Egyptian Stories,* BAe I
MÄS	Münchner Ägyptologische Studien
MDAIK	Mitteilungen des Deutschen Archäologischen Instituts, Abt. Kairo
MIFAO	Memoires publiés par les Membres de l'Institut français d'Archéologie orientale du Caire
MIO	Mitteilungen des Instituts für Orientforschung
MMAF	Mémoires publiés par les Members de la Mission Archéologie française au Caire
MSL	Materialen zum Sumerischen Lexicon
MVEOL	Mededeelingen en Verhandelingen van het Vooraziatisch-Egyptisch Genootschap (Gezelschap) "Ex Oriente Lux"
NAWG	Nachrichten von der Akademie der Wissenschaften zu Göttingen, Phil.-hist. Kl.
OLZ	Orientalistische Literaturzeitung

OMRO Oudheidkundige Mededeelingen uit het Rijksmuseum van Oudheden te Leiden
OIP Oriental Institute Publications
PRU *Le Palais royal d'Ugarit*
PdÄ Probleme der Ägyptologie
PSBA Proceedings of the Society of Biblical Archaeology
Pyr. Kurt Sethe, *Die altägyptischen Pyramidentexte*
Pyr.Über. Kurt Sethe, *Übersetzungen und Kommentar zu den altägyptischen Pyramidentexen,* 6 vols.
RÄRG Hans Bonnet, *Reallexikon der ägyptischen Religionsgeschichte*
RdÉ Revue d'Égyptologie
RGAÄ S. Morenz, *Religion und Geschichte des alten Ägyptens*
RHR Revue de l'Histoire de Religions
RT Recueil de Travaux Rélatifs à la Philologie et à l'Archéologie Égyptiennes et Assyriennes
SAK Studien zur altägyptischen Kultur
SAOC Studies in Ancient Oriental Civilizations
SPAW Sitzungsberichte der Preußischen Akademie der Wissenschaften, Phil.-hist. Kl.
TÄB Tübinger Ägyptologische Beiträge
TAVO Tübinger Atlas des Vorderen Orients
UGAÄ Untersuchungen zur Geschichte und Altertumskunde Ägyptens
Urk. I *Urkunden I, Urkunden des Altens Reichs*
Urk. IV *Urkunden des aegyptischen Altertums IV, Urkunden des 18. Dynastie*
VESO W. F. Albright, *The Vocalization of Egyptian Syllabic Orthography*
VIO Deutsche Akademie der Wissenschaften zu Berlin, Institut für Orientforschung, Veröffentlichungen
WZKM Wiener Zeitschrift für die Kunde des Morgenlandes
Wb Adolf Erman and H. Grapow, *Wörterbuch der ägyptischen Sprache*
WdO Die Welt des Orients
ZÄS Zeitschrift für ägyptische Sprache
ZAW Zeitschrift für die Alttestamentliche Wissenschaft
ZDMG Zeitschrift der Deutschen Morgenländischen Gesellschaft

Notes

Introduction

1. My translation of the tale follows the introduction. Other common translations are available in *ANET*³, pp. 23–25 (John A. Wilson, trans.) and in Miriam Lichtheim's *Ancient Egyptian Literature* (hereafter *AEL*), 2:203–11. The latter reference also contains a solid bibliography, p. 203, as does Gaston Maspero, *Les Contes populaires de l'Égypte ancienne,* 4th ed. (1911), pp. 1–3; Gustave Lefèbvre, trans. and comm., *Romans et contes de l'époque pharaonique* (1949), pp. 140–42; and Emma Brunner–Traut, "Papyrus d'Orbiney," *LÄ* IV, col. 702–704.

2. An exact translation of the word "Märchen" is impossible. It has variously been translated "fairy tale," "legendary fiction," and the like. I prefer to translate it as "folktale," given that "Märchen" may or may not have actual fairy characters, but in the long run it seems best simply to use "Märchen" and leave the precise translation alone or to the reader's sensibility.

3. Jacques Vandier, *Le Papyrus Jumilhac* (1960).

4. This study originated as the author's dissertation, which is available as "The New Egyptian 'Tale of Two Brothers': A Mythological, Religious, Literary, and Historico-Political Study of the Papyrus d'Orbiney," Ann Arbor, MI: University Microfilms International, 1982.

5. For a more historical approach to the scholarship of the Papyrus d'Orbiney, see the author's dissertation, "The New Egyptian 'Tale of Two Brothers'," pp. 1–69.

6. For comments on this issue see Richard Dorson, "Introduction," in *Folklore and Folklife,* ed. Richard Dorson (1972), pp. 1–50; Linda Dégh, "Folk Narrative" in *Folklore and Folklife,* pp. 53–83; and most recently, Lutz Röhrich, "The Quest of Meaning in Folk Narrative Research," in *The Brothers Grimm and Folktale,* ed. James M. McGlathery with

Larry W. Danielson, Ruth E. Lorbe, and Selma K. Richardson (1988), pp. 1–15.

7. The author is greatly indebted to the thought of Albert B. Lord for this idea. He states it most explicitly in *Singer of Tales* (1960), p. 148.

"The Tale of Two Brothers"

1. Bata.
2. Anubis.
3. Bata.
4. Literally, what is in your heart.
5. The day began at sunset, and Anubis's return was after sundown, hence the "yesterday" in this passage.
6. Bata.
7. The sun-god.
8. Bata.
9. The nine gods, those who created and ruled the land.
10. The potter god and a creator god.
11. Goddesses of fate.
12. The Bata-bull.
13. The noblewoman, the king's wife (who is Bata's wife).
14. The infant son, Bata, of course.
15. These two special types of nurses are the subject of discussion in Chap. 6.
16. The son.
17. An administrative title in the New Kingdom which does not imply royalty in any way.
18. An ancient title which, in the time of the New Kingdom, was reserved solely for the crown prince.
19. A euphemism for dying.
20. Bata.
21. "A single line of large writing across the top of the page," (Gardiner, *LES,* p. 29a).
22. The thirteenth crown prince and successor of Merneptah (possibly with Amenmesse in between).
23. "Upside down from the standpoint of the recto" (Gardiner, *LES,* p. 30a).
24. "Two lines of large writing transversely across the papyrus. Beginning of the same entry as in recto, 20, 1" [see appendix above], (Gardiner, *LES,* p. 30a).

Chapter 1

1. Emmanuel de Rougé, *Notice sur un manuscrit égyptien en écriture hiératique écrit sous le règne de Merienphthah, fils du grand Ramses vers le*

XVe siècle avant l'ère chrétienne, extrait de *Revue Archéologique* (1852), pp. 1–15. This article actually appeared in three different publications during 1952 and was later included in his *Oeuvres diverses.* See Gaston Maspero, *Les Contes populaires de l'Égypte ancienne,* 4th ed. (1911), p. 1, for details.

2. W. Mannhardt, "Das älteste Märchen," *Zeitschrift für deutsche Mythologie und Sittenkunde* (1859), pp. 232–59. It must be noted that this publication seems to have escaped the notice of Egyptologists. The earliest reference to it was made by Sir Peter Le Page Renouf, "Parallels in Folklore," *PSBA* XI (Apr. 1889), pp. 177–89, rpt. in *The Life Work of Sir Peter Le Page Renouf,* 3 vols., eds. Gaston Maspero and Harry Rylands (1902–1905), Vol. 3, pp. 311–27, and Maspero did not include it in his bibliography until his fourth edition of *Les Contes populaires* in 1911.

3. The papyrus was originally purchased in Italy by Madame d'Orbiney, who asked de Rougé to read it. From this reading he published the initial article, but only later were the circumstances surrounding this event revealed, first by Henri Brugsch in 1864 and then more fully by Maspero (1871). According to Brugsch, Madame d'Orbiney had attempted to sell the papyrus to various museums with no success because of the high price, and so she settled for having de Rougé read it. Its eventual purchase by the British Museum was possible because of that institution's wealth. In 1870 Maspero modified this note by explaining that the museum's purchase took place following Madame d'Orbiney's death in 1857, and so it was purchased from the administrators of her estate rather than from her. Soon after its acquisition by the museum, Samuel Birch published it in facsimile edition, making the text available to scholars generally for translation and study. Various hieratic copies and hieroglyphic transcriptions have been published since, the most significant being that of Alan Gardiner in 1932, the hieroglyphic text in standard use today.

4. The "New Egyptian" dialect represents the vernacular of the late eighteenth through twenty-fourth dynasties, in which letters and business documents as well as some literary works, such as this one, were written.

5. Birch, *Select Papyri,* part ii, pp. 7–9 and Plates 9–19.

6. Maspero, *Contes populaires,*[1] p. ii.

7. Charles E. Moldenke, "The Oldest Fairy Tale," *The Transactions of the Meriden (Conn.) Scientific Association* 7 (1895), pp. 32–81.

8. Other biblical parallels cited include Esther 2:15–18, the episode in which she has her time with the king (first cited by de Rougé, p. 13, n. 18, later by Mannhardt, and most recently by Donald B. Redford, *A Study of the Biblical Story of Joseph: Genesis 37–50,* Supplements to *Vetus Testamentum* 20 [1970], pp. 91–93), and Matthew 14:6–11, with its parallel, Mark 6:22–24, which relates the promise that Herodias's

daughter Salome extracted from Herod the tetrarch (cited by William M. Flinders Petrie, *Egyptian Tales. Series II: XVIII–XIX Dynasties* [1895], pp. 36–86).

9. In those days, the field of Egyptology justified its work "with a view to the elucidation of the History and Arts of Ancient Egypt and the illustration of the Old Testament narrative, so far as it had to do with Egypt and the Egyptians," to quote from the 1882 organizing principles of the Egyptian Exploration Fund (quoted by John A. Wilson, *Signs & Wonders upon Pharaoh: A History of American Egyptology,* [Chicago, 1964], p. 72). Indeed, de Rougé's publication makes prominent mention of the tale as from the time of Merneptah, whose father Ramesses II was thought to be the pharaoh feared by Moses and from whom the latter fled. Biblical apologetics as the basis for Egyptology soon lessened, however, especially with the 1885 publication of a work on life in ancient Egypt by Adolf Erman (this work is available in English in a reprint of the 1894 English translation: Adolf Erman, *Life in Ancient Egypt,* trans. by H. M. Tirard with a new introduction by Jon Manchip White [New York: Dover Publications, 1971]), along with the observation that despite the proliferation of materials from ancient Egypt, none of them mentioned any of the Egyptian-based events recorded in the Hebrew text. Thus, by the turn of the century, the study of ancient Egypt had begun to exist for itself.

10. Mannhardt 1859, pp. 248–49.

11. "A type is a traditional tale that has an independent existence" (Stith Thompson, *The Folktale* [1946], p. 415).

12. "A *motif* is the smallest element in a tale having the power to persist in tradition" (Thompson 1946, p. 415).

13. Mannhardt 1859, pp. 248–50. This is a tale from Siebenburgen (Transylvania) (cf. p. 250, n. 1) and is not the same tale as that of the Grimm brothers' tale with the same title, KHM 85.

14. Mannhardt 1859, p. 249.

15. Georg Ebers, *Aegypten und die Bücher Mose's: sachlicher Commentar zu den aegyptischen Stellen in Genesis und Exodus* (1868), vol. 1, pp. 311–16.

16. One should note that late twentieth-century biblical scholarship would certainly date the written version of the Joseph story after the thirteenth century BCE, when the Papyrus d'Orbiney was written down.

17. See Richard Dorson, "The Eclipse of Solar Mythology" in *The Study of Folklore,* ed. Alan Dundes (1965), pp. 57–83.

18. François Lenormant, "Le Roman des deux frères" in *Les Premières civilisations: études d'histoire et d'archéologie* (1874), vol. 1, pp. 375–401.

19. An idea incorrect even then, for according to Maspero, *Popular Stories of Ancient Egypt,* pp. x and 115, by 1874, the story of Satni-Khamois with the mummies (Cairo No. 30646) was known. Found in 1864, by 1872 it had been published by de Rougé and analyzed by Brugsch, Mariette, and Maspero. It is, however, written in demotic and

of Ptolemaic date. This tale is easily available in *AEL* III, pp. 127–38 and in Brunner-Traut, *Altägyptischen Märchen*[5] #33, pp. 171–92.

20. Lenormant, "Le Roman des deux frères," p. 378.

21. Hyacinthe Husson, *La Chaîne traditionnelle: contes et légendes au point du vue mythique* (1874), pp. 78–102.

22. See *The Panchatantra,* trans. Arthur W. Ryder (1935), p. 381ff.

23. Actually *pꜣ ym,* "the sea," in the tale.

24. E. Cosquin, "Un Problème historique à propos du conte égyptien des deux frères," *Revue des Questions Historiques* 22 (1877), pp. 502–16.

25. Dégh, "Folk Narrative," p. 56.

26. E. Cosquin, "Le Conte égyptien des deux frères" in *Contes populaires de Lorraine* (1886), vol. 1, Appendix B, p. lvii ff.

27. Sir Peter Le Page Renouf, "Parallels in Folklore," *PSBA* XI (April 1889), pp. 177–89.

28. Ibid., p. 317.

29. In written form, the tale of Meleager dates to the eighth and seventh centuries BCE, some centuries after the 1215 BCE date of the Papyrus d'Orbiney.

30. See n. 19 above.

31. See n. 13 above.

32. Renouf, "Parallels," p. 324.

33. Michael C. Astour, *Hellenosemitica: An Ethnic and Cultural Study in West Semitic Impact on Mycenaean Greece* (1965), pp. 256–61.

34. Ibid., p. 259.

35. John D. Yohannan, ed. and comm., *Joseph and Potiphar's Wife in World Literature: An Anthology of the Story of the Chaste Youth and the Lustful Stepmother* (1968).

36. Ibid., p. 2.

37. Ibid., pp. 7–9.

38. Theodor Gaster, *Myth, Legend, and Custom in the Old Testament,* 2 vols. (1969), Vol. 1, pp. 217–18, and nn. p. 379.

39. Donald B. Redford, *A Study of the Biblical Story of Joseph: Genesis 37–50,* Supplements to *Vetus Testamentum 20* (1970), pp. 91–93.

40. Ibid., p. 92.

41. Ibid., p. 93. See also n. 3, p. 93.

42. Ibid., pp. 180–82.

43. In each edition, the "Tale of Two Brothers" occupied the premier spot in the collection and received a great deal of attention in the introduction to the book. The thoughts about the story that Maspero expressed in the general introductions along with the copious and detailed notes accompanying it contributed a great deal to the understanding of the tale and of ancient Egypt.

44. Maspero, *Contes populaires,*[1] p. vii.

45. Maspero, *Contes populaires,*[1] p. ix; *Les Contes populaires,*[2] p. xi; *Les Contes populaires,*[3] p. xiv; states they "auraient pu fournir la matière

de deux romans différents." In *Les Contes populaires,*[4] p. xiv, he speaks of "l'étoffe de deux romans distincts."

46. Maspero, *Les Contes populaires,*[4] p. xiv, and *Popular Stories,* p. xvii.

47. Maspero, *Contes populaires,*[1] p. 18.

48. Maspero, *Popular Stories,* pp. xviii–xxiv.

49. Ibid., p. xvii.

50. Alfred Wiedemann, *Altägyptische Sagen und Märchen* (1906), pp. 58–77.

51. Ibid., pp. 58–59.

52. Alfred Wiedemann, *Popular Literature in Ancient Egypt,* trans. J. Hutchinson, *The Ancient East* (1902), vol. 5, p. 2ff.

53. Ibid., p. 47.

54. Hermann Schneider, *Kultur und Denken der alten Ägypter* (1907), pp. 252–63. This reference came from Otto Rank, *Psychoanalytische Beiträge zur Mythenforschung: Gesammelte Studien aus den Jahren 1912 bis 1914* (1919), p. 365.

55. Max Pieper, "Aegyptische Literatur," in *Handbuch der Literaturwissenschaft,* ed. Oskar Walzel (1927), pp. 78–81.

56. Ibid., p. 78.

57. Equals the search for the owner of the hair.

58. See Grimm tale #47, "The Juniper Tree" (AT 720: My mother slew me, my father ate me).

59. Pieper, "Aegyptische Literatur," p. 79.

60. Ebers was also concerned with the wickedness of the women and collected several references about women as perceived by the Egyptians, one from the Prisse Papyrus X, 3, 4, describing a woman as "a collection of all baseness and a sack full of all intrigues" and another from Chabas's *Monuments égyptiens von Prisses d'Avennes,* plate 45, where the epithets accompanying the pictures of women being beset by all manner of wild beasts call them "a spying woman" and "an uppity wife," indicating that they are women who should be "muzzled" (Ebers, *Aegypten und die Bücher Mose's,* pp. 314–16.). Unfortunately, current understanding of the Egyptian words in the Prisse is that it is greed or covetousness rather than a woman who is the collection (cf. Lichtheim, *AEL,* vol. 1, p. 69; Erman, *AE,* p. 60). Prisse X, 3–4 reads:

> *pw bint nbt ṯ3wt*
> it is a seizing of every evil thing,

where the *pw* refers to *wn-ib* "avarice" of Prisse X,1 (Zbynek Žába, *Les Maximes de Ptahhotep* [Prague, 1956], pp. 39–40). To Posener's mind, the story is clearly addressed to a male audience, and he observed that "the view of the weaker sex is scarcely flattering."

61. Leonard Lesko, "Three Late Egyptian Stories Reconsidered," in

Egyptological Studies in Honor of Richard A. Parker. Presented upon the Occasion of His 78th Birthday December 10, 1983 (1986), pp. 98–103.

62. See Lichtheim, *AEL,* vol. 2, pp. 211–14 for a translation.

63. Ibid., pp. 214–23 for a translation.

64. Posener also noted the unflattering view of women in the "Tale of Two Brothers," though he did not attempt to see the story as unified by them (Georges Posener, "Literature," in *The Legacy of Egypt,* 2d ed., ed. J. R. Harris [1971], pp. 220–56, esp. pp. 239–40).

65. Walter Scherf, *Lexikon der Zaubermärchen* (1982), p. 462.

66. For general discussions, see Thompson, *The Folktale,* pp. 367–461, and Dégh, "Folk Narrative."

67. Stith Thompson, *The Types of the Folktale: A Classification and Bibliography,* FFC 183 (1964).

68. Stith Thompson, *Motif-Index of Folk-Literature,* revised and enlarged (1955–1958).

69. Between 1955 and 1964, revisions of the Aarne-Thompson motif classification appeared, and in 1962 Walter Liungman published a classification of Swedish folktales (*Die schwedischen Volksmärchen: Herkunft und Geschichte* [1961]) which included a section entitled "Das Batamärchen," type number GS 367 (pp. 78–80). The Swedish story tells of two brothers, a life-sign, a dragon (with two variants), a wonderful sword, revivification, transformations, and final vengeance. Liungman related it to the Egyptian story, which he supposed came from Asia Minor or North Syria. The result is that the tale from the Papyrus d'Orbiney is often classified as GS 367.

70. Thompson, *The Folktale,* pp. 275–276 lists the following motifs for the Egyptian "Tale of Two Brothers":

1. Potiphar's Wife (K 2111);
2. Advice from a Speaking Cow (B 211);
3. Obstacle Flight (separating river) (D 672);
4. Separable Soul (E 710);
5. Evil Prophecy (M 340);
6. Love through Sight of Hair of Unknown Woman (T 11.4.1 and H 1213.1.1);
7. Betrayal of Husband's Secret by His Wife (K 2213.4);
8. Life Token: Foaming Beer (E 761.6.4);
9. Resuscitation by Replacing Heart (E 30);
10. Repeated Reincarnation (E 670); and
11. Person Transforms Self, Is Swallowed and Reborn in New Form (E 607.2).

Thompson does not include the (self-) castration motif. The appropriate references in the index (S 176, mutilation: sex organs cut off, and S 176.1, mutilation: emasculation) refer only to Indian or Irish examples.

Thompson, *The Types of the Folktale,* gives the Egyptian "Tale of Two

Brothers" as a primary example of AaTh 318 (Faithless Wife = AaTh 590 A [Treacherous Wife]); earlier AaTh 318 was AaTh 315 B. Other types included in the tale are as follows:

1. AaTh 870 C* (Stepmother makes love to stepson);
2. AaTh 302 B (Hero with life dependent on sword); and
3. AaTh 516 B (Abducted princess—love through sight of floating hair).

It is important to note these last three classifications are not indexed by Thompson, but are included by other commentators.

71. Cosquin, "Un problème historique." The five motifs with which he worked were 1) transformation, 2) external heart, 3) life sign, 4) lock of hair, and 5) Potiphar's wife.

72. J. Bolte and G. Polivka, *Anmerkungen zu den Kinder- und Hausmärchen der Brüder Grimm* (1930), vol. 4, pp. 95–98, adding 6) the protective stream, and 7) animal warning.

73. Carl Wilhelm von Sydow, "Den fornegyptiske Sagan om te tvä Brüderna," *Yearbook of the New Society of Letters at Lund,* 1930, pp. 53–89, résumé in French on pp. 84–89 noted the following "national" motifs: Potiphar's wife, the names of the heroes, self-castration, and sacrifice of the bull-transformed hero.

74. Carl Wilhelm von Sydow, "On the Spread of Tradition (1932)," *Selected Papers on Folklore,* ed. Laurits Bodker (1948), pp. 11–43.

75. According to Alan Dundes, Von Sydow borrowed this term, also written *oicotype,* "from the science of botany where it denoted a genetic variety of plant that adapted to a certain environment (e.g., seashore, mountains) through natural selection and thus differed somewhat from other members of the same species. In folklore, the term refers to local forms of a tale type, folksong, or proverb, with 'local' defined in either geographic or cultural terms . . . [T]he oicotype is tied by definition to a very specific locale" (Alan Dundes, Introduction to "Folktale Studies and Philology: Some Points of View" by C. W. von Sydow in Alan Dundes, *The Study of Folklore* [1965], pp. 219–20).

76. von Sydow, "On the Spread of Tradition" (1932).

77. Carl Wilhelm von Sydow, "Märchenforschung und Philologie," *Universitas* 3 (1948), pp. 1047–1058, rpt. in *Wege der Märchenforschung,* ed. Felix Karlinger (1973), pp. 177–93. The English translation of this article appears in the following collections: Carl Wilhelm von Sydow, "Folktale Studies and Philology: Some Points of View," in Alan Dundes (1965), pp. 219–42, and in von Sydow, *Selected Papers on Folklore,* pp. 189–219.

78. Vladimir Vikentiev, *Skazka o dvuh bratjah* (Moscow, 1917), which is a translation into Russian with commentary and a study of its folklore.

79. Vladimir Vikentiev, "Nâr-Ba-Thai," *JEA* 17 (1931), pp. 67–80.

80. Vladimir Vikentiev, "Le Conte égyptien des deux frères et quelques histoires apparentées," *Bulletin of the Faculty of Arts, Fouad I University, Cairo* 11, part 2 (1949), pp. 67–111, is the article most pertinent here, but there are many others. Vikentiev made liberal reference to any story which seemed to fit his purpose when discussing particular comparisons.

81. For fine translation with commentary, see John Gardiner and John Maier, *Gilgamesh: Translated from the Sin-Leqi-Unninni Version* (1984).

82. Vikentiev, "Le Conte égyptien des deux frères," p. 102. There is no question that the earliest written version of *Gilgamesh* predates the Papyrus d'Orbiney. To my knowledge, Vikentiev is the only commentator to compare the entire *Epic of Gilgamesh* to the d'Orbiney.

83. Gustav Lefèbvre, "Bata and Ivan," *CdÉ* 25 (1950), pp. 17–26.

84. Warren R. Dawson and Eric Uphill, *Who was Who in Egyptology,* 2d ed. (London: Egypt Exploration Society, 1972), pp. 293–94.

85. Kurt Ranke, *Die zwei Brüder,* FFC 114 (1934), pp. 38–40, 282–83.

86. Ibid., p. 39.

87. *Das Fischer Lexikon: Literatur 2/1,* ed. Wolf-Hartmut Friedrich and Walther Killy (1965), pp. 188–89. (According to Karol Horálek, "Brüdermärchen: Das ágyptische B.," *Enzyklopädie des Märchens* [1978], vol. 1, col. 939, n. 1, hereafter *EM* 1, Kurt Ranke is responsible for the section from *Das Fischer Lexikon.*) Kurt Ranke, "Brüder: Die zwei B. (AaTh 303)," *EM* I, cols. 912–19.

88. Friedrich von der Leyen, *Die Welt der Märchen* (1953), vol. 1, pp. 121–48, esp. 133–40.

89. For this tale, see Lichtheim, *AEL* III, pp. 138–51.

90. Jan de Vries, *Betrachtungen zum Märchen,* FFC 150 (1954), pp. 50–60.

91. E 761.1.4. See above and Ranke, *Die zwei Brüder,* p. 39.

92. D 762.

93. De Vries drew this conclusion from his work with Helmut Jacobsohn's study (Helmut Jacobsohn, *Die dogmatische Stellung des Königs in der Theologie der alten Ägypter* [1939] and the materials of the historian of religions Brede Kristensen.

94. de Vries, *Betrachtungen zum Märchen,* p. 60.

95. Horálek, "Brüdermärchen: Das ägyptische B.," col. 925–40.

96. AaTh 302 B is often linked with AaTh 516 B, and Horálek has chosen to treat them as one under AaTh 302 B.

97. Horálek, "Brüdermärchen: Das ägyptische B.," col. 938. The German reads, "eine literarische Bearbeitung dreier vershiedener Märchentypen, die noch in der neuzeitlichen Tradition leben: AaTh 870 C*, 302 B, und 318. Die ursprüngliche Form ist besonders gut im dritten Teil erhalten. Der Einfluß anderer Märchentypen ist nicht ausgeschlossen,

konnte aber nur unbedeutende Details betreffen. Es ist auch mit einer sekundären Mythologisierung (wahrscheinlich durch den ägyptische Bearbeiter) zu rechnen. In diesem Sinn kann das Brüdermärchen als ein Zeugnis der altägyptischen Mythologie gewertet werden."

98. Max Pieper, "Das ägyptische Märchen," *Morgenland* 27 (1935), pp. 33–40.

99. Adolf Erman, *Die Literatur der Aegypter: Gedichte, Erzählungen und Lehrbücher aus dem 3. und 2. Jahrtausend v. Chr.* (1923), translated into English in 1927 by A. M. Blackman as *The Literature of the Ancient Egyptians,* and reprinted with a new introduction in 1966: Adolf Erman, *The Ancient Egyptians: A Source Book of their Writings,* trans. Aylward M. Blackman, introd. William Kelly Simpson (1966); hereafter *AE.*

100. *AE,* p. 150.

101. Hermann Kees, "Aegypten," in *Kulturgeschichte des Alten Orients,* 1. Abschnitt, *Hdb. d. Altertumswissenschaft* 3. Teil, 1. Teil, 3. Band (1933), pp. 287–88.

102. Ibid., p. 287. The German reads: "alte Göttergeschichten stecken auch im bekanntesten Märchen des N.R., der Erzählung von den zwei Brüdern . . . aber welche Wandlung haben im Volksmund die Mythen durchgemacht, wenn man den dunklen Ton erhaltener Stücke aus der religiösen Literatur vergleicht!"

103. Lenormant, "Le Roman des deux frères," p. 376. Stith Thompson, "Studying the Folktale," *The Folktale* (1946), pp. 367–461, especially p. 370, discusses this concept in the course of a survey of the history of the study of the folktale. Linda Dégh, "Folk Narrative" in *Folklore and Folklife: An Introduction,* ed. Richard M. Dorson (1972), pp. 53–83, gives a fine and more recent survey of the different schools of folklore theory. Her discussion on p. 55 concerns the particular idea, propounded by the Grimm brothers and their disciples, that folktales are relics of ancient Indo-Germanic mythology.

104. William M. Flinders Petrie, *Egyptian Tales, Series II: XVIII–XIX Dynasties* (1895), pp. 36–86.

105. Ibid., p. 67.

106. *AE,* p. 150, n. 3 and p. 281, n. 1. He refers to Edinburgh Ostracon 916 discussed in Chapter 2 of this study.

107. Pieper 1927, p. 79.

108. Pieper, "Aegyptische Motive."

109. Ranke, *Die zwei Brüder,* p. 39.

110. de Vries, "Betrachtungen zum Märchen," FFC 150 (1954), pp. 50–60.

111. C. W. Goodwin, "Hieratic Papyri," *Cambridge Essays,* 1858, pp. 232–39.

112. Mannhardt, "Das älteste Märchen," p. 244, n. 3.

113. Ebers, *Aegypten und die Bücher Mose's,* p. 315.

114. de Rougé, *Notice,* p. 6, n. 4.

115. Ibid., p. 13, n. 19.

116. C. W. Goodwin, "Hieratic Papyri," *Cambridge Essays,* 1858, pp. 232–39.

117. Mannhardt, "Das älteste Märchen," p. 245.

118. Birch, *Select Papyri,* p. 9.

119. See Husson, *La Chaîne traditionnelle,* for this discussion.

120. Petrie, *Egyptian Tales,* pp. 36–86.

121. Petrie (ibid., p. 66) wrote, "The present translation is . . . a fresh one made by Mr. (F. L.) Griffith word for word and shaped as little as possible by myself in editing it." He gives no reference.

122. This meaning for *Ḥwt-Ḥr* appears to be unique to Petrie. Neither the *Wörterbuch* (*Wb,* III, 5) nor the *Concise Dictionary* (p. 166) shows "goddess" or any related word in reference to it. Even Budge, *Hieroglyphic Dictionary* (p. 455b) makes no such suggestion.

123. Pieper, "Das ägyptische Märchen," pp. 33–40.

124. The concept of sympathetic magic states that when a person has a personal article belonging to another person, be it a piece of clothing or something more personal like a strand of hair, the possessor has power over the one to whom it belongs. For a full discussion of magical practices, see Sir James G. Frazer, *The Golden Bough,* abr. (1922), pp. 12–52. For a concise, up to date discussion of Egyptian magic, see J. F. Borghouts, "Magie," *LÄ* III, cols. 1137–1151, although sympathetic magic is not a part of his discussion. A collection of magical texts translated into English can be found in J. F. Borghouts, *Ancient Egyptian Magical Texts,* Nisaba 9 (1978). Spell 91 of this collection, "How Isis rescued her son Horus from a scorpion bite" (p. 62ff.) provides an excellent example of sympathetic magic.

125. Maspero, *Les Contes populaires,*[2] p. 22, n. 1; *Les Contes populaires,*[3] p. 13, n. 2; *Les Contes populaires,*[4] p. 14, n. 1; and *Popular Stories,* p. 13, n. 2.

126. Pieper, "Das ägyptische Märchen," p. 37.

127. Pieper, "Aegyptische Literatur," p. 79, and Pieper, "Das ägyptische Märchen," p. 40, says that Maspero propounded this idea, but with no reference to where Maspero states the idea, and I have not been able to find it.

128. For one discussion of the many of this view of myth, see Lauri Honko, "The Problem of Defining Myth" in *Sacred Narrative,* ed. by Alan Dundes (1984), pp. 49–50.

129. See the New Egyptian narratives "Truth and Falsehood" in *Ancient Egyptian Literature,* trans. and ed. Miriam Lichtheim, vol. 2 (1976), pp. 211–14, and the story Isis told Seth on the Island in the Midst in the "Contendings of Horus and Seth," (Lichtheim, vol. 2, pp. 214–23, especially p. 217). See also John Gwyn Griffiths' commentary to his edition of *Plutarch's "De Iside et Osiride"* (1970), pp. 100–101.

130. Philippe Virey, "Influence de l'Égypte ancienne sur les transformations du paganisme," *Revue des Questions Historiques* 53 (1893), pp. 336–43.

131. Philippe Virey, *La Religion de l'ancienne Égypte* (1910), pp. 193–202.

132. Virey, "Influence de l'Égypte ancienne," p. 339.

133. Ibid., p. 338.

134. Ibid., p. 338, n. 3.

135. Ibid., pp. 339–40.

136. Ibid., p. 340. Virey makes this equation with no explanation.

137. Virey, *La Religion de l'ancienne Égypte,* p. 197.

138. Virey, *La Religion,* pp. 201–202. A thoughtful look at Virey's discussion suggests that he may have been influenced by the solar mythology school of Max Müller.

139. Otto Rank, "Die ägyptischen Sagen von Osiris und Bata," in *Die Bedeutung der Psychoanalyse für die Geisteswissenschaft,* 2d ed., eds. O. Rank and H. Sachs (1913), pp. 36–57, published as "Das Brüdermärchen" in Rank, *Psychoanalytische Beiträge zur Mythenforschung,* pp. 355–80.

140. Otto Rank, "Traum und Mythus" in Sigmund Freud, *Die Traumdeutung,* 6th ed., Anh. 2 (1921), pp. 368–80. The relevant paragraph appears on p. 374.

141. Plutarch, *De Iside et Osiride,* 18. The translation used for this study is that of J. G. Griffiths, ed. and trans., *Plutarch's "De Iside et Osiride"* (1970).

142. Bruno Bettelheim, *The Uses of Enchantment: The Meaning and Interpretation of Fairy Tales* (1977), pp. 90–96.

143. Ibid., p. 92.

144. Ibid., p. 92.

145. Carl Jung, *Studien über alchemistische Vorstellungen,* in *Gesammelte Werke,* vol. 13 (1978), §401.

146. Ibid., §458.

147. Carl Jung, *Mysterium Conjunctionis,* in *Gesammelte Werke,* vol. 14 (1968), part IV, §§11–12. This text was found by Jung in H. Kees, *Der Opfertanz des ägyptischen Königs* (1912), p. 60, an Edfu text. See below, Chap. 4, "Bata's Heart and Egyptian Beliefs about the Heart," for further discussion of it.

148. Bernd Sledzianowski, "Notizen zum Zweibrüdermärchen," *GM* 4 (1973), pp. 35–40, especially 38–40.

149. Miriam Lichtheim, *Ancient Egyptian Literature,* 3 vols. (1973/80); William Kelly Simpson, *The Literature of Ancient Egypt: An Anthology of Stories, Instructions, and Poetry* (1972); Gustave Lefèbvre, trans. and comm., *Romans et contes de l'époque pharaonique* (1949); and Emma Brunner-Traut, *Altägyptische Märchen* (1963) and six editions since.

150. Lefèbvre, *Romans et contes,* introduction and pp. 137–50.

151. Ibid.

152. Gustave Lefèbvre, "Bata et Ivan," *CdÉ* 25(1950):17–26; Alfred Rambaud, *La Russie épique,* Paris (1876), pp. 377–80.

153. Fritz Hintze, *Untersuchungen zu Stil und Sprache neuägyptischer Erzählungen,* VIO 2 and 6 (1950–52).

154. The Nitokris motif is the same as the Cinderella motif in European literature.

155. See n. 58 above.

156. Hintze, *Untersuchungen zu Stil,* p. 25.

157. Ibid., p. 25, n. 2.

158. Walther Wolf, *Kulturgeschichte des alten Ägypten* (1962), pp. 400–401.

159. Helmut Brunner, *Grundzüge einer Geschichte der altägyptischen Literatur* (1966), pp. 77–78.

160. Joachim Spiegel, "Göttergeschichte, Erzählungen, Märchen, Fabeln," *HO*[2] I. Abt; I. Band; 2. Abschn. (1970), pp. 147–68, especially 163–64.

161. Ibid., p. 163.

162. G. Posener, *De la Divinité du pharaon* (1960), p. 90.

163. Georges Posener, "Literature," in *The Legacy of Egypt,* 2d ed., ed. J. R. Harris (1971), pp. 220–56, especially pp. 239–40.

164. Ibid., p. 240.

165. Posener, *De la Divinité du pharaon,* pp. 91–93.

166. Brunner-Traut, *Altägyptische Märchen,* 5th ed. (1979), pp. 28–40 and 258–60 were used in this study. In it the "Tale of Two Brothers" is number 5. The seventh edition of this work, which I have not seen, was published in 1986, so I do not know what, if any, changes she made in her commentary on the "Two Brothers."

167. Emma Brunner-Traut, "Ägypten," *EM* I, col. 175–214.

168. Emma Brunner-Traut, "Altägyptische Literatur" in *Altorientalische Literaturen,* ed. Wolfgang Röllig, *Neues Handbuch der Literaturwissenschaft,* ed. Klaus von See (1978), vol. 1, pp. 25–99, especially 35–44.

169. Eberhard Otto, *Wesen und Wandel der altägyptischen Kultur* (1969), p. 146.

170. Brunner-Traut, *Altägyptische Märchen,* p. 259.

171. Brunner-Traut, "Altägyptische Literature," p. 35.

172. Brunner-Traut, *Altägyptische Märchen,* p. 259.

173. Ibid., p. 260.

174. Brunner-Traut, "Altägyptische Literature," p. 36.

175. Elke Blumenthal, "Die Erzählung des Papyrus d'Orbiney als Literaturwerk," *ZÄS* 99 (1972), pp. 1–17.

176. Jan Assmann, "Das ägyptischer Zweibrüdermärchen (Papyrus d'Orbiney)," *ZÄS* 104 (1977), pp. 1–25, and Jan Assmann, "Textanalyse auf verschiedenen Ebenen: zum Problem der Einheit des Papyrus d'Orbiney," in *XIX Deutscher Orientalistentag vom 28. September bis 4. Oktober 1975,* ZDMG Suppl. III, 1 (1977), pp. 1–15.

177. As analysis, her approach consisted of dealing with what has become and therefore is, that is, a synchronic approach, using the New

Egyptian corpus which she defined as Gardiner's *Late Egyptian Stories.* In it she found two thematic spheres: mythical and historical. The former includes the d'Orbiney and the "Contendings of Horus and Seth" while the latter consists of "Apophis," the "Taking of Joppa," and "Wenamun." Stories of questionable theme include "Truth and Falsehood," "Doomed Prince," and "Ghost Story," though the latter draws close to the mythic with the theme of the cult of the dead.

178. Blumenthal, "Die Erzählung des Papyrus d'Orbiney," p. 7.

179. Ibid., p. 7.

180. Ibid., p. 10. The German reads: "spielt . . . mit den Elementen theologischer Überlieferung, verbindet sie zu einer ergötzlichen Geschichtenfolge und würzt das Ganze mit einem kräftigen Schuß Ironie, mit dem Ergebnis, daß sich der Leser auf Kosten des höchsten Götterkollegiums blendend amüsiert."

181. Emma Brunner-Traut, "Papyrus d'Orbiney," *LÄ,* cols. 697–704.

182. cf. *AEL* II, pp. 211–14.

183. Assmann, "Das ägyptischer Zweibrüdermärchen."

184. Assmann perseveres in calling it the Valley of the Cedar despite evidence known for some years that the *ʿš*-tree is really the pine. See Chap. 4, "The Valley of *ʿš* and Its Significance," for discussion.

185. V. Propp, *Morphology of the Folktale,* trans. L. Scott, 2d ed., revised and edited by Louis Wagner, new introduction by Alan Dundes (1968).

186. V. Propp, "Transformation von Zaubermärchen," trans. Maria-Gabriele Wosien, in *Morphologie des Märchens,* herausgegeben von Karl Eimermacher (1972), p. 156. Assmann has concluded that although such an analysis is not feasible for the whole text, it is possible for what he terms the second and third parts, Chaps. 9–24, d'Orbiney 8,8 to the end. His analysis runs as follows:

$$\alpha\beta^1\ \gamma^1\ \delta^1 \quad \begin{matrix} \mathrm{I}\ \varepsilon^1\ \zeta^1\ \eta^1\ \theta^3\ \mathrm{A}^1 \\ \mathrm{a}^1\ \mathrm{B}^4\ \mathrm{C}\ \mathrm{K}^9 \mid \mathrm{o\ Q\ Ex\ M\ T\ U} \\ \mathrm{II}\ \varepsilon^1\ \zeta^1\ \mathrm{A}^{13} \end{matrix}$$

The meanings of the symbols used are as follows, including interpretations relative to the story:

α—the initial situation: at the separation
β^1—absentation (departure) of elders: Anubis
γ^1—prohibition: Bata to his wife
δ^1—transgression: wife
I.
   ε^1—inquiry by villain: the king of his sages
   ζ^1—betrayal: the information given to the king
   η^1—deceitful persuasion: woman with jewels to wife
   θ^3—hero gives in or reacts mechanically: Bata
   A^1—villainy: kidnapping of wife

II.

ε[1]—inquiry by villain: king of wife
ζ[1]—betrayal: information given by wife
A[13]—command for death: king to men
a[1]—lack of an individual: Bata dead
B[4]—announcement of misfortune: sign to Anubis
C—consent to counteraction: Anubis leaves
K[9]—revival and abolition of misfortune: resuscitation and revival of Bata
l—return: Bata and Anubis to Egypt
o—unrecognized arrival: Bata as bull
Q—recognition: Bata reveals himself to his wife
Ex—exposure of false hero: conviction
M—difficult task: attempts to kill Bata fail
T—new form: ascends the throne
U—punishment: wife is judged

187. In a note in "Textanalyse auf verschiedenen Ebenen" (p. 15, n. 51), Assmann understands Jacobsohn to speak of a royal initiation rite, an idea Assmann does not pursue.

188. Ibid., pp. 10–11.

189. Brunner-Traut, "Papyrus d'Orbiney," *LÄ,* cols. 697–704.

190. The portions of the Papyrus Jumilhac which have a bearing on a study of the Papyrus d'Orbiney appear in an English rendition in the Appendix of the present study.

191. Alan H. Gardiner, "The Hero of the Papyrus d'Orbiney," *PSBA* 27 (1905), pp. 185–86. See Chap. 2 for discussion.

192. Vandier, *Le Papyrus Jumilhac,* pp. 3–4.

193. Jum. III, 21–22; XX, 18. Vandier (Vandier, *Le Papyrus Jumilhac,* p. 46) feels that the equation existed "de tout temps," despite the fact that Bata has the tendency to be an Osirian symbol. Since Vandier's publication of the Jumilhac, scholars have generally accepted the Seth-Bata equation with virtually no question.

194. Vandier, *Le Papyrus Jumilhac,* p. 26. The earlier standard showed a falcon with wings that were represented folded, while the wings appeared extended in later times.

195. Ibid., p. 31.

196. Ibid., p. 32.

197. Ibid., p. 33.

198. Ibid., p. 33, n. 12.

199. Altenmüller, "Bemerkungen zum Hirtenlied," pp. 219–20, recognizing the etiological strain in the Jumilhac, postulated that the Papyrus d'Orbiney is also etiological. He looked for a place with the persea tree and a bull as sacred animal, and ended by locating the origin of the New Kingdom tale in the Herakleopolitan nome, since the persea is sacred there, and Edfu I, 343, 5 mentions that *Bt* was located there as a divinity. As I show below, the identification of this *Bt* and Bata is far from assured.

200. See Chap. 2, Sec. 4 for a discussion.

Chapter 2

1. Assmann, "Textanalyse auf verschiedenen Ebenen," p. 13, n. 32.

2. Gardiner states ("The Hero of the Papyrus d'Orbiney," p. 185) that Bata must have been a well-known god to the nineteenth dynasty Egyptians. Alan H. Gardiner, *Ancient Egyptian Onomastica,* 3 vols. (1948), hereafter *AEO,* p. 104* notes that personal names were compounded with Bata's name in this period, e.g., Bataemḥab, Bataḥotep.

3. Franz Joseph Lauth, *Aegyptische Chronologie* (1877), pp. 30–31. Manetho's writings, including histories of Egypt, survive only in fragments as transmitted by others, among whom is Eusebius.

4. Gardiner, "The Hero of the Papyrus d'Orbiney," pp. 185–86.

5. Alan H. Gardiner, *The Wilbour Papyrus,* 4 vols. (1948–1952), vol. 2, p. 49.

6. Abd el Mohsen Bakir, *The Cairo Calendar, No. 86637* (1966), p. 27 and plates XVII and XVII A, lines 1 and 2.

7. Labib Habachi, *The Second Stela of Kamose and His Struggle Against the Hyksos Ruler and his Capital,* ADAIK 8 (1972), p. 41, line 41, attests to Saka as a place of some significance, for the text indicates that Saka and its nome had been in Hyksos possession and was rescued by Kamose, a town which is unattested in Egypt prior to Kamose (Vandier, *Le Papyrus Jumilhac,* p. 46).

8. d'Orb. 1,1; 9,4; 9,6; 10,4; 11,9; 12,6; 12,8; 14,1; 14,5; 15,1; 15,9; 17,7.

9. W. R. Dawson and T. E. Peet, "The So-called Poem on the King's Chariot," *JEA* 19 (1933), pl. XXVI, line 8.

10. Bakir, pl. XVII A, 1.

11. Gardiner, *The Wilbour Papyrus,* A 40, 3; A 52, 46; A 65, 37; A 77, 38 (without the male determinative), Bata-em-ḥab, a personal name.

12. Ibid., A 77, 45, Bata-ḥotep, a personal name.

13. Ibid., A 89, 25, Pa-an-bata, a personal name.

14. Ibid., B 9, 18; B 9, 23; B 23, 1, Pen-aa-bata, a place-name.

15. Ibid., B 3, 4, Per Bata, a sanctuary name.

16. Ibid., A 25, 26; A 38, 36; A 62, 24; A 99, 11; A 99, 22, Per Bata, Lord of Saka, a sanctuary name.

17. William F. Albright, *The Vocalization of the Egyptian Syllabic Orthography,* American Oriental Series, vol. 5 (1934); hereafter *VESO.* See particularly p. 40, #15 for Bata. Also see p. 63, D for the second syllable.

18. William F. Albright, "Historical and Mythical Elements in the Story of Joseph," *JBL* 37 (1918), p. 121.

19. William F. Albright and Thomas O. Lambdin, "New Material for Egyptian Syllabic Orthography," *JSS* 2 (1957), p. 127.

20. Ibid., p. 116.

21. See below for discussion.

22. Albright, *VESO,* pp. 39–40.
23. Wolfgang Helck, *Die Beziehungen Ägyptens zu Vorderasien im 3. und 2. Jahrtausend v. Chr.,* 2d ed., Äg.Ab. 5 (1971), p. 549.
24. *Urk.* IV, 1567, 9 and H. Gauthier, *Temples immergés de la Nubie. Le Temple d'Amada* (1913).
25. Elmar Edel, *Altägyptische Grammatik,* 2 vols. An.Or. 34/39 (1955/64), vol. 1, p. 66, §151.
26. F. W. F. von Bissing and Hermann Kees, *Das Re-Heiligtum des Ne-Woser-Re (Rathures)* (1905–1928), vol. 3, Blatt 15.
27. Edouard Naville, *The Festival Hall of Osorkon II with the Great Temple of Bubastis* (1892), pl. XI, 5.
28. Gardiner's Sign list, F 28.
29. J. Lopez, "Inscriptions de l'Ancien Empire à Khor el-Aquiba," *RdÉ* 19 (1967), p. 57.
30. Altenmüller, "Bemerkungen zum Hirtenlied des Alten Reichs," p. 212.
31. H. K. Jacquet-Gordon, *Les Noms des domaines funéraires sous l'Ancien Empire égyptien,* BdÉ 34 (1962), p. 260, 1. See also Edward Brovarski, "Two Old Kingdom Writing Boards from Giza," *ASAÉ* LXXVI (1987), p. 32.
32. Jacquet-Gordon 1962, p. 264, 3.
33. Ibid., p. 175, 60.
34. Paule Posener-Kriéger and Jean Louis de Cenival, *Hieratic Papyri in the British Museum. Fifth Series* (1968), pl. 62, name 36. See pp. xv–xvii for dating.
35. Lopez, "Inscriptions," p. 52, fig. 3.
36. Peter Kaplony, *Die Inschriften der ägyptischen Frühzeit,* Äg.Abh. 8/9, 3 vols. and suppl. (1963/64), vol. 1, pp. 473–74; hereafter *IÄF.* He also included two damaged examples, but both lack the first elements of the name and so are not helpful as examples.
37. H. W. Fairman, "Notes on the Alphabetic Signs employed in the Hieroglyphic Inscriptions of the Temple of Edfu," *ASAÉ* 43 (1943), p. 244, #294.
38. Ibid., p. 244, #289.
39. Pierre Montet, *Géographie de l'Égypte ancienne,* 2 vols. (1957/61), vol. 1, p. 148.
40. Vandier, *Le Papyrus Jumilhac,* III, 22; XX, 18; Vignette for XX.
41. *Edfu* I, 343, 5.
42. Alan H. Gardiner, T. Eric Peet, and J. Cerny, *The Inscriptions of Sinai,* 2 vols., 2d ed. (1952/55), vol. 1, pp. 92–94.
43. Jean Yoyotte, "Sur Bata, maître de Sako," *RdÉ* 9 (1952), p. 158, n. 5. See Sir Alan Gardiner, *Egyptian Grammar,* 3d ed. (1957), Sign List E 10 and R 7.
44. Gardiner, Peet, and Cerny 1952/55, vol. 1, plate XXIII, #85.
45. Gardiner, *The Wilbour Papyrus,* vol. 2, p. 49.

46. Ibid., A 38, 36; A 77, 51; B 21, 11.

47. Gardiner, *AEO,* vol. 1, pp. 51–53.

48. P. A. A. Boeser, *Beschreibung der ägyptischen Sammlung des Niederländischen Reichsmuseums der Altertümer in Leiden: Die Denkmäler des Neuen Reiches* (Haag, 1913), Band IV, 3. Abt., pp. 1–2 and pl. 1, 1, 16.

49. Dawson and Peet, "The So-Called Poem on the King's Chariot," pl. XXVI, 7–9. The transliteration and translation is mine. See also Alan R. Schulman, "The So-Called Poem on the King's Chariot Revisited," *JSSEA* XVI (1989), pp. 40 and 45.

50. My transliteration follows the ideas of Albright, *VESO,* p. 62 and differs from Dawson and Peet. Schulman transliterates the hieroglyphic as *bt.w.*

51. Contrary to Dawson and Peet, p. 171, I am reading the bird as a *s3*-bird, the pintail duck of Gardiner's sign list, G 39 rather than reinterpreting it as the *b3*-bird, the jabiru bird, sign list G 29, which makes no sense in the orthography. See also Jean Yoyotte, "Sur Bata, maître de Sako," *RdÉ* 9 (1952), pp. 158–59. Gardiner does not even acknowledge his own reinterpretation (cf. Gardiner 1905, p. 186).

52. There has been some debate over the meaning of *m3wḏ.* Peter Kaplony, "Bata," *LÄ* I, col. 635, n. 6, argues *m3wḏ* does not mean "arms," but is derived from *m3wḏ* "to furnish, provide." He does not, however, elaborate on how he would then translate the clause. Vikentiev "Nâr-Ba-Thai," pp. 78–79, suggests the word has to do with hand rhythms, but he also does not say how he would translate the clause.

53. *PRU* V, p. 129, #105, 1, 2.

54. *CAD* N, I, 1, pp. 359–60.

55. *MSL* VI, p. 6, #15 and p. 36, #7.

56. Cyrus Gordon, *Ugaritic Textbook,* An.Or. 38 (1965), p. 288.

57. Schulman, translating the word *btw,* sees more than one *b3ti* to a chariot and speculates they might have been its outer facings, "a wild guess" (1989, p. 27).

58. M. Calverley and M. F. Broome, *Temple of King Sethos I at Abydos,* ed. A. H. Gardiner (1933–1938), vol. 2, pl. 29.

59. Eberhard Otto, "Bastet," *LÄ* I, col. 629.

60. R. O. Faulkner, *The Ancient Egyptian Pyramid Texts* (1969) (hereafter *AEPT*) serves as the basis for the translations of the texts from the pyramids that occur throughout the present study.

61. Bakir, *The Cairo Calendar, No. 86637,* pl. XVII and XVII A, lines 1 and 2.

62. My translation differs from that of Bakir, p. 27, in treating *št3w* as a substantive rather than as an adjective, which I do because of the presence of the third-person singular masculine pronoun.

63. Ibid., p. 72, n. 1 for Recto XVII.

64. Nicholas Millet, "The Reserve Heads of the Old Kingdom" in

Studies in Ancient Egypt, the Aegean, and the Sudan, ed. Wm. Kelly Simpson and Whitney M. Davis (1981), pp. 129–31.

65. E. A. Wallis Budge, *Facsimiles of Egyptian Hieratic Papyri in the British Museum, 2nd Series* (1923), p. 36 and pl. XCVII. See also François Chabas, *Oeuvres diverses IV,* BÉ XII (1905), p. 170.

66. Altenmüller, "Bemerkungen zum Hirtenlied," p. 221, n. 3, would restore the damaged section to read "Bata," but says the restoration of "Osiris" cannot be excluded.

67. *Urk.* IV, 1567, 9.

68. Ibid., 1566–67.

69. Ibid., 1567, 14.

70. Kaplony, *IÄF,* 473.

71. Lana Troy, *Patterns of Queenship in Ancient Egyptian Myth and History* (1986), p. 152, No.1.14.

72. *IÄF* I, p. 473.

73. Peter Seibert, *Die Characteristik: Untersuchungen zu einer altägyptischen Sprechsitte und ihren Ausprägungen in Folklore und Literature,* I, Äg.Ab. 17 (1967), p. 61.

74. See for examples, Hermann Ranke, *Die ägyptischen Personennamen,* 2 Vols. (1935–1952), vol. 1, p. 39, 25–27.

75. Lopez, "Inscriptions de l'Ancien Empire à Khor el-Aquiba," p. 52.

76. Jacquet-Gordon, *Les Noms des domaines funéraires,* p. 260 and 264.

77. Ibid., p. 175.

78. Posener-Kriéger and de Cenival (1968), p. 25.

79. For specific Old Kingdom examples with similar orthography but other gods, see Hermann Ranke, *Die ägyptische Personennamen,* vol. 1 (1935), p. 263.

80. R. O. Faulkner, *A Concise Dictionary of Middle Egyptian* (1962), p. 185; hereafter *CD.*

81. It could also refer to the accession of Bytis, the demi-god who ruled on earth according to Manetho's king list and who may be related to *Bt/Biti.* See below.

82. The discussion accompanying Gardiner's sign F 28 and the entry for *Wb,* IV, 17 indicate that the cow's-skin determinative usually occurs with the sense of "colored, dappled." On the other hand, the nature of a piece of skin suggests a dead animal, as does the mummiform ram (see below), and it is not difficult to equate the two. It is important to note, however, that Posener-Kriéger and de Cenival, *Hieratic Papyri in the British Museum. Fifth Series,* pl. 62A, include question marks with each of the relevant signs: the *b,* the *t,* and the cow's-skin determinative.

83. von Bissing and Kees, *Das Re-Heiligtum des Königs Ne-Woser-Re (Rathures),* vol. II, 11, 27. Heinrich Schäfer, ed. Emma Brunner-Traut, *Principles of Egyptian Art,* trans. and ed. by John Baines (1974), §4.4.7,

pp. 230–34, discusses the importance of relative sizes in ancient Egyptian depictions. In the examples from the Sed-fest scenes, *Bt* is better than a third again as large as those accompanying him.

84. Naville, *The Festival Hall of Osorkon II,* pl. 11.

85. W. W. F. von Bissing and Hermann Kees, *Untersuchungen zu den Reliefs aus dem Re-Heiligtum des Rathures,* ABAW XXXII, 1 (1922), p. 81, suggest that this cord is the loop a shepherd carries on his staff. Peter Kaplony goes further in "Das Hirtenlied und seine fünfte Variante," *CdÉ* 44 (1969), pp. 42–44, and argues that the cord is a symbol of office for the shepherd. He thus equates the person of the Sed-fest representation with the shepherd of *Ḫrty* by means of his interpretation of the meaning of *Bt* in the "Shepherd Song." His discussion indicates that the lasso of the hunter (Wolfgang Decker, "Lasso," *LÄ* III, col. 938, adds that it belongs to the guard as well) and this cord are the same. The lasso is not attested for the shepherd, however, and indeed the flail and the crook are the normal symbols of that office (A. Moret, *La Mise à mort du dieu en Égypte,* [1927], pp. 34–35). Kaplony also notes the interchange of the cord with a sack in other presentations, citing the Pyramid Texts in particular. He does not speak of the fact that this sack is always on a stick, the "Tragstange mit Matte" mentioned as a characteristic of the shepherd by Wolfgang Helck, "Hirt," *LÄ* II, col. 1221. The discussion is provocative, for Kaplony's sources show *s3w* with this determinative, which suggests more guarding, waiting for, than herding as one of the functions of the lasso.

86. Although the example from Osorkon II shows almost the same orthography as that of Tuthmosis IV from Amada, it is hard to say the two mean the same thing or that the twenty-second dynasty interpretation of the fifth-dynasty word from Abu Gurob is not influenced by intervening interpretations. It is significant that the Amada example occurs in a list of deities, while that of Osorkon strongly militates against an interpretation of the figure as a deity. There remains the possibility that it can be related to the Middle Kingdom example, but clear evidence is lacking.

87. Edouard Naville, "Le dieu *Bat,*" *ZÄS* 43 (1906), pp. 77–88. *Pyr,* 1096b reads:

> *RN pw B3t ḥrwy.s snw*
> The king is Bat with her two faces.

Naville read this text (p. 77), "le roi est le dieu *bat,* celui qui a deux faces," and he went on to equate *B3t* with Bata, even though the latter was clearly a normal bull with one head, as indeed Naville acknowledged. He found the necessary duality in the two drops of blood growing into two trees. He further related *B3t* to the two-headed bull from the well-known Hunter's Palette (BM 20790, BM 20793, Louvre E 11254, cf. Cyril Aldred, *Egypt to the End of the Old Kingdom* [1965 (1982)] ill. 38), although he acknowledged that others called this bull *ḫns.*

88. Maspero, *Les Contes populaires,*[4] p. 4, n. 1; *Popular Stories,* p. 3, n. 3.

89. Kurt Sethe, *Zur altägyptischen Sage vom Sonnenauge,* UGAÄ 5, fasc. 3 (1912), p. 32.

90. H. G. Fischer, "Bat," *LÄ* I, col. 631, and H. G. Fischer, "The Cult and Nome of the Goddess Bat," *JARCE* 1 (1962), p. 7.

91. Careful copies of the text may be found as follows: Peter Kaplony, "Das Hirtenlied und seine fünfte Variante," *CdÉ* 44 (1969), p. 30 and Hartwig Altenmüller, "Bemerkungen zum Hirtenlied des Alten Reichs," *CdÉ* 48 (1973), p. 212.

92. This line is found only in the Chapel of *Sḫm-ʿnḫ-Ptḥ* and is restored by William Kelly Simpson, *The Offering Chapel of Sekhem-Ankh-Ptah in the Museum of Fine Arts, Boston* (1967), pp. 12–13 and plates XIII and D.

93. Kaplony, "Das Hirtenlied und seine fünfte Variante," p. 29. It must be stated here that Kaplony's views are difficult to discuss, for his paper is quite confused, and as P. Derchain observed in his summary in *Annual Egyptian Bibliography,* 1969, pp. 87–88, Kaplony depends very largely on his own previous works and his opinions expressed in them. Furthermore, the paper is heavily interspersed with suppositions and is a collection of a large number of ideas which are of questionable significance to the discussion at hand.

94. Altenmüller, "Bemerkungen zum Hirtenlied des Alten Reichs," p. 213.

95. Pierre Montet, *Les Scènes de la vie privée dans les tombeaux égyptiens de l'Ancien Empire* (1925), p. 191 and pl. XV for the scene from Ty.

96. Simpson, *The Offering Chapel of Sekhem-Ankh-Ptah,* pp. 12–13 and plates XIII and D. On p. 12, n. 3, Simpson speaks of the puzzling "shepherd's implement" carried in the *Sḫm-ʿnḫ-Ptḥ* depiction, a stave with some kind of circlet of "thongs, spikes or streamers," whose identification poses a problem.

97. Prentice Duell, *The Mastaba of Mereruka,* OIP 39 (1938), vol 2, plates 169–70. See also H. Wild, *Le Tombeau de Ti,* MIFAO 65, 2 (1963), Taf. CXIII.

98. Kaplony, "Das Hirtenlied und seine fünfte Variante," p. 29.

99. G. Maspero, *Études égyptiennes* (1888), vol. 2, p. 71 and p. 73, n. 3.

100. Kaplony, "Das Hirtenlied und seine fünfte Variante," pp. 27–59; Peter Kaplony, "Hirtenlied, Harfnerlieder und Sargtext-Spruch 671 als verwandte Gattungen der ägyptische Literatur," *CdÉ* 45 (1970), pp. 240–43.

101. Altenmüller, "Bemerkungen zum Hirtenlied des Alten Reichs," pp. 211–31.

102. See also Susan T. Hollis, "On the Nature of Bata, the Hero of the Papyrus d'Orbiney," *CdÉ* LIX, 118 (1984), pp. 248–57.

103. Maspero, *Études égyptiennes,* vol. 2, p. 71 and p. 73, n. 3. *Wb* I,

415, 12–17 transliterates the word written with the *b3*-bird as *b3* and defines it as "to hoe, hoe up." None of the examples uses any kind of ram, though one variant (uncited) shows it written with only a *b* and a double weak aleph, but accompanied by the characteristic hoe determinative.

104. H. Goedicke, "Eine Variante des 'Hirtenliedes'," *WZKM* 54 (1957), p. 50.

105. Kaplony, "Das Hirtenlied und seine fünfte Variante," p. 34.

106. Kaplony, "Das Hirtenlied und seine fünfte Variante," p. 37. He acknowledges that **b3t* is an unattested word until this point.

107. Jacquet-Gordon, *Les noms des domaines funéraires,* p. 94; H. Altenmüller, "Bemerkungen zum Hirtenlied," p. 214.

108. Note, however, that Jan Bergman, *Isis-Seele und Osiris-Ei,* Acta Universitati Upsaliensis: Historia Religionum 4 (1970), p. 61, speaks of a priest *b3ty* of the *b3t* when he mentions the hall of Osorkon II, observing the lack of understanding of form or function of the *b3t* and the *b3ty*.

109. Maspero, *Etudes égyptiennes,* 2, p. 73, n. 3 and p. 71.

110. Adolf Erman, *Reden, Rufe, und Lieder auf Gräberbilden des Alten Reichs,* APAW 1918, p. 19, n. 10 and p. 20, n. i (three times).

111. Although Maspero, *Études égyptiennes,* vol. 2, p. 74 translates *bt* as "the picker," in n. 3 on the same page, he refers to two previous translations, one by Brugsch and one by Erman, in which *bt* was translated as Hirt. This helps account for von Bissing's and Kees' translation as "shepherd."

112. von Bissing and Kees, *Untersuchungen zu den Reliefs,* p. 81.

113. Kaplony views it instead as an ideogram for *Ḫrty* and in *IÄF,* §43, p. 391, states, "The ideogram of the recumbent ram is to be read *Ḫrty* with or without sense signs," giving no further explanation. This leads him to deal with *Bt* as a priest or servant of *Ḫrty*, functioning as the shepherd of the **b3t*. In his discussion of the "Shepherd Song" (Kaplony, "Das Hirtenlied und seine fünfte Variante," p. 35), he goes further and says that *Ṯ3i-sp.f* is also linked with *Ḫrty*, since he too has the recumbent ram with his name.

114. R. Weill, "Le Dieu *Ḫrty*" in *Miscellanea Gregoriana* (1941), pp. 381–91, especially pp. 384–87 and p. 391. Other discussions of *Ḫrty*, each dependent on Weill's work, can be found in *RÄRG,* p. 135, and Peter Kaplony, "Cherti," *LÄ* I, cols. 944–45.

115. Kaplony, *IÄF,* p. 455. He discusses the god in the name *Ṯ3i-sp.f.*

116. cf. Gardiner, *Egyptian Grammar*^{3}, §§6 and 22–24.

117. Kurt Sethe, *Urgeschichte und älteste Religion der Ägypter,* AKM 1930, §11.

118. Weill, "Le Dieu *Ḫrty*," p. 385.

119. Note that Osiris almost invariably appears with his lower body unarticulated as if wrapped like a mummy.

120. Jacquet-Gordon, *Les Noms,* p. 94.

121. Cecil M. Firth and J. E. Quibell with plans by J.-P. Lauer, *The Step Pyramid* (1936), vol. 3, pl. 90, 7.

122. Kaplony, *IÄF* I, p. 455. See also Abb. 366.

123. Sethe, *Urgeschichte und älteste Religion der Ägypter,* §11.

124. Gardiner, *Egyptian Grammar,* Sign List E 10.

125. Ahmed Mohamad Badawi, *Der Gott Chnum* (1937), especially Chap. I, Part 1.

126. Hermann Ranke, *Die ägyptische Personennamen,* 2 vols. (1935/52), shows the following *Bt* names: vol. 1, 10, 3; 89, 10; 89, 11; 89, 12; 97, 22; 98, 31; 99, 1; 99, 2; 93, 3; 171, 7; 258, 13; 266, 22; 418, 9; vol. 2, 308, 24; 275, 29; 275, 30; 275, 31; 276, 1; 276, 2; 277, 17; 277, 18; 277, 19. For Chnum, see Badawi, *Der Gott Chnum,* pp. 5–7. See also Ranke, *Die ägyptische Personennamen,* vol. 1, 126, 4; 171, 21; 171, 22; 173, 5; 173, 8; 173, 9; 228, 8; 275, 5; 275, 6; 275, 10; 275, 12; 276, 1; 276, 6; 284, 6; 292, 24; 293, 1; 413, 5; vol. 2, 311, 9; 383, Nachträge to vol. 1, 276, 6.

127. Montet, *Géographie de l'Égypte ancienne,* vol. 1, p. 148, has identified the Ram of Mendes as being the same genus, the *ovis longipedis,* as the rams depicted in the sowing/threshing scenes of *Ty* and *Mrrw-k3* which accompany the "Shepherd Song."

128. *Wb* I, 414, 8–14.

129. Papyrus Berlin 3024, l. 66. See I. Gamer-Wallert, *Fische und Fischekult im alten Ägypten,* Äg.Ab. 21 (1970), pp. 122–23.

130. Seibert, *Die Charakteristik,* p. 63 with n. 70.

131. Moret, *La mise à mort du dieu en Égypte,* pp. 34–35.

132. This refers to the story as it appears in *DIO* 18.

133. Moret, *La mise à mort du dieu en Égypte,* p. 35.

134. Pierre Montet, *Everyday Life in Ancient Egypt in the Days of Ramesses the Great,* trans. A. R. Maxwell-Hyslop and Margaret S. Drower, with new introd. by David B. O'Connor (1981), p. 112.

135. Kaplony, "Das Hirtenlied und seine fünfte Variante," pp. 38–42.

136. Altenmüller, "Bemerkungen zum Hirtenlied," p. 222.

137. The sources cited by Altenmüller for this information are R. B. Onians, *The Origin of European Thought* (1951), p. 109, n. 4 and H. te Velde, *Seth, God of Confusion,* PdÄ 6 (1967), p. 42. See also B. Stricker, *Die Geboorte van Horus,* MVEOL XIV (1963), vol. 1, p. 30. According to these sources, the ancients perceived that the testicles were the repository of the semen, and they knew the effects of gelding.

138. Altenmüller, "Bemerkungen zum Hirtenlied," p. 231.

139. *CT* II, 100a.

140. Montet, *Géographie de l'Égypte ancienne,* vol. 2, p. 189.

141. See the Appendix for the relevant texts.

142. Altenmüller, "Bemerkungen zum Hirtenlied," pp. 219–20.

143. The following represents a loose translation of the chart from Altenmüller, "Bemerkungen zum Hirtenlied," pp. 217–18. For the rele-

vant tales from the Jumilhac, see the appendix. Note that the explanations are more extensive in Jum. XX, 1–22, which includes parts not found in the simpler version from Jum. III, 12–25.

144. Altenmüller observed that the "fairy tale-like traits" of the 2d part of the d'Orbiney showed its different purpose from that of the Jumilhac.

145. Altenmüller did not include the fact that Seth changed his form in order to appear like Anubis and fool the guard (Jum. III, 13–15).

146. The exact meaning and, thus, translation of this frequently recurring phrase is unknown. The *ḫt-m-ḫftyw* may be magical objects, but the lack of a determinative in the writing makes interpretation virtually impossible.

147. My quotes.

148. Note the divine intervention that resulted from Bata's prayer to Pre-Harakhti for aid in the form of the water, a stream with crocodiles.

149. Jumilhac XX, 1-22 includes a number of interpolations.

150. Actually d'Orbiney 7,9 says that Bata threw his phallus into the water, after which a *nʿr*-fish swallowed it.

151. Vandier, *Le Papyrus Jumilhac,* p. 21, mentions the accompanying demotic inscription which he identifies as misplaced since it reads,

> *ky ḏmʿ ḥr msḥ,*
> another chapter on the crocodile.

152. Despite the time difference, it is generally recognized that Ptolemaic texts very often reflect the much older (Old Kingdom) stratum of Egyptian culture. In dealing with them, however, it is important to recall that Greek interests and Greek culture often intermingle with and color the Egyptian materials, and furthermore, many of these late texts contain much of an etiological nature, as is the case with the Jumilhac.

153. The phallus of Osiris is reported to have been guarded by the Ram of Mendes (H. Brugsch, *Dictionnaire géographique de l'ancienne Égypte* [1879], p. 219 and 635; *Edfu* I, 334; Jumilhac IV caption, 20–22, and Vandier, *Le Papyrus Jumilhac,* pp. 233–34, note 900).

154. Seth also appears as a bull in *Pyr.* Utt. 580, where he is the sacrificial animal.

155. *Pyr.* §581*a.*

nḏr.n Ḥr Stš	Horus has laid hold of Seth;
d.n.f n.k sw ḫr.k	he has set him under you
wṯs.f ṯw	that he may lift you up.

Pyr. §642*a*

d.n n.k Ḥr ḫfti.k ḫr.k	Horus has set your foe under you
wṯs.f ṯw	that he may lift you up.

Pyr. §649*a*

rdi.n Ḥr wṯsf ṯw	Horus has caused him to lift you up
m rn.k n wṯs wr	in your name of the Great Lifted One.

Pyr. §§651*b–c*

rdi.n Ḥr int n.k Ḏḥwty	Horus has caused Thoth to bring
ḫfti.k	your foe to you,
d.n.f kw ḥr sꜣ.f	and he has set you on his back.

156. *Pyr.* §§1007*c* and 1977*c*

qꜣs.n.f n.k	He has bound for you
qꜣs ṯw	the one (ox/wild bull) who bound you.

157. *Pyr.* §418*a*

ḥr Ḥr n irt.f	Horus fell because of his eye;
sbn kꜣ/Stš n ẖrwy.f	the bull/Seth crawled away because of his testicles.

Pyr. §679*d*

ḥr Ḥr n irt.f	Horus fell because of his eye;
pꜣsḫ Stš ḥr ẖrwy.f	Seth suffered because of his testicles.

158. Although Seth is commonly referred to in animal forms other than that of a bull (*RÄRG,* p. 702), only once does he appear as a ram. This occurs in a myth derived from Canaanite material (Rainer Stadelmann, *Syrisch-Palästinensische Gottheiten in Ägypten,* PdÄ 5 [1967], pp. 131–32) in which Seth mounts the goddess Anat, springing as a ram springs (A. H. Gardiner, *Hieratic Papyri in the British Museum,* 3d series, Chester Beatty Gift [1935], Chester Beatty VII, Verso I, line 6). A parallel version found on an ostracon in the Ramesseum relates that Seth springs as a bull springs (ibid., p. 62, n. 8). A minor point here is that in the former Seth acts *mi . . . rhn* (ibid., pl. 36, Vs. I, line 6), "like a ram," while in the latter he behaves *m . . . kꜣ* (ibid., p. 62, n. 8), "as a bull," a clearer equation.

159. Maspero, *Contes populaires,*[1] p. xx and p. 6, n. 2. The second and third editions duplicate the statement in the introduction of the first edition in their respective introductions. The note accompanying the beginning of the story of the first edition is exactly the same in the second edition, and slightly varied for the third edition to include the Greek name of Bytis. The fourth edition differs radically, as does the English edition, apparently as a direct result of Naville's 1906 article on the goddess Bat mentioned above (see note 87).

160. Gardiner, "The Hero of the Papyrus d'Orbiney," p. 185. In 1940, H. G. Waddell, trans., *Manetho,* Loeb Classical Library 350

(1940), p. 5, suggested that Bites may be no more than *bity*, the Egyptian word for the king of Lower Egypt. Without an underlying hieroglyphic text for Manetho, we cannot determine the validity of this suggestion. Perhaps it is sufficient to note that the orthography of Bata's name with the *bꜣ*-bird and the *tꜣ*-bread contrasts sharply with the bee of *bity*.

161. Wolfgang Helck, *Untersuchungen zu Manetho und die ägyptischen Königslisten,* UGAÄ 18 (1956), p. 5.

162. Ursula Köhler, *Das Imiut: Untersuchungen zur Darstellung und Bedeutung eines mit Anubis verbundenen religiösen Symbols,* GOF IV, 4 (1975), pp. 328ff; 363–64.

163. Hermann Kees, "Anubis, Herr von Sepa und der 18. oberägyptische Gau," *ZÄS* 58 (1923), pp. 79–91, and "Der Gau von Cynopolis und seine Gottheit," *MIO* 6 (1958), pp. 157–75.

164. Montet, *Géographie de l'Égypte,* vol. 2, p. 164. See also Hermann Kees, *Der Götterglaube im alten Ägypten,* 2d ed. (1956), pp. 28–30.

165. Gardiner, *AEO* II, pp. 98*–103*; Vandier, *Le Papyrus Jumilhac,* pp. 38–39, 41–43.

166. Gardiner, *AEO* II, pp. 107*–110* and map p. 99*; Vandier, *Le Papyrus Jumilhac,* pp. 39–43; Montet, *Géographie de l'Égypte,* vol. 2, p. 175.

167. Gardiner, *AEO* II, p. 103*; Vandier, *Le Papyrus Jumilhac,* p. 45; Montet, *Géographie de l'Égypte,* vol. 2, p. 166.

168. Jum. VI, 17–18.

169. Gardiner, *AEO* II, p. 110*. For a similar reference from Edfu, see Montet, *Géographie de l'Égypte,* vol. 2, p. 166.

170. Gardiner, *Wilbour Papyrus,* vol. 2, p. 50.

171. Vandier, *Le Papyrus Jumilhac,* p. 46.

172. Maspero, *Popular Stories,* p. 3, n. 1, considered the emphasis unnecessary, referring to permitted polygamy (i.e., allowing a man to pass his wife on to a subordinate). This same note appears in each of the four French editions.

173. In another form, this Ennead had Horus as a third brother who was also the offspring of Geb and Nut.

174. J. Gwyn Griffiths, *The Conflict of Horus and Seth from Egyptian and Classical Sources: A Study in Ancient Mythology* (1960), pp. 1–22, especially 12–22. I observed in Chap. 1 that Altenmüller ("Bemerkungen zum Hirtenlied des Alten Reiches," p. 224, n. 2) suggests that the conflict between Anubis and Bata reflects the Horus-Seth conflict displaced into the Other World.

175. Calverley and Broome, *Temple of King Sethos I at Abydos,* pl. 29. A Ptolemaic papyrus reports the same, for which see P. Barguet, *Le Papyrus N 3776 (S) du Musee du Louvre,* BdÉ 37 (1962), col. II, 9, cf. p. 6 and p. 8, which reads:

ink Inp sꜣ Bꜣstt
I am Anubis, son of Bastet.

176. Köhler, *Das Imiut.* For the particular relation with Hesat see pp. 327f, 410ff, and 438ff. See also Vandier, *Le Papyrus Jumilhac,* p. 65. According to A. M. Blackman and H. W. Fairman, "The Significance of the Ceremony of *ḤWT-BḤSW* in the Temple of Horus at Edfu," *JEA* 36 (1950), p. 65, n. 14. Ptolemaic tradition refers to Anubis as *nb wp,* "Lord of the Kine." This is apparently derived from his sonship to Hesat, though he is also referred to as the son of Isis in the passage.

177. J. Gwyn Griffiths, "Hesat," *LÄ* II, col. 1170.

178. Helmut Brunner, *Die Geburt des Gottkönigs,* Äg.Ab. 3 (1960), p. 131ff. See also pl. XII D and p. 122ff. Because of these last functions, it is tempting to see in her also the mother of Bata, both in his bull form and as crown prince, especially in her relation to Hathor and her depiction as mummiform (cf. Sethe, *Urgeschichte und älteste Religion,* §11), similar to *Bt* and suggesting mortuary implications. While the idea cannot be discounted, no evidence has been found to support it.

179. Jum. V, 6; VI, 2, 5–6, 11–12, 14–16.

180. F. Ll. Griffith and H. Thompson, *The Demotic Magical Papyrus of London and Leiden* (1904), 20, 2–4, 9–10, 25.

181. Köhler, *Das Imiut,* p. 313, for F2, II.

182. H. O. Lange, *Der magische Papyrus Harris* (1927), col. VII, 7–8 (p. 61).

183. *DIO* 14.

184. R. O. Faulkner, *The Ancient Egyptian Coffin Texts* (1973–1980), hereafter *AECT,* serves as the basis for the translations from the Coffin Texts.

185. Alan H. Gardiner, "Hymns to Sobk in a Ramesseum Papyrus," *RdÉ* 11 (1957), p. 50, lines 64–65 and pl. 3, lines 64–65. For other references to Osiris as the father of Anubis, see John Gwyn Griffiths, trans. and ed., *Plutarch's "De Iside et Osiride"* (1970), p. 318, hereafter *DIO.*

186. Gardiner's note here states that *Inpw* here represents "the name or status of a youthful prince or of the heir to the throne," referring to *Wb* I ,96, 5,6; and though he observes the relationship to Anubis "the dog deity," he says he is unable to offer an explanation. See below for a possible explanation.

187. Jum. VI, 4, again in a context recalling Horus.

188. *DIO* 14.

189. Köhler, *Das Imiut,* p. 352.

190. Köhler, *Das Imiut,* pp. 340–343, 350.

191. The meaning of the name *Inpw,* Anubis, has been the subject of discussion over the years, but no scholarly consensus has been reached. For the different arguments, see the following references: Sethe, *Urgeschichte und älteste Religion,* §17; Erik Hornung, *Der Eine und die Vielen: Ägyptische Gottesvorstellungen* (1973), pp. 57, 272; Hornung, *Conceptions of God in Ancient Egypt: The One and the Many,* trans. John Baines (1982), pp. 67, 275; Brunner, *Die Geburt des Gottkönigs,* pp. 27–29;

Elke Blumenthal, *Untersuchungen zum ägyptischen Königtum des Mittleren Reiches I: Die Phraseologie,* ASAW 61, 1 (1970), pp. 35–36; J. Gwyn Griffiths, *The Origins of Osiris and his Cult,* Studies in the History of Religions (Supplement to Numen) XL (1980), p. 6; Dmitri Meeks, "Notes de Lexicographie," *RdÉ* 28 (1976), pp. 87–92; Pierre Lacau, *Études égyptologie II,* BdÉ 60 (1972), pp. 67–75; Kurt Sethe, *Pyr.Über.* vol. 5, pp. 197–98 (§ 1282b).

192. Winfried Barta, *Aufbau und Bedeutung des altägyptischen Opferformel,* Äg.For. 24 (1968), p. 289. Though not indicating possible gods, he does propose *sdi, wpiw, mniw, št3,* and even *s3b,* the proper word for jackal, as possible readings. Köhler acknowledges the problem, especially where there is no evaluative context such as a characteristic epithet, since *Ḫnty-imnty(w)* also appears as a recumbent jackal from the first dynasty on (Köhler, *Das Imiut,* p. 341). Walter Federn, "*Ḥtp (r)di(w) (n) 'Inpw:* zum Verständis der vor-osirianischen Opferformel," *MDAIK* 16 (1958), p. 130, n. 1, states simply that it is not certain that these canidae represent Anubis, a question which is discussed by Kees, *Der Götterglaube,* pp. 26–32.

193. Köhler, *Das Imiut,* Excurs I, pp. 328–32 with n. 1, p. 332.

194. Ibid., pp. 345–46; Kees, *Der Götterglaube im alten Ägypten,* p. 30.

195. Köhler, *Das Imiut,* pp. 345–48.

196. Ibid., pp. 340–44, especially n. 2 on p. 343.

197. Ibid., Abb. 1.

198. Ibid., pp. 363–64.

199. Ibid., p. 363.

200. Ibid., pp. 383–84. Federn, "*Ḥtp (r)di(w) (n) 'Inpw,*" p. 130, n. 1, implies a different order in suggesting that Anubis was the son of Osiris who became Horus when Osiris was assimilated into the Heliopolitan system.

201. Köhler, *Das Imiut,* p. 365, n. 2. On p. 419, n. 4, Köhler refers to *BD* 17, in which the sun god incorporates the new being: tomorrow is Re. *DIO* 44 refers to Anubis as the horizon, an equation which Virey uses in his allegorical summary of the "Tale of Two Brothers" (Virey, "Influence de l'Égypte," pp. 339–40), as described above in Chapter 1.

202. Köhler, *Das Imiut,* p. 407.

203. Ibid., pp. 376–77. This kind of identification was not limited to Anubis (cf. Pyr. Utt. 215) or to the mortuary world, as is shown by Wolfgang Helck, "Herkunft und Deutung einiger Züge des frühägyptischen Königsbildes," *Anthropos* 49 (1954), pp. 961–91. See especially pp. 964–70 for the king's identification with animals and animal parts to gain their powers.

204. *Pyr.Übers,* I, p. 61. See also *CT* VI, 391*g* and 392*a*, for back and legs, and *Book of the Dead,* Ch. 181c. T. G. Allen, *The Book of the Dead, or Going Forth by Day,* SAOC 37 (1974) provides the base for

translation and the sections of the Book of the Dead cited in this book, hereafter *BD*.

205. For the hieroglyphic text see E. A. Wallis Budge, *The Book of the Dead,* 3 vols. (1898), text vol., p. 112, line 11. For other examples see *BD* Ch. 151a §2, Ch. 172, §§3–4; Budge, *The Book of the Dead,* text vol. p. 447, lines 2–3, 10. See also Budge, *The Chapters of Coming Forth by Day or the Theban Recension of the Book of the Dead. The Egyptian Hieroglyphic Text Edited from Numerous Papyri,* 2d ed. London, 1910, 3 vols. Books on Egypt and Chaldaea XXVII–XXX, rpt. AMS 1976, vol. 1, p. 146, line 15.

206. The dead king also assumes Anubis's powers in "as Anubis . . ." references, often with one or more of his characteristic epithets (*Pyr.* §§727*c*; 793*c*; 1564*c*; 1713*c*; 1867*b*; 2150*c*; 2241*c*). Some of these references cite Anubis in his commanding role in the Otherworld (*Pyr.* §§57*d*; 220*c*; 1552*c*), the role which the king seeks to assume and which lies behind these identifications. See also *CT* VI, 384*p–q*; 386*d–e*.

207. See also *BD* Ch. 179a and Ch. 188, Budge, *The Book of the Dead,* text vol., pp. 491–92, and Budge 1910, vol. 3, pp. 90–91 and 111–12.

208. In these texts, "N" stands for the name of the deceased.

209. Köhler, *Das Imiut,* p. 356.

210. Barta, *Aufbau und Bedeutung des altägyptischen Opferformel,* pp. 8–9.

211. *Pyr.* §§745*a*, 806*c*, 807*a*.

212. *CT* V, 165*a;* VI, 354*j–q;* VII, 112*h–m;* VII, 121*g*.

213. For example, *BD* 17, 18, 122, 142, and 144.

214. Barta, *Aufbau und Bedeutung des altägyptischen Opferformel,* p. 8, and Faulkner, *AEPT,* Index "Anubis." This list also gives *ḫnty tꜣ wʿb* (*Pyr.* 804*d*), a much less common epithet. At the same time it omits *ḫnty tꜣ ḏsr*, which actually appears in *Pyr.* 1552*c*.

215. The epithet *ḫnty-imntyw* was assumed by Osiris as he rose to prominence in the mortuary formulas beginning in the late Old Kingdom. For this development, see Barta, *Aufbau und Bedeutung des altägyptischen Opferformel,* p. 8, where he shows Anubis as the sole god of the fourth dynasty formulas, a position which he shares increasingly with Osiris in the fifth (p. 15) and sixth (p. 25) dynasties, but a position he never completely loses despite the ascendancy of Osiris. See also Griffiths, *The Origins of Osiris,* pp. 60, 145, and 175.

216. Köhler, *Das Imiut,* p. 368.

217. *CD,* p. 293, with references.

218. *Wb.* V, p. 228, 6, 8, 9, 12.

219. Alan H. Gardiner, "The Great Speos Artemidos Inscription," *JEA* 32 (1946), p. 51.

220. Wolfgang Helck, "Wirtschaftliche Bemerkungen zum privaten

Grabbesitz im Alten Reich," *MDAIK* 14 (1956), pp. 63–64.

221. Jurgen Settgast, *Untersuchungen zu altägytischen Bestattungsdarstellungen,* ADAIK 3 (1963), pp. 48–50.

222. Hartwig Altenmüller, *Die Texte zum Begräbnisritual in den Pyramiden des Alten Reiches,* Äg.Ab. 24 (Wiesbaden: Otto Harrassowitz, 1972), p. 213. The texts pertaining to the rites cited by Altenmüller, which are Pyramid Utterances 321, 317, 318–20, 277–301, and 226–43, make no reference to Anubis, which is rather curious considering that Anubis is *ḫnty/nb tȝ ḏsr.*

223. Köhler, *Das Imiut,* p. 368.

224. Köhler, *Das Imiut,* pp. 378–379.

225. Auguste Mariette, *Les Mastaba de l'ancien empire* (1884), A 2, B 1, B 2, C 4, C 9, C 11, C 18, C 19, C 22, D 18, E 1 & 2, E 17.

226. *Pyr.* §§ 896*c,* 897*d,* 1287*c,* 1364*c,* 1909*a,* 2012*b.*

227. Hartwig Altenmüller, "Die Bedeutung der 'Gotteshalle des Anubis' im Begräbnisritual," *JEOL* 22 (1971–72), pp. 307–317. See also Settgast, *Bestattungsdarstellungen,* pp. 94–104.

228. Hartwig Altenmüller, "Balsamierungsritual," *LÄ* I, col. 615–17, and Altenmüller, *Die Texte zum Begräbnisritual,* p. 170, n. 148.

229. *Pyr.* 1549*b.*

230. Mariette, *Les Mastaba de l'ancien empire,* p. 130, C 9; p. 22f, D 18; p. 368, D 69; p. 375 and 377, E 1 & 2; p. 424, E 17.

231. Joachim Spiegel, *Die Götter von Abydos,* GOF IV, 1 (1973), p. 42. In his study of Middle Kingdom stelae from Abydos, Spiegel found that this epithet accompanies Anubis's name in 132 of 197 occurrences. No other epithet comes close in number: *imy-wt* appears 84 times and *nb tȝ ḏsr* 88 times, while the strongly predominant *ḫnty sḥ nṯr* of the Old Kingdom shows up only 20 times. He links this predominance with the presence of canidae in the border mountains of the Nile valley, especially located around the twelfth Upper Egyptian nome.

232. Kees, "Der Gau von Cynopolis und seine Gottheit," p. 158, and Jean-Claude Grenier, *Anubis alexandrin et romain,* ÉPRO 57 (1977), p. 5.

233. Spiegel, *Die Götter von Abydos,* p. 42.

234. Other unmentioned epithets relate Anubis directly with specific necropolis areas, especially *R-stȝw* (*CT* III, 325*j*), the necropolis area of Giza, and *R-qrrt* (*CT* I, 228*b*), the necropolis area of Assiut. He is also called *nb spȝ,* Lord of the Centipede (*CT* VI, 213*e* and frequently in *BD*) in his cult at Tura, the limestone quarries east of the Nile from which stone for the pyramids at Giza and Saqqara was obtained (Kees, "Anubis, Herr von Sepa und der 18. oberägyptische Gau," pp. 79–82 and pp. 90–91). Tura was not a necropolis, however, despite its being the source of necropolis material, and an understanding of the title remains incomplete, even with the references relating to Anubis and the Day of the Centipede in the Coffin Texts (*CT* III, 265*a*) and the Book of the Dead,

BD Chaps. 31b; 69a, §S 4). Jum. V, 1–6, 2 lists these and other epithets as gods who are transformed into Anubis.

235. *Pyr.* §1122*c.*

236. *CT* I, 223*f–g.*

237. *CT* IV, 375*a* and *f;* IV 377*c; BD* Ch. 99b; *BD* Ch. 151a.

238. *CT* III, 107*a–c;* VI, 123*b–c; BD* Ch. 26b.

239. *CT* I, 195*g* ff.

240. In *BD* 168B, S 12, Anubis is called the embalmer, and in *BD* 172, S 7, he is said to swathe the deceased.

241. J.-C. Goyon, *Rituels funéraires de l'ancienne Égypte* (1972), p. 26. See Jan Assmann, "Neith spricht als Mutter und Sarg," *MDAIK* 28,2 (1973), pp. 124–25 for three texts which state that Anubis mummified and restored the deceased. The specifics of the embalming ritual are little known since the relevant texts within the mortuary literature have not been identified (H. Altenmüller, "Balsamierungsritual," col. 615–17). It seems reasonable to speculate that there existed a certain reluctance to depict and describe the details of the embalming ritual due to the inherent danger perceived in the actions of cutting, cleaning, and generally treating the deceased.

242. R. Weill, *Recherches sur la* 1re *dynastie et les temps prépharaoniques,* BdÉ 38,2 (1961) pp. 147–70. See also *CD,* p. 248.

243. This text recalls *Pyr.* 134*a:*

> *hꜣ RN*
> *n sm.n.k is mt*
> *sm.n.k ʿnḫ*
> O, King,
> you have not left dead;
> you have departed alive.

244. Faulkner's translation, *AECT,* vol. 2, p. 307, Spell 785, the only sensible way to interpret what is clearly a scribal error.

245. Jum. IV, 11; VII, 9–11; XI, 12–14.

246. Jum. vignette V.

247. Jum. III, 12–25; XX, 1–22; I, x + 4–11, 20. See n. 146 to this chapter for discussion.

248. Köhler, *Das Imiut,* Chapter I, pp. 324–39. The Egyptian *imy-wt* can be translated "the one who is in the wrappings."

249. *Pyr.* §§ 1280*b–c;* 835*a–c;* 1981*a–c.*

250. *Pyr.* §§ 1683*b*–1685*a.*

251. Brigitte Altenmüller-Kesting, *Reinigungsriten im ägyptischen Kult* (1968), p. 80; Altenmüller, "Die Bedeutung der 'Gotteshalle des Anubis' im Begräbnisritual," p. 309.

252. See *Pyr.* 1995*b* and Eberhard Otto, *Das ägyptische Mundöffnungsritual,* 2 vols., Äg.Ab. 3 (1960), vol. 2, pp. 83–84.

253. Otto, *Mundöffnungsritual,* vol. 2, pp. 37–42.

254. Jum. V, 1–2. See Grenier, *Anubis,* pp. 13–14 and n. 56.

255. Wolfgang Helck, *Untersuchungen zu den Beamtentiteln des ägyptischen Alten Reiches,* Äg.For. 18 (1954), p. 17. See also Altenmüller-Kesting, *Reinigungsriten,* pp. 6–7. The *sm*-priest also was a functionary related to Sokar and to Ptah of Memphis. See H. de Meulenaere, "Un Titre memphit méconnu" in *Mélanges Mariette,* BdÉ 32 (1961), pp. 289–90, for discussion; and Grenier, *Anubis,* p. 4, n. 56.

256. Otto, *Mundöffnungsritual,* vol. 2, Abb. 7.

257. Ibid., Abb. 12.

258. Ibid., p. 18.

259. Ibid., pp. 18 and 83–84; Goyon, *Rituels funéraires,* pp. 25–26.

260. Köhler, *Das Imiut,* pp. 350–51.

261. See Jumilhac XX, 13–14 and VI, 17–VII, 1 for such a transferral to Seth in Ptolemaic period.

262. Köhler, *Das Imiut,* Chapter 3, § 5 is especially concerned with its form, and Chapter 4 deals with the name.

263. Ibid., p. 352.

264. *Pyr.* §1282*b*. See Köhler, *Das Imiut,* p. 358, n. 3.

265. *CT* VI, 386*f–g*.

266. *CT* II, 134*h*.

267. Köhler, *Das Imiut,* p. 358ff, n. 3.

268. Ibid., p. 358ff, n. 3. See Bernard Bruyère, *Rapport sur les fouilles de Deir el Médineh (1924–25),* FIFAO III, 3 (1926) p. 128, fig. 88, p. 129, and p. 161, fig. 108 and Bernard Bruyère, *Rapport sur les fouilles de Deir el Médineh (1927),* FIFAO V, 2 (1928) pl. 3.

269. Erik Hornung, *Buch von den Pforten,* I, Aeg.Hel. 7 (1979), pp. 195–96; Erik Hornung, trans., *Ägyptische Unterweltsbücher* (1972), p. 240.

270. Alexandre Piankoff, *The Tomb of Ramesses VI,* ed. N. Rambova, Bollingen Series XL, 1 (1954), pl. 139; Köhler, *Das Imiut,* pp. 388–89.

271. Köhler, *Das Imiut,* p. 389. The following is taken directly from Köhler's outline of the passage.

272. Köhler, *Das Imiut,* pp. 393–95.

273. Ibid., pp. 399–401.

274. Jum. XV, 9–XVI, 8; Köhler, *Das Imiut,* pp. 407–10.

275. Köhler, *Das Imiut,* pp. 401–403.

276. Ibid., pp. 405–406.

Chapter 3

1. For a description at some length of everyday life in ancient Egypt, see Montet, *Everyday Life in Ancient Egypt,* and Maspero, *Popular Stories,* notes to pp. 3–5.

2. W. Westendorf, "Beiträge aus und zu den medizinischen Texten," *ZÄS* 92 (1966), pp. 142–43, from *Wb* I, 539. Brunner-Traut, "Papyrus

d'Orbiney," col. 702, n. 3, suggests that *pḥty*, sexual power, is used in place of the later *ṯnr*, physical power, and may be intended as a contrast, though she says that this is conjecture. It must be noted, however, that the two words occur in the same passage in d'Orbiney 3,5–6, leading me to think that the contrast is intentional. See also Hintze, *Untersuchungen zur Stil und Sprache,* p. 75.

3. Westendorf, "Medizinischen Texten," p. 143.

4. Chester Beatty I, 4, 3–4; Georges Nagel, "Set dans la barque solaire," *BIFAO* 28 (1929), p. 36, which is cited in J. Zandee, "Seth als Sturmgott," *ZÄS* 90 (1962), p. 155. See also W. Barta, *Untersuchungen zum Götterkreis der Neunheit,* MÄS 28 (1973), p. 24, and *CT* VI, 266*f*.

5. *CT* VII, 154*j*.

6. *CT* VI, 272*e*.

7. *CT* IV, 92*i*.

8. *Wb* I, 539, 21 gives Mariette's *Abydos III* as a thirteenth-dynasty example and states "und oft D 18–20" without further citations.

9. At times even the deceased bears it, e.g., *CT* VI, 97*b;* VI, 414*s,* presumably referring to his/her transliteration to the other world, i.e., the world of the gods. In relation to the deceased, the epithet contains reflexes of the older royal tradition in which the king becomes a god, especially evident in the Pyramid Texts.

10. The king is considered to be divine.

11. W. Guglielmi, *Reden, Rufe, und Lieder auf altägyptische Darstellungen der Landwirtschaft, der Viehzucht, des Fisch- und Vogelfangs vom Mittleren Reich zur Spätzeit,* TÄB I (1973), pp. 95–100.

12. Montet, *Everyday Life in Ancient Egypt,* p. 123. According to Montet, the cattle herders lived in the stables or byres, both to guard the herd and to be ready to get to the pastures early in the morning.

13. B 211. Advice from a Speaking Cow.

14. Erich Lüddeckens, *Untersuchungen über religiösen Gehalt, Sprache und Form der ägyptischen Totenklagen,* MDAIK 11 (1943), p. 180.

15. Emma Brunner-Traut, *Die alten Ägypter: Verborgenes Leben unter Pharaonen* (1971), p. 39.

16. See Lichtheim, *AEL* II, pp. 200–203.

17. Lüddeckens, *Totenklagen,* p. 147f, #73. See also p. 180 for a general description and p. 93f, #38; p. 154f, #77; p. 73f, #28, and p. 75, #29 for other examples. A. Hermann, *Altägyptische Liebesdichtung* (1959), p. 43, n. 29, suggests this type of expression is "eine rein literarische Weiterbildung." Even if it is purely literary, its customary usage reflects some sense of a special relationship.

18. For a discussion of this mixed form, see Lüddeckens, *Totenklagen,* p. 148, note to c.

19. *Wb* I, 465, 12.

20. *Wb* III, 330, 3.

21. *CT* V, 57*c*.

22. *BD* Ch. 125c, § S4.

23. *Urk.* IV, 236–38 and 239–40. Emma Brunner-Traut, *Altägyptische Tiergeschichte und Fabel: Gestalt und Strahlkraft* (1968), p. 33, feels that this example reflects less myth than "eine lyrische Empfindung für die Kreatur."

24. A previously unmentioned parallel as far as I know.

25. H. Brunner, "Fruchtbarkeit," *LÄ* II, col. 339.

26. Merikare, lines 130–31.

27. Dieter Müller, "Der gute Hirte: Ein Beitrag zur Geschichte ägyptischer Bildrede," *ZÄS*, 86 (1961), p. 131.

28. See Müller, "Der gute Hirte," p. 133. The document, which dates to Sesostris I, is translated in Erman, *AE,* p. 49.

29. The god, Horus of the Two Horizons.

30. See Müller, "Der gute Hirte," p. 133. An English translation of the extant fragments of this hymn can be found in Erman, *AE,* p. 137.

31. See Erik Hornung, *Conceptions of God in Ancient Egypt: The One and the Many* (1982) p. 193.

32. Müller, "Der gute Hirte," pp. 134–136.

33. Ambrose Lansing, "The Museum's Excavations at Thebes," *BMMA* (Nov. 1935), Sec. II, *The Egyptian Expedition 1934–1935,* fig. 9. See Müller, "Der gute Hirte," p. 138.

34. Although it has been called the most ancient scene of its kind by Philippe Derchain, "La Perruque et le cristal," *SAK* 2 (1975), p. 55, the attempt of Ishtar to seduce Gilgamesh in Tablet VI of the *Epic of Gilgamesh* is older. See Tzvi Abusch, "Ishtar's Proposal and Gilgamesh's Refusal: An Interpretation of the *Gilgamesh Epic,* Tablet 6, Lines 1–79," *History of Religions,* vol. 26, #2 (November 1986), pp. 143–87, and Samuel Noah Kramer, *History Begins at Sumer* (1959), pp. 190–91, for a discussion of the Sumerian antecedent to the Old Babylonian version. For a discussion of the similarities and the very significant differences between the scene in the d'Orbiney and that involving Gilgamesh, see Susan Tower Hollis, "The Woman in Ancient Examples of the Potiphar's Wife Motif," in *Gender and Difference in Ancient Israel,* ed. Peggy L. Day, pp. 28–42 (Minneapolis: Fortress, 1989), especially pp. 36–38.

35. See below, Excursus I: The Papyrus d'Orbiney and Genesis 39, for a full discussion of the relationship between the episodes.

36. Derchain, "Le Perruque et le cristal," p. 59.

37. Ibid., p. 67.

38. Philippe Derchain, "Snéfrou et les rameuses," *RdÉ* 21 (1969), pp. 21–25; Derchain, "La Perruque et le cristal," p. 59; Aylward M. Blackman, "The Story of Sinuhe and other Egyptian Texts," *JEA* XXII (1936), p. 41.

39. For translations and commentaries on Egyptian love songs, see Michael V. Fox, *The Song of Songs and the Ancient Egyptian Love Songs* (1985). Translations of some of the love songs appear in the collections

of Lichtheim, vol. 2; Simpson, *LAE;* and Erman, *AE.* In addition, John L. Foster, *Love Songs of the New Kingdom* (1974) provides illustrated translations of many of the songs, some accompanied by hieroglyphic transcriptions.

40. *CT* II, 282*a.* See also *BD* Ch. 115.

41. Fox, *The Song of Songs and the Ancient Egyptian Love Songs,* pHarris 500, Group A, #3. See also Group B, #10, #16, and pChester Beatty I, Group C, #43 (= Simpson *LAE,* #43, p. 324). Another poem describes the hair as "true lapis lazuli" (Fox, pChester Beatty I, Group A, #31 = Simpson, *LAE,* #32, pp. 315–16.), and a third mentions "hair laden with balm" (Fox, pHarris 500, Group A, #8).

42. The papyrus describes the original situation as *iw.tw ḥms ḥr nbd st* (d'Orb. 2,10), "one was sitting, braiding her hair."

43. Translators vary in how they interpret *wnḫw.* E. F. Wente, Jr., "The Tale of Two Brothers" in *The Literature of the Ancient Egyptians,* ed. Wm. Kelly Simpson with translations by R. O. Faulkner, E. F. Wente, Jr., and Wm. K. Simpson (1973), p. 97 translates d'Orbiney 5,2 as, "You shall put on your braids"; Lichtheim, *AEL* II, p. 205 reads it, "Loosen your braids"; Brunner-Traut, *Altägyptische Märchen,*[5] p. 31 translates it, "Setz deine Perücke auf"; and Lefèbvre, *Romans et contes,* p. 146, reads, "Mets ta perruque." The verb carries the sense of dressing or adorning, putting on, but it is difficult to relate to dressing one's hair.

44. Erman restores *mtn* in A. Erman, *Die Märchen des Papyrus Westcar,* (1890), p. 23. On p. 24, he draws an analogy with d'Orbiney 3,7 and 5,1, describing the expression as "erotic."

45. This consequence is what the instructional literature teaches. For instance, the "Instruction of Ptahhotep" from the Old Kingdom warns a man to be wary of women in a friend's house for:

> *n nfr n bw irw.st im*
> . . .
> *ꜣt ktt mitt rswt*
> *iw pḥ.tw mt ḥr rḫ st* (lines 282, 287–88)
> unhappy is the place where it is done,
> . . .
> a short moment is like a dream,
> one achieves death because of knowing her.

In the "Instruction of Any," dating from the eighteenth dynasty, a father warns his son about strange women:

> *m ir rḫ sw im ḥꜥwt*
> . . .
> *st-ḥmt wꜣwy.tw r hꜣy.st*
> . . .

iw.st ꜥḥꜥ tw sḫty tw(=st)
btȝ ꜥȝ mt
m-ḫt sḏmw.tw.f (Any 3,14–16)
do not know her carnally
. . .
for the woman is one far from her husband
. . .
she will ensnare you,
a great and deadly crime
after it is heard.

46. S. Allam, "Ehe," *LÄ* I, col. 1174.

47. J. Vergote, *Joseph en Égypte,* Orientalia et Biblica Louvaniensia III (1959), pp. 22–23, suggests that this behavior was possible on the woman's part because of the equality or near equality of a woman with her husband. F. Jesi, "It tentato adulterio mitico in Grecia e in Egitto," *Aegyptus* 42 (1962), p. 292, disagrees, saying that it happened in Greece as well, where women clearly lacked equality.

48. Hieroglyphic copies of the story may be found in A. H. Gardiner, *Die Erzählung des Sinuhe und die Hirtengeschichte,* Hieratische Papyrus aus der königlichen Museen zu Berlin V, ed. A. Erman (1909) pl. 16–17, and Hans Goedicke, "The Story of the Herdsman," *CdÉ* 90 (1970), pp. 245–47. Different translations of the story may be found in Erman, *AE,* p. 35; Brunner-Traut, *Altägyptische Märchen,*[5] p. 10f; Lefèbvre, *Romans et contes,* p. 26ff.

49. Goedicke, "The Story of the Herdsman," p. 244; Rosemarie Drenkhahn, "Hirtengeschichte," *LÄ* II, col. 1223.

50. Goedicke, "The Story of the Herdsman," pp. 249, 258.

51. Erman, *AE,* p. 35.

52. A. Hermann, *Altägyptische Liebesdichtung,* p. 18 with n. 44.

53. Ibid., p. 18; Lefèbvre, *Romans et contes,* p. 26, calls her "une nymphe ou fée des étangs," and Brunner-Traut, *Altägyptische Märchen,*[5] p. 254, terms her "eine Wassernixe," though also referring to her as a goddess.

54. For example, "The Contendings of Horus and Seth," pChester Beatty I, 4, 1–3. See Chap. 5 below.

55. Goedicke, "The Story of the Herdsman," p. 249.

56. Goedicke, "The Story of the Herdsman," p. 260. See Chap. 5 concerning Hathor and Bata's wife.

57. V. Vikentiev, "L'Énigme d'un papyrus (Berlin P. 3024)" (Cairo, 1940), has stated otherwise, feeling that both are of Asiatic origin and are related to the *Epic of Gilgamesh,* and that the "Story of the Herdsman" and the "Shipwrecked Sailor" together "devait former une version complète de la 'légende des Deux Frères'" (p. 13).

58. In ancient myths and epic tales, sexual relations between the divine and human worlds carry a great deal of danger—strange destiny, odd births, and so forth—even death.

59. Labib Habachi, "Amenwahsu Attached to the Cult of Anubis, Lord of the Dawning Land," *MDAIK* 14 (1956) pp. 52–62, especially p. 60. See also Allam, *Hathorkult,* p. 97.
60. *Wb* I, 415, 4–6.
61. *Wb* I, 7, 11–12.
62. Westendorf, "Medizinischen Texten," p. 133.
63. B. Schmitz, "Sem(priester)," *LÄ* V (1984), cols. 833–36.
64. Westendorf, "Medizinischen Texten," pp. 131–33.
65. G. Posener, "La Piété personelle avant l'âge amarnien," *RdÉ* 27 (1975), pp. 195–210.
66. A. Erman, "Denksteine aus der thebanischen Gräberstadt," *SPAW* 1911, pp. 1086–1110. For Amarna, see M. Sandman, *Texts from the Time of Akhenaton* (Bibliotheca Aegyptiaca, 8 Brussels, 1938) 100, 12; 101, 10. See also Jan Assmann, "Aton," *LÄ* V, col. 534; and Helmut Brunner, "Persönliche Frommigkeit," *LÄ* IV (1982), cols. 951–63.
67. Erman, "Denksteine aus der thebanischen Gräberstadt," pp. 1108–1110; Jan Assmann, *Ägyptische Hymnen und Gebete,* (1975), pp. 349–417, which is a whole section of hymns and prayers of personal piety, an expansion of Erman's work.
68. E. Brunner-Traut, "Krokodil," *LÄ* III, col. 793. Amenemope XXII, 9–10, Chap. 21 reports that dread of the crocodile is "ancient."
69. A. H. Gardiner, *Admonitions of an Egyptian Sage* (1909), p. 29, states that *ḏs iry* = *ḏs.sn.*
70. *BD* Ch. 17a, §13. Ammut (*ʿm-mwt,* "the swallower of the dead"), the devouring animal of the Tribunal, is a mixed creature with a crocodile snout.
71. Jum. XXII, 20.
72. Brunner-Traut, "Krokodil," col. 795.
73. Ibid., col. 796.
74. A. Théodoridès, "De la prétendue expression juridique *pnʿ r mdt,*" *RdÉ* 19 (1967), p. 113, n. 3.
75. See Susan T. Hollis, "The Cartonnage Case of Pa-di-mut, Harvard Semitic Museum 2230" in "*Working with No Data,*" Semitic and Egyptian Studies Presented to Thomas O. Lambdin, ed. David M. Golomb with assistance of Susan T. Hollis, 1987 (1988), pp. 165–79 for a twenty-second-dynasty example. Though one sees Osiris as the god of judgment in the burial scenes more often than one sees Re/Pre, a parallel exists in ancient Mesopotamia, where the sun god Shamash also acts as the god of justice, e.g., the depiction on the stela of the Code of Hamurappi.
76. Any (eighteenth dynasty) and Amenemope (Ramesside).
77. See Ptahhotep 479–80, Any 7,12, Any 8,14–15, and Amenemope IV, 10–13, for pertinent examples.
78. See Lichtheim, *AEL* II, p. 141.
79. See below, Chap. 4, "Bata's Phallus."
80. See above, Chap. 1, "Myth or Folktale? The Folklorists' Views."

81. Maspero, *Popular Stories,* p. 10, n. 3; Assmann, "Zweibrüdermärchen," p. 23.
82. Assmann, "Textanalyse," p. 10 and p. 15, n. 52.

Excursus I

1. The following discussion is drawn from my article entitled "The Woman in Ancient Examples of the Potiphar's Wife Motif, K2111" (see Chap. 2, n. 34 for the full reference).
2. Thompson, *Motif Index,* p. 474.
3. E.g., Child Ballad 291, "Child Owlet."
4. In 1973, in the Festschrift for Cyrus Gordon, Delbert Hillers examined the seduction theme in an article entitled "The Bow of Aqhat: The Meaning of a Mythological Theme" (*Orient and Occident: Essays Presented to Cyrus Gordon on the Occasion of his Sixty-fifth Birthday,* ed. by Harry A. Hoffner [1973] pp. 71–81), limiting his study to ancient Near Eastern sources. From his work, he derived a pattern somewhat similar to that of Yohannan (see Chaps. 1, 3 above), but with more details, especially in its sexual connotations.
5. Hillers, "The Bow of Aqhat," p. 75.
6. Ibid., pp. 75–76. In an editorial note to the article (n. 30, p. 76), Hoffner cites the Elkunirsa myth as an additional example.
7. Donald Redford, *A Study of the Biblical Story of Joseph,* Supplements to *Vetus Testamentum* 20 (1970), p. 92.
8. J. Robin King, "The Joseph Story and Divine Politics," *JBL* 106, (Dec. 1987), pp. 577–94.
9. Cf. Hillers, "The Bow of Aqhat," 76–78; King, "The Joseph Story," pp. 580–85.
10. Arnold van Gennep, *The Rites of Passage* (Chicago: University of Chicago, 1960).
11. Victor Turner, *The Ritual Process* (Ithaca, NY: Cornell, 1969), especially chap. 3.
12. Redford, *A Study,* p. 183; W. Lee Humphreys, *Joseph and His Family: A Literary Study* (Columbia, S.C.: University of South Carolina, 1988), p. 204.
13. E.g., G. Coats, *From Canaan to Egypt: Structural and Theological Context for the Joseph Story,* CBQMS 4 (Washington, DC: Catholic Biblical Association, 1976), pp. 28–29.
14. The numbers in brackets designate the part of the pattern to which the description refers.
15. Normally, death, not prison, was the sentence for adultery in Egypt, and few commentators on Genesis 39 fail to mention this fact. Von Rad, for instance, feels that the narrator, if questioned, would have explained the situation simply by saying, "Yahweh was with Joseph" (Gerhard von Rad, *Genesis: A Commentary,* 3d rev. ed. [OTL; London: SCM, 1972], p. 367), and Speiser points out that one should not "over-

look the simple point that had Joseph been subjected to the [normal] fate . . . the Joseph story itself would have died an untimely death (E. A. Speiser, *Genesis: A New Translation with Introduction and Commentary,* 3d ed., [AB I; Garden City, NY: Doubleday 1987], p. 304).

16. See Louis Ginzberg, *The Legends of the Jews,* vol. 2 (Philadelphia: The Jewish Publication Society, 1910) pp. 39–58, for a legendary account of the Joseph and Potiphar's wife episode; and Thomas Mann, *Joseph and His Brothers* (New York: Knopf, 1971), pp. 667–840, for a novelistic rendering of the episode, perhaps reflecting the legendary account.

17. For a fine discussion of transition in terms of symbolic death, see Victor W. Turner, *The Forest of Symbols: Aspects of Ndembu Ritual* (Ithaca: Cornell University, 1967), Ch. 7; Turner, *The Ritual Process,* Chap. 4, pp. 93–111; and Victor W. Turner, "Betwixt and Between: the Liminal Period in *Rites de Passage,*" in *Reader in Comparative Religion*[4], ed. by William A. Lessa and Evon Z. Vogt (New York: Harper & Row, 1979), pp. 234–43.

18. Joseph Vergote, *Joseph in Égypte: Genèse Chap. 37–50 à la lumière des études égyptologiques récentes* (Louvain-Leuven: Publications Universitaires/Institutut voor Oriëntalisme, 1959), pp. 146–48. See also Hermann Ranke, *Die ägyptische Personennamen,* vol. 1 (Glückstadt: J. J. Augustin, 1935), p. 123, 11; and Adolf Erman and Hermann Grapow, *Wörterbuch der ägyptischen Sprache,* vol. 1 (Leipzig: J. C. Hinrichs'sche, 1925), p. 492, 6.

19. Although references to this myth appear in all periods of Egyptian history, no complete rendition of it dates earlier than that of Plutarch, about 120 CE. For a translation and commentary, see J. Gwyn Griffiths, *Plutarch's "De Iside et Osiride"* (Cardiff: University of Wales, 1970), Chaps. 12–20.

20. This represents the Kamutef (bull of his mother) concept discussed in Chap. 6 "Kamutef."

21. With specific regard to the role of the women in the Egyptian tale, Leonard Lesko has suggested recently that this tale, along with the "Contendings of Horus and Seth" and the "Blinding of Truth by Falsehood," two other New Egyptian tales, reflects not only the succession to kingship but also presents a negative attitude toward queens (Leonard Lesko, "Three Late Egyptian Stories Reconsidered" [see note 61 to Chap. 1 above for the full reference]). He argues that the strength of Hatshepsut and eighteenth-dynasty queens in general led to the attempt by the nineteenth dynasty to avert any challenge to the throne by their surviving relations. Though he has a point, I am inclined to think the issue is far more complex and refers even more strongly to a basic ambivalence expressed by men towards women in all times and all places. See also Barbara S. Lesko, "Women of Egypt and the Ancient Near East," in *Becoming Visible: Women in European History.* 2d ed., ed. by Renate Bridenthal, Claudia Koonz, Susan Stuard (Boston: Houghton Mifflin, Co., 1987),

p. 52. For another more popularized discussion of women in ancient Egypt, see B. S. Lesko, *The Remarkable Women of Ancient Egypt,* 2d rev. ed. (Providence, RI: B.C. Scribe, 1987). For a discussion of queens and the mythology surrounding them, see Lana Troy, *Patterns of Queenship in Ancient Egyptian Myth and History,* BOREAS 14 (Uppsala, 1986).

22. David O'Connor ("New Kingdom and Third Intermediate Period, 1552–664 BC" in *Ancient Egypt: A Social History,* B. G. Trigger, B. J. Kemp, D. O'Connor, and A. B. Lloyd [Cambridge: Cambridge University, 1983], p. 223) states that Amenmesses usurped Seti II's position as king for a time during the latter's reign, while K. A. Kitchen (*Pharaoh Triumphant: The Life and Times of Ramesses II* [Mississauga, Canada: Benben, 1982], p. 216) suggests that Amenmesses, probably a lesser son, ruled for a very short time before Seti II, the crown prince (see the colophon to the papyrus), acceded to the throne.

23. This knowledge may challenge commentators to look more deeply into tales of other apparently negative or destructive women.

Chapter 4

1. G. Ebers, *Aegypten und die Bücher Mose's,* p. 314.
2. Griffiths, *Plutarch's "De Iside et Osiride",* p. 343.
3. Redford, *A Study of the Biblical Story of Joseph,* p. 91, n. 6.
4. Hillers, "The Bow of Aqhat," p. 78.
5. Gerald Kadish, "Eunuchs in Ancient Egypt," in *Studies in Honor of John A. Wilson, September 12, 1969,* SAOC 35 (1969), p. 62. He does not expand on how this acts as a "literary device," an explanation of which might prove elucidating to the concept of Egyptian tale-telling if it could be confirmed from Egyptian sources.
6. *Pyr.* § 1061*b.*
7. pChester Beatty, I, lines 3–4.
8. *Pyr.* § 510*b.*
9. *Pyr.* § 1248*a–b.*
10. H. Grapow, *Grundriß der Medizin der alten Ägypter,* 8 vols. (1954–73), vol. 1, p. 85; hereafter referred to as *GMAÄ,* See also Lothar Störk, "Kastration," *LÄ* III, col. 355. Of interest is the fact that in the First Division of the Book of Caverns, the bound enemies are shown naked and lacking sexual organs. For reference, see Piankoff, *The Tomb of Ramesses VI,* fig. 10, and Hornung, *Ägyptische Unterweltsbücher,* p. 320. This last reference is a description of the vignette.
11. D. Müller, "Die Zeugung durch das Herz in Religion und Medizin der Ägypter," *Orientalia* 35 (1966), p. 273, and Stricker, *Die Geboorte van Horus,* I, p. 30, show the emendation, presumably on the basis of Grapow's discussion in *GMAÄ* I, p. 73, in which he discusses how all the vessels of a man lead to his heart, even those of the testicles. Ebers 103, 2–3, is the appropriate textual citation.

12. Grapow, *GMAÄ* I, p. 85, states that Bata's castration included the testicles, although nothing in the text indicates that such was the case.

13. Jacobsohn, *Die dogmatische Stellung des Königs,* p. 14.

14. Elfiede Reiser, *Der königliche Harim im alten Ägypten und seine Verwaltung,* Dissertationen der Universität Wien (1972), p. 117; Andrew T. Sandison, "Eunuchen," *LÄ* II, col. 46–47; and Kadish, "Eunuchs in Ancient Egypt," pp. 55–62, especially 59–61.

15. Reiser, *Der königliche Harim,* p. 106. Reiser (pp. 108–13) discusses the terms *sẖty, ḥm,* and *ḥmty,* the terms commonly thought to have been used to designate a eunuch. See also Kadish, "Eunuchs in Ancient Egypt," pp. 59–61, and Vergote, *Joseph en Égypte,* p. 41.

16. H. te Velde, *Seth, God of Confusion,* PdÄ 6 (1967, rpt. with corrections 1977), p. 40; J. Gwyn Griffiths, *Conflict of Horus and Seth* (1960) p. 37. Griffiths notes that there are many allusions to the restoration of the eye of Horus and the testicles of Seth, which may explain the lack of reference to Seth as a eunuch.

17. Griffiths, *Conflict of Horus and Seth,* pp. 41–46; te Velde, *Seth,* pp. 32–46 and pp. 53–59. Te Velde chooses not to separate the quarrel of Horus and Seth from Seth's homosexuality.

18. H. Attridge and R. Oden, eds., *The Syrian Goddess (De Dea Syria),* Texts and Translations 9, Graeco-Roman Series 1 (1976), p. 29ff.

19. A. D. Nock, "Eunuchs in Ancient Religion," in *Arthur Darby Nock: Essays in Religion and the Ancient World,* ed. Z. Stewart (Cambridge, Mass.: Harvard University Press, 1972), I, pp. 7–12.

20. Maspero, *Contes populaires,*[1] p. 14, n. 1, and K. Sethe, "Zur ältesten Geschichte des ägyptischen Seeverkehrs mit Byblos und dem Libanongebiet," *ZÄS* 45 (1908) p. 13, n. 2. A. Blackman, "Some Remarks on an Emblem upon the Head of an Egyptian Birth Goddess," *JEA* 3 (1916), p. 205, n. 2, spoke of Bata-Osiris relative to this episode. All three of these scholars make their references on the basis of Plutarch's *De Iside et Osiride,* Chap. 18, where Isis is reported to have gathered all of Osiris's dismembered parts save his phallus, which was swallowed by the lepidotus, phagros, and oxyrhynchos fish.

21. A. Moret, "La Légende d'Osiris à l'époque thébaine d'après l'Hymne à Osiris du Louvre," *BIFAO* 30 (1931), pp. 741–44.

22. A. Erman, "Gebete eines ungerecht Verfolgte und andere Ostraka aus den Königsgräbern," *ZÄS* 38 (1900), p. 30. An English translation of the prayer appears in Erman, *AE,* p. 304.

23. For instance, see E. A. Wallis Budge, *Osiris and the Egyptian Resurrection,* 2 vols. (1911), vol. 2, p. 42, from Dendera. Two other depictions show Osiris holding his clenched fist in the appropriate location for his phallus (pp. 25 and 30). See also Theodor Hopfner, *Plutarch über Isis und Osiris,* 2 vols. (1940), vol. 1, pp. 81–84; and Eberhard Otto and Max Hirmer, *Osiris und Amun. Kult und heilige Stätten* (1966), plates 16–20.

24. Griffiths, *Plutarch's "De Iside et Osiride"*, p. 343.
25. Sethe, *Pyr.Über.* IV, p. 35 re *Pyr.* § 805*c*.
26. Faulkner, *AEPT,* pp. 145, 171, 250.
27. *Pyr.* § 805*c* writes *dmꜣt,* the singular, in all three copies. Whether this is the "correct" text and refers to the phallus can only be a matter of speculation. All copies of the other references clearly represent the plural.
29. pChester Beatty VIII, 6,5ff.
29. Jum. IV, 21–23 reports it to be found in the temple of the white ram, which Vandier interprets as Mendes, while noting no confirmation of the designation. Furthermore, the Mendes location of the Jumilhac occurs in the context of the finding of the phallus, in this case on the twenty-eighth day of the fourth month of *ꜣḫt,* while an alternative tradition from the same papyrus reports the phallus to have been found on the twenty-fifth day without specifying the location (Jum. IV, 16). Kees also locates the phallus at Mendes (Hermann Kees, "Die 15 Scheintüren an Gräbmal," *ZÄS* 88 [1963], p. 106).
30. Hopfner, *Plutarch,* I, p. 99.
31. In Theban Tomb 87 (Robert Mond, "Report of Work in the Necropolis of Thebes during the Winter of 1903–1904," *ASAE* VI [1905] pl. V, lines 6–7), the text reads *ḥḏt ḫnt qnt* as in B2Bo, B4Bo, B9c, and B2p.
32. K. Sethe, "Die Sprüche für das Kennen der Seelen der heiligen Orte," *ZÄS* 57 (1922), p. 27, n. 21, translates *wrmty* as "testicles," while Faulkner, *AECT,* vol. I, p. 133, adds "(?)" following the same word. Köhler, *Das Imiut,* p. 361ff, uses other variants and emends them so that the sense is that of Anubis inflicting harm to the corpse.
33. "Injured privy parts" is Faulkner's translation of *bꜣgw* (*AECT* I, p. 26). His note to the translation (n. 24, p. 27) observes the absence of the word in the *Wb,* but he finds a similar sense in *CT* II, 162*i*.
34. Lothar Störk, "Kastration," *LÄ* III, col. 355, has stated outright that Osiris is a castrated god.
35. G. Elliot Smith, *The Royal Mummies* (1912), p. 61.
36. Ibid., p. 67; see also James Harris and Kent R. Weeks, *X-Raying the Pharaohs* (1973), p. 157.
37. A.-P. Leca, *The Egyptian Way of Death,* tr. Louise Asmal (1981), p. 151. Sethe, "Kennen der Seelen," p. 32, n. 24, states that sometimes the phallus was severed and interred separately (without reference), and similar general references were made by Hopfner, (*Plutarch,* I, p. 100), and Störk ("Kastration," col. 355). Harris and Weeks do not even discuss it, and neither does Zaky Iskander, "Mummification in Ancient Egypt: Development, History, and Techniques," in *An X-Ray Atlas of the Royal Mummies,* ed. by James Harris and Edward Wente (1980), pp. 1–28.
38. My interpretation differs from those of Sethe, *Pyr.Über.* V, 390–91, re §1450*b* and Griffiths, *The Origins of Osiris,* p. 211. Sethe suggested it is a common person, not the king, who "did not swallow the member." That is to say that the deceased has not acted in such a way as

to be unworthy of the state of blessedness in the Otherworld. One could say Sethe's deceased commoner speaks to the human side of the king, his mortal aspect. Griffiths states that by not swallowing the member the deceased "has not shown proper respect to the realm of the dead," which appears to contradict the sense of safely gaining the next world.

39. An unknown word for fish or anything else.

40. *LES,* p. 17a, re d'Orb. 7,9.

41. Gamer-Wallert, *Fische und Fischkulte,* p. 9ff. See also M. Claude Gaillard, *Recherches sur les poissons,* MIFAO 51 (1923), pp. 50–60.

42. In taxonomic language, "family" ranks below "order" and above "genus" (plural "genera"), the latter ranking above "species."

43. Gaillard, *Poissons,* p. 57.

44. Gamer-Wallert, *Fische und Fischkulte,* Abb. 9 and 10 (p. 31f), and Gaillard, *Poissons,* fig. 32, 33, and 35. One should observe that Gerard Godron, "A propos du nom royal " *ASAÉ* 49 (1949), pp. 217–20 and plate I, gives twenty-four examples of the name, with many of the inscriptions showing an indistinctness of the dorsal fin structure, the fish being characterized most clearly by the head and beard.

45. The presence of the bi-dorsal *Heterobranchus* in Narmer's name might suggest an Upper Egyptian origin for this king, if indeed the modern observation that this fish did not appear commonly on the Nile of Egypt was a fact about the fish five millennia ago. Such an origin may be thought to be the case, since the detailed paintings of fish in the fifth dynasty tomb of *Ty* and the sixth dynasty mastaba of *Mrrw-kꜣ* do not show the *Heterobranchus,* while each clearly exhibits both species of *Clarias* (Gaillard, *Poissons,* fig. 1–6 in the text and Gamer-Wallert, *Fische,* Tafel I and II, with accompanying lists identifying the fish).

46. Gaillard, *Poissons,* pp. 53–54. François Daumas, "Quelques remarques sur les représentations du pêche à la ligne sous l'ancien empire," *BIFAO* 62 (1964), p. 79, states this too.

47. Godron, "A propos du nom royal," pp. 219–20.

48. Jean Capart, "Cultes d'el Kab et préhistoire," *CdÉ* XIV (1939), pp. 213–17.

49. Georg Möller, "Die Ägypter und ihre libyschen Nachbarn," *ZDMG* 78 (1924), p. 38 and Tafel 2.

50. Gamer-Wallert, *Fische und Fischkulte,* pp. 116–17.

51. Erik Hornung, *Das Amduat,* 2 vols., Äg.Ab. 7 (1963), II, p. 145. Hornung shows both examples in *Ägyptische Unterweltsbücher* with pictures on pp. 143 and 343 and text on pp. 145 and 341 respectively.

52. Piankoff, *Ramesses VI,* I, fig. 12 opp. p. 66 and text on p. 68.

53. Capart, "Cultes d'el Kab," fig. 2, 3, and 4. See also Gamer-Wallert, *Fische und Fischkulte,* p. 116, n. 321, p. 117, and Tafel XII, 2. It is difficult both to compare the examples from the different periods and to be certain that the *nʿr* is acting in a protective fashion, and so the question whether it was protective must remain open. Even the Edfu text in which wels-headed figures appear in the following of the white goddess

and are called the *nʿr* of *Wsrt* and the brother of *ʿꜣ pḥty* does not help (Capart, "Cultes d'el Kab," pp. 214–15).

54. Gamer-Wallert, *Fische und Fischkulte,* pp. 109–13.

55. Ibid., p. 117, n. 330.

56. Ibid., p. 118 and Taf. XIII, 2.

57. As was shown in Ch. 2, "Contexts of the Biconsonantal Nams Related to Bata," above, Altenmüller has suggested that *Bt,* whom he perceives as *Btjj(.j),* "my-what-belongs-to-*Bty,*" is the phallus, the same phallus as that of Bata. Because he sees *Bt* in the water as representing fertilization, he considers that Bata's phallus in the water likewise represents fertilization (Altenmüller, "Bemerkungen zum Hirtenlied," pp. 222–24).

58. Helck, "Herkunft und Deutung einiger Züge des frühägyptischen Königsbildes," p. 969.

59. Daumas, "du pêche à la ligne," pp. 79–80, points out that a mallet or club in fishing was portrayed, a practice used in certain types of fishing today, and it is not impossible that the wels carrying the club may be a humorous *captatio benevolentiae.*

60. Daumas, "du pêche à la ligne," pp. 67–85, especially 76–83. Daumas, a scholar who has written most explicitly on the maliciousness of the wels, largely used the work of Hasselquist of the eighteenth century, Geoffroy Saint-Hilaire of the early nineteenth century, and three first-century classical writers, Strabo, Seneca, and Pliny the Elder.

61. Gamer-Wallert, *Fische und Fischkulte,* p. 113.

62. Ibid., p. 7.

63. Gaillard, *Poissons,* p. 113.

64. Gamer-Wallert, *Fische und Fischkulte,* pp. 88–90.

65. Kaplony, "Das Hirtenlied," p. 49. His reason for regarding the wels as the enemy of Osiris is that the wels swallowed the phallus of Osiris, for which see the discussion below.

66. A. H. Gardiner, *Hieratic Papyri in the British Museum. Third Series,* 2 vols. (1935), vol. 1, p. 16, vol. 2, pl. 7.

67. Altenmüller, "Bemerkungen zum Hirtenlied," pp. 225–27.

68. Gamer-Wallert, *Fische und Fischkulte,* pp. 101–107, especially p. 102; Altenmüller, "Bemerkungen zum Hirtenlied," pp. 225–27.

69. If Altenmüller's reasoning is correct, it may explain the Edfu statement concerning the fifteenth Lower Egyptian nome:

> *bwt.f nʿr . . . m niwt.f* (*Edfu* I, 334,1)
> he detests the *nʿr* . . . in his town,

for such would be the case if the wels were one of the fish to have swallowed Osiris's phallus. See also Gamer-Wallert, *Fische und Fischkulte,* pp. 33 and 119, and Pierre Montet, "Le fruit défendu," *Kemi* 11 (1950) p. 99.

70. D'Arcy Wentworth Thompson, "On Egyptian Fish Names used by

Greek Writers," *JEA* 14 (1927), p. 27, outlines the tradition of the *phagros* as voracious, but he suggests it encompasses fish other than the wels.

71. This type of act is typical of modern folktales, e.g., Grimm tale #31, "The Girl without Hands," AaTh 706.

72. Assmann, "Textanalyse," p. 8, suggests that the weakness is due both to impotence and to the external soul. At this point in the tale, however, Bata still has his heart in his body; he does not remove it until he gets to the Valley.

73. B. Altenmüller, *Synkretismus in den Sargtexten,* GOF IV/7 (1975), p. 266, lists ten different references.

74. Gardiner, *Hieratic Papyri in the British Museum. Third Series,* vol. 1, p. 67, vol. 2, pl. 39.

75. I.e., life, liberty.

76. Moret, "La légende d'Osiris à l'epoque Thébaine d'après l'Hymne à Osiris du Louvre," p. 743, and A. de Buck, *Egyptian Readingbook* (1948), p. 111, line 15.

77. The citations given in *CD* and in *GMAÄ* were examined and in only two could anything like death be construed, and even in those it was problematical. *Urk.* IV, 1280, 2, "The Great Sphinx of Amenhotep II" (lines 13–14) states that men, having rowed a half mile, were *ẖsyw* and *gnnw* in their limbs and they did not *tpi ṯȝw,* breathe air. That they were deceased is doubtful, but rather they were most likely winded. The Berlin Medical Papyrus (15, 1–5) speaks of a king *m-ḫt ẖsf,* after he became weak. The context does not make it clear whether he is dead or not at the time, this being a magical text in which the name of the king, in addition to that of an apparently later king, were both written with *mȝʿ ḫrw,* deceased.

78. van Gennep, *Rites of Passage,* pp. 70–75, 81; Turner, *The Forest of Symbols,* pp. 151–279, esp. 152–53 and 267–68.

79. I. Jesi, "Il tentato adulterio mitico in Grecia e in Egitto," *Aegpytus* 42 (1962), p. 292.

80. Ibid., p. 288.

81. See the following section for a discussion of this concept.

82. Hermann te Velde, *Seth, God of Confusion* (1977), pp. 41–42.

83. See Excursus I, n. 17 for anthropological references.

84. Maspero, *Contes populaires,*[1] p. 13, n. 1.

85. P. Virey, "Influence de l'Égypte ancienne sur les transformations du paganisme," *Revue des Questions Historiques,* 1893, p. 338ff, and Virey, *La Religion,* pp. 194–97.

86. Maspero, *Les Contes populaires,*[2] p. 14, n. 1; *Les Contes populaires,*[3] p. 8, n. 3; *Les Contes populaires,*[4] p. 9, n. 1; and *Popular Stories,* p. 9, n. 1.

87. V. Vikentiev, "Nâr-Ba-Thai," *JEA* 17 (1931) pp. 74–78.

88. A. H. Gardiner, "Tanis and Pi Raʿmesse: A Retraction," *JEA* 19 (1933) p. 128.

89. V. Vikentiev, "Le Conte égyptien des deux frères et quelques histoires apparentées," *Bulletin of the Faculty of Arts,* Fouad I University, Cairo, 11, No. 2 (1949), pp. 71–84.

90. K. A. Kitchen, ed., *Ramesside Inscriptions: Historical and Biographical* (1969), vol. 2, p. 14.

91. Gardiner, "Tanis and Pi Raʿmesse," p. 128. A brief discussion can also be found in Pierre Montet, "Notes et documents pour servir à l'histoire des relations entre l'Égypte et la Syrie," *Kemi* 16 (1962), p. 78. See too Sir Alan Gardiner, *The Kadesh Inscriptions of Ramesses II* (1960), p. 8, P35 and p. 16, P35. H. Goedicke, "Considerations on the Battle of Kadesh," *JEA* 52 (1966), p. 73, n. 12, states that the *int p3 ʿš* in the d'Orbiney "refers to a place outside the dominion of the Pharaoh."

92. E. Chassinat, *Le Mystère d'Osiris au mois de Khoiak* (1968), p. 701, n. 4.

93. Wolfgang Helck, *Die Beziehungen Ägyptens zu Vorderasien im 3. und 2. Jahrtausend v. Chr.,* 2d ed., Äg.Ab. 5 (1971), p. 495.

94. Otto Weber, "Anmerkungen," in J. Knudtzon, *El-Amana-Tafeln* (1915), p. 1112.

95. *CAH*³ II/2, maps opp. p. 17 and p. 103.

96. *^{mâtu}am-ki* occurs in EA 53, 58; 170, 16; 173, 2; 174, 9; 175, 8; 176, 8; and 140, 27 and 30, these last two written: *^{mâtati}am-ki.* Three occurrences are virtually identical, though not from the same correspondents:

> *a-mur-mi ni-e-nu e-ba-ša-nu a-na ^{mâtu}am-ki*
> *alani šarri bêli-ia* (EA 174,9; 175,8; 176,8)
> See, we are in Amki,
> the cities of the king, my lord.

EA 170 tells of taking Amki; EA 53 mentions people of Amki; EA 140 reports Aziru's action against the lands of Amki; while EA 173 is so broken as to give no information.

97. A. Lucas, *Ancient Egyptian Materials and Industries,* 4th ed. revised and enlarged by J. R. Harris (1962), pp. 319–20. For a discussion of the use of resin in mummification, see James Hamilton-Patterson and Carol Andrews, *Mummies: Death and Life in Ancient Egypt* (1980), pp. 44, 47, 48, 49, 51.

98. Helck, *Die Beziehungen*², p. 23 and p. 73.

99. Helck, *Die Beziehungen*², pp. 376–77.

100. *Urk.* I, 236, 12. Cf. Helck, *Die Beziehungen*², p. 26. From the hieroglyphic text, it appears that what may have been brought is some kind of oil of the *ʿš*-tree.

101. Habachi, *The Second Stela of Kamose,* pp. 37, 53.

102. *Pyr.* 519*b.* Pierre Montet, "Le pays de Negau, près de Byblos, et son dieu," *Syria* IV 1923, pp. 184–85 gives five examples of *Ng3w,* including the two used that clearly link the *ʿš*-tree with it.

103. *Urk.* IV, 1237, 9ff. Cf. *ANET*[3], p. 243, and Helck, *Die Beziehungen*[2], p. 375.
104. *Urk.* IV, 1232, 2ff.
105. *Pyr.* 53*b.*
106. Otto, *Das Mundöffnungsritual,* vol. 2, pp. 122–23. See also Goyon, *Rituals funéraires de l'ancienne Égypte,* p. 149.
107. See Lichtheim, *AEL* I, p. 52, and Helck, *Die Beziehungen*[2], p. 28.
108. Maspero, *Les Contes populaires*[4], p. 9, n. 1, and *Popular Stories,* p. 9, n. 1.
109. V. Loret, "Quelques notes sur l'arbre âch," *ASAÉ* XVI (1916), pp. 33–51.
110. Lucas, *Ancient Egyptian Materials,* p. 319, and Helck, *Die Beziehungen*[2], pp. 26–27.
111. J. A. Wilson in *ANET*[3], p. 25.
112. Helck, *Die Beziehungen*[2], pp. 26–27, using Loret.
113. It is *mrw*-wood, which is cedar.
114. Helck, *Die Beziehungen*[2], p. 495.
115. Kitchen, "Interrelations of Egypt and Syria" in *La Siria nel Tardo Bronzo,* ed. Mario Liverani, Orientis Antiqui Collectio 9 (1969), p. 88.
116. For example, "Sinuhe," "The Doomed Prince," and "The Taking of Joppa."
117. Altenmüller, "Bemerkungen zum Hirtenlied," p. 219, n. 1.
118. Jürgen von Beckerath, "Die 'Stele der Verbannten' im Museum des Louvre," *RdÉ* 20 (1968), pp. 11, 14, 35. See also John Baines, "Interpreting *Sinuhe,*" *JEA* 68 (1982), p. 41, n. 41.
119. Baines, "Interpreting *Sinuhe,*" p. 37.
120. A. Piankoff, *Le "Coeur" dans les textes égyptiens* (1930), p. 72.
121. Helmut Brunner, "Das Herz in ägyptischen Glaubens," in *Das Herz im Umkreis des Glaubens* (1965), p. 93.
122. Blumenthal, "Papyrus d'Orbiney," p. 3. Recall that Thompson included it in his *Motif Index* as motif E 710: Separable Soul.
123. *GMAÄ* I, p. 73.
124. Brunner, "Das Herz," p. 81.
125. Ibid., p. 87.
126. *CT* I, 265*f.*
127. Brunner, "Das Herz," p. 85. W. Spiegelberg, "Das Herz als zweites Wesen des Menschen," *ZÄS* 66 (1930), p. 36, thinks that this second being and also the *bꜣ* of a man live as the *kꜣ,* a discussion of which lies outside the scope of this inquiry.
128. Found in Aylward M. Blackman, *Middle Egyptian Stories,* Bibliotheca Aegyptiaca II (1972).
129. Brunner, "Das Herz," p. 84.
130. Diodorus Siculus I, 91, 5.
131. E.g., G. E. Smith and W. R. Dawson, *Egyptian Mummies* (1924), pp. 81, 94, 99, 125.

132. Brunner, "Das Herz," pp. 102–103.
133. J. Zandee, *Death as an Enemy* (1960), p. 180.
134. *BD,* Chaps. 27, 28, 30.
135. Zandee, *Death as an Enemy,* pp. 20, 174ff, 180.
136. The phrase *m ẖt.k* is something of a problem. In the many cases in which it occurs (see following note), Faulkner tends to translate it "in your body." However, *m* can also mean "from" in the sense of separation (Gardiner, *Grammar,*[3] §162), and so the phrase can be read "from your body." In this case, the sense is that of returning the previously separated heart (his own heart) to the deceased.
137. *Pyr.* §§ 3 (×2), 1640*a;* 1786*b;* 1885; 1891; 1892*a;* 1916*b;* and 2097*c.*
138. *CT* I, 80*a–b; CT* I, 265*e–f; CT* V, 332*h.*
139. *BD* Ch. 26.
140. A. Moret, *Rituel du culte divin journalier en Égypte,* Annales du Musée Guimet 14 (1902), p. 63.
141. K. Sethe, "Zur Vorgeschichte der Herzskarabäen" in *Mélanges Maspero,* MIFAO LXVI (1935), p. 119; Brunner, "Das Herz," pp. 102–103.
142. Smith and Dawson report the heart in situ in an early twelfth-dynasty example, but none earlier.
143. Erika Feucht-Putz, "Hertzskarabäus," *LÄ* II, col. 1168–1170.
144. Ibid., col. 1168–1170.
145. K. Sethe, "Zur Geschichte der Einbalsamierung bei den Ägypten," *SPAW* 1934, No. 13, pp. 236–39, especially 239.
146. *šdi* is used particularly in the sense of cutting out/away parts of the body, especially in animal slaughter. On this use, see K. Sethe, "Zur Vorgeschichte der Herzskarabäen," p. 119. See also Zandee, *Death as an Enemy,* pp. 154–55.
147. Sethe, *Pyr.Über.* V, pp. 60–62.
148. Budge, *Book of the Dead,* Text Vol., p. 502.
149. The translation follows Allen, *The Book of the Dead,* p. 40 (Ch. 30, T 1).
150. Hermann Kees, *Totenglauben und Jenseitsvorstellungen der alten Ägypter,* (1956), p. 55.
151. Brunner, "Das Herz," pp. 100–101, and see fig. 3 between pp. 94–95. The deceased is represented as watching it, although in one example on a twenty-second-dynasty coffin in the Semitic Museum at Harvard University, the deceased himself is depicted as holding the balance. On this example, see J. Capart, "Livres," *CdÉ* V (1930), pp. 106–108; J. Capart, "Ra, juge des morts," *CdÉ* XIV (1939), pp. 233–36; and Susan T. Hollis, "The Cartonnage Case of Pa-di-mut, Harvard Semitic Museum 2230," in *"Working with No Data," Semitic and Egyptian Studies Presented to Thomas O. Lambdin,* ed. David M. Golomb with the assistance of Susan T. Hollis, Winona Lake, in Eisenbrauns, 1987.

152. Edouard Naville, *Das ägyptische Todtenbuch der XVIII bis XX Dynasties,* 2 vols. (1886), I, pl. XLIII.

153. See Christine Seeber, *Untersuchungen zur Darstellung des Totengerichts in Alten Ägypten,* MÄS 35 (1976), Excurs, pp. 187–92 for discussion of the representation in the Book of Gates.

154. E. Otto, "Ein Beitrag zur Deutung der ägyptischen Vor- und Frühgeschichte," *WdO* 1 (1952), pp. 431–53, especially 432–35.

155. R. Weill, "Ceux qui n'avaient pas de tombeau dans l'Égypte ancienne," *RHR* 118 (1938), pp. 31–32, reports the apparent continuation of this practice into the modern period, at least until the 1930s.

156. In the Pyramid Texts, there are over thirty references to reassembling the bones or the body members: *Pyr.* §§ 9; 364–65; 585; 592; 616; 617; 635; 639; 654; 735; 828; 830; 840; 843; 858; 980; 1036–1037; 1297; 1368; 1514; 1675; 1684; 1732; 1896; 1908; 1916; 1947; 1952; 2008; 2086; 2097; 2182. In *RÄRG,* Bonnet states that these writings reflect the natural disintegration of the corpse, although earlier in the same article (p. 421), he says that the unnatural position of the bones in some grave finds is due to dismemberment or mutilation. He noted that some scholars, like Kees, have suggested Bedouins or the predatory animals of the waste or even secondary burials to account for the position of the bones. See also Kees, *Totenglauben,* pp. 17–19, especially p. 19.

157. M. Burchardt, "Das Herz des Bata," *ZÄS* 50 (1912), p. 118, cited the Hottentot parallel, which was noted previously by Hyacinthe Husson in 1874 (cf. Chapter 1, "The Nineteenth-Century Search for Origins," above).

158. See also *Pyr.* §§ 1180*b*–1181*a,* which is cited in Chap. 2 of this study, and Altenmüller-Kesting, *Reinigungsriten,* pp. 52–55, especially p. 53.

159. The correction of *k* to *s* is made by Faulkner following Mercer, *AEPT,* p. 288, n. 3.

160. Budge, *The Book of the Dead,* Text Vol., p. 454. See p. 452, n. 1 for explanation of the introductory line v.

161. H. Kees, *Der Opfertanz des ägyptischen Königs* (München: n.p., 1912), pp. 65–66 and p. 273, No. 20a from *Edfu* I, 116, 7–9.

162. Kees, *Der Opfertanz,* p. 66. The god's parts as meaning the Nile is Kees's interpretation, the discussion of which falls properly within a major study of the Sed-fest.

163. This theme corresponds to AaTh 302B, Hero's life dependent upon his sword. See Chap. 1, "Twentieth-Century Ideas on Structure and Origins," above. Most commonly the separately preserved heart on which the hero's life depends involves a sinister figure such as a giant or an ogre.

164. Blumenthal, "Papyrus d'Orbiney," p. 4. In actuality, the blossom of the pine is very small, making this image quite unrealistic and

showing the Egyptian writer's lack of firsthand knowledge of the tree.

165. Hermann Schlögl, *Der Sonnengott auf der Blüte,* Aeg. Hel. 5 (1977). This work builds on and expands the classic work of S. Morenz and J. Schubert, *Der Gott auf der Blume,* Artibus Asia Supplementum XII (1954).

166. Schlögl, *Der Sonnengott auf der Blüte,* p. 11. See also Altenmüller-Kesting, *Reinigungsriten,* pp. 74–75.

167. Schlögl, *Der Sonnengott auf der Blüte,* p. 17. Schlögl cites two examples, one belonging to Tuthmosis IV and the other to Tutankhamon. The Tutankhamon example may be seen in Christiane Desroches-Noblecourt, *Life and Death of a Pharaoh: Tutankhamon,* (Boston: The New York Graphic Society, 1963), pl. XLb.

168. Ali Radwan, "Der Königsname: Epigraphisches zum göttlichen Königtum in alten Ägypten," *SÄK* 2 (1975), p. 231.

169. Schlögl, *Der Sonnengott auf der Blüte,* pp. 19–20. In this way it is possible to see the deceased (Osiris) appear as Re (*CT* I, 191*g*–192*b*), and to perceive a clear fusion of the two, Osiris and Re, thus the deceased king and the sun, a concept most vividly expressed in the joint visit of Osiris and Re to the Underworld, as depicted in the scenes from the Underworld Books (J. Gwyn Griffiths, "Osiris," *LÄ* IV, col. 629).

170. Edmund Hermsen, *Lebensbaumsybolik im alten Ägypten: Eine Untersuchung* (1981), p. 139.

171. Literally, "reported."

172. Judges 16:15–19.

173. H. Brunner, "Das Herz als Sitz des Lebensgeheimnis," *AfO* 17 (1954/56), p. 140.

174. *Urk.* IV, 219, 15–220, 2.

175. Müller, "Die Zeugung durch das Herz," p. 258.

176. Ibid., p. 259; Jan Assmann, *Ägyptische Hymnen und Gebete* (1972), no. 212; hereafter *ÄHG.*

177. This is my emendation and translation on the basis of Müller, "Die Zeugung durch das Herz," and the texts cited on copulation. Faulkner, *AECT* II, p. 181, reads "DESIRE SHALL COME TO THE WOMAN BENEATH HIM WHENEVER HE COPULATES."

178. See Sigfried Morenz, "Wortspiele in Ägypten," *RGAÄ,* pp. 329–42.

179. Piankoff, *Le "Coeur,"* p. 104.

180. Ebers 103, 2–3 reads:

> *ir s iw mt 22 im.f n ḥ3ty.f*
> *nt sn dd n ʿwt.f nbt*
> As for the man, there are twenty-two vessels in him to the heart which give to all his body parts.

181. Brunner, "Das Herz" (1968), p. 93.

182. Helck, *Die Beziehungen,*[2] p. 495. His agreement on the shape is found on p. 27.

183. An exhibit of New Kingdom arts at Boston's Museum of Fine Arts in the spring of 1982 actually contained several examples of New Kingdom models of grape clusters, and a heart could be likened to one very easily, as could be said of a pinecone as well. See *Egypt's Golden Age: The Art of Living in the New Kingdom, 1558–1085 B.C., Catalogue of the Exhibition* (Boston: Museum of Fine Arts, 1982), p. 168, #190, Bottle in the form of a bunch of grapes, and p. 92, #12, Grape Cluster.

Excursus II

1. Sethe, "Zur ältesten Geschichte des ägyptischen Seeverkehrs mit Byblos und dem Libanongebiet," *ZÄS* 45 (1908), p. 13.
2. Emile Chassinat, *Le Mystère d'Osiris au mois de Khoiak* (Le Caire: Imprimerie de l'Institut français d'Archéologie orientale, 1968), p. 701.
3. Griffiths, *Plutarch's "De Iside et Osiride",* p. 320.
4. Sethe, "Byblos und dem Libanongebiet," pp. 13–14.
5. Griffiths, *Plutarch's "De Iside et Osiride",* p. 323.
6. Chassinat, *Khoiak,* p. 699. The Hebrew form *'oren* corresponds to the Northwest Semitic **'urn.* The Akkadian word *erenu,* Sumerian *erinnu* (cedar) would suit Chassinat's hypothesis better, but it would be difficult to account for its use in this locale.
7. Chassinat, *Khoiak,* p. 699.
8. Griffiths, *The Origins of Osiris,* p. 28.
9. Helmut Brunner, "Osiris in Byblos," *RdÉ* 27 (1975), pp. 37–40.
10. Griffiths, *The Origins of Osiris,* pp. 30–32.
11. Ibid., pp. 26–28.
12. W. Hermann, "Isis in Byblos," *ZÄS* 82 (1958), pp. 54–55.
13. Griffiths, *Plutarch's "De Iside et Osiride",* p. 321.
14. Christine Strauss, "Ertrinken/Ertränken," *LÄ* II, col. 18.
15. See also *Pyr.* §§ 24*d* and 615*c–d.*
16. E. Chassinat, "Les Papyrus magiques 3237 et 3229 du Louvre," *RT* 14 (1893), pp. 14–15 (lines 6–7).
17. H. Junker, *Die politische Lehre von Memphis,* APAW 1941, 6, p. 36. Although commonly dated to the Old Kingdom, note that in his 1973 article, "Zur Fehldatierung des sog. Denkmals memphitischer Theologie oder Der Beitrag der ägyptischen Theologie zur Geistesgeschichte der Spätzeit" (MDAIK 29, 195–204), F. Junge identifies this work as pseudepigraphic, dating it almost certainly to the twenty-fifth dynasty (753–656 BCE).
18. C. E. Sander-Hanson, *Die Texte der Metternich Stele,* An.Aeg. VII (1956), p. 30.
19. Griffiths, *Plutarch's "De Iside et Osiride",* p. 323.
20. Sethe, *Pyr.Über.* V, p. 442.

21. Chassinat, *Khoiak,* p. 702.
22. Ibid., p. 700.
23. The text can be found in Paul Pierret, *Études égyptologiques* (Paris: Librarie A. Frank, 1873), p. 44, l. 13. It is translated by Sethe, "Osiris und die Zeder von Byblos," *ZÄS* 47 (1910), p. 72.
24. Jean-Claude Goyon, *Rituels funéraires de l'ancienne Égypte* (Paris: Les Éditions du Cerf, 1972), p. 44.
25. Ibid., p. 22.

Chapter 5

1. Helmut Jacobsohn, "Der altägyptische, der christliche, und der modern Mythos," *Eranos Jahrbuch* 1968, p. 416. See also Hartwig Altenmüller, "Jagd," *LÄ* III, col. 221.
2. E. Otto, "An Ancient Egyptian Hunting Ritual," *JNES* 9 (1950), pp. 164–77, and H. Altenmüller, "Jagd," col. 221.
3. H. Altenmüller, "Jäger" *LÄ* III, col. 220.
4. E. Otto, "Ein Beitrag zur Deutung der ägyptischen Vor- und Frühgeschichte," *WdO* I/6 (1952), p. 439.
5. Sethe, *Pyr.Über.* IV, pp. 109–11, in reference to Pyr. §851*b*. The difficulty lies in the presence of the determinative for "hill country" in some versions and its absence in others. There is also at least one where it is replaced by a canid-type animal.
6. *AEPT,* p. 74, n. 5 says, "presumably *Reʿ*," although in the later parallel Horus appears to be the speaker.
7. Sethe, *Pyr.Über.* IV, 110.
8. Otto, "Vor- und Frühgeschichte," pp. 431–53, especially pp. 432–35.
9. W. Barta, "Königsdogma," *LÄ* III, col. 490–91, and W. Barta, "Königskronung," *LÄ* III, col. 531.
10. S. Morenz, *Egyptian Religion,* trans. Ann E. Keep (1973), pp. 40–41; H. Brunner, "Konig-Gott-Verhältnis," *LÄ* III, col. 462–63; S. Sauneron, *The Priests of Ancient Egypt,* trans. Ann Morrissett (1980), pp. 33–34. See also Philippe Derchain, "Le Role du roi d'Égypte dans le maintien de l'ordre cosmique," in *Le Pouvoir et le sacré,* Annales du Centre d'Étude des Religions, 1 (1962), pp. 61–73; Georges Posener, *De la Divinité du Pharaon* (Paris: Imprimerie National, 1960); and Blumenthal, *Untersuchungen zum ägyptisches Königtum,* p. 134.
11. The only clear members of this Ennead are Khnum and Pre, from which it is impossible to be sure which Ennead is represented here. It is well known that various towns in Egypt had local Enneads, although we are not generally able to determine definitively their members (H. Brunner, "Neunheit," *LÄ* IV, col. 475), and it is equally well known that even the Ennead of Heliopolis was composed of different members, depending on the source used. W. Barta, *Untersuchungen zum Götterkreis der Neun-*

heit, MÄS 28 (1973), pp. 65–73, shows eighty-four permutations. Brunner, "Neunheit," col. 476, states that at least from the time of the Middle Kingdom, *psḏt,* Ennead, also means *nṯrw nbw,* all the gods. Thus it is difficult to define the Ennead of the d'Orbiney more precisely than to say it is a body of gods among whom are Pre and Khnum.

12. Maspero, *Contes populaires,*[1] p. 16, n. 1, and *Les Contes populaires,*[2] p. 18, n. 1, draws an analogy between this activity of the Ennead and the report of the Homeric gods walking on their way to eat with the Ethiopians (*Ody.* I, 22; V, 282; etc.). The third (p. 11, n. 1), fourth (p. 11, n. 1), and English (p. 11, n. 2) editions cite F. Chabas, *Oeuvres diverses IV,* BÉ 12 (1905), p. 161, "Le calendrier des jours fastes et néfastes" as another Egyptian source for the earthly activity of the Ennead, in this instance, the Ennead in the form of a bull. In this reference, Chabas translates the text for the twenty-fifth day of Paopi, i.e., the second month of *ꜣḫt,* as follows: "Quiconque rencontre les dieux en ce jour sous forme de taureau mourra ce jour-là." Bakir, *Cairo Calendar,* provides no precise parallel, though in it, the nineteenth day of the second month of Shomu reads:

> *sqddy.t psḏt*
> *msꜥ.sn m tꜣ r ḏrf* (vs. IV, 3–4)
> The Ennead sails,
> they (the sailings) are much in the whole land.

Two other references from the Cairo Calendar report the movement of the Ennead to or from Nun (II *ꜣḫt,* 17 and IV *ꜣḫt,* 1), and one tells of the Ennead going before Re (I *ꜣḫt,* 2). These three do not say "on the land."

13. Sethe, *Pyr. Über.,* I, p. 306, relative to *Pyr.* § 276*a.*

14. Ibid., III, p. 325 relative to *Pyr.* § 717*a.*

15. Brunner, "Neunheit," col. 476.

16. Helmut Jacobsohn, *Die dogmatische Stellung des Königs in der Theologie der alten Ägypter,* Ag. For. 8 (1939), p. 22.

17. Barta, *Götterkreis der Neunheit,* p. 36. Jacobsohn sees the Ennead's address to Bata as "Bull of the Ennead" as reflecting this form rather than as referring to a deceased (Helmut Jacobsohn, *Die dogmatische Stellung* [1939] p. 22).

18. For instance, *CT* II, 52*g,* "Bull of the Sky"; *CT* II, 53*f,* "Bull of the Enneads"; *CT* V, 386*c–d,* "Bull who is in charge of the Ennead"; "N. is Bull of the gods"; *CT* V, 377*b–c,* "I am a Bull, lord of the gods."

19. Budge, *Book of the Dead,* p. 230, 44, the Papyrus of *Nbsny;* see also p. 228, 33.

20. Brunner-Traut, *Altägyptische Märchen,*[5] p. 259, has suggested that the sense of its not being good to live alone recalls the paradisiacal. In Geness 2:18, one reads, "The Lord God said, 'It is not good that the man should be alone. I will make him a helper fit for him'" (RSV).

21. Helmut Brunner, *Die Geburt des Gottkönigs,* Äg.Ab. 3 (1964),

p. 68ff; James Henry Breasted, *Ancient Records of Egypt,* 5 vols. (1906), vol. 2, pp. 81–82.

22. Westendorf, "Medizinischen Texten," p. 136, explains that the Seven Hathors appear to announce the fate of children, and correspond to Seshat when she assigns the length of life to the royal heir at his entrance to maturity. Brunner, *Die Geburt,* p. 163, briefly discusses the Hathors relative to the birth scenes. They also appear in "Doomed Prince" to decree the fate of the king's son (Papyrus Harris 500, 4, 3–4). F. W. von Bissing and H. P. Blok, "Eine Weihung an die Sieben Hathoren," *ZÄS* 61 (1927), p. 88, refer to the example from the Papyrus Harris and note three other examples from the Middle Kingdom as well as examples from mortuary offering formulas dating from the Ramesside period.

23. *tꜣ špst* has been considered as a royal title and is discussed in Chap. 6, "Bata's Wife Goes to Egypt," in this work.

24. Anonymity in itself is not an unusual phenomenon. Knowledge of the name gives the knower power over the named. Conversely, especially relative to gods, there can be danger inherent in the knowledge and/or use of a god's name (E. Brunner-Traut, "Anonymität [der Götter]," *LÄ* I, col. 281–91, especially 281 and 284). For instance, in a "Hymn to Amun" (A. H. Gardiner, "Hymns to Amun," *ZÄS* 42 (1905), pp. 33–34 [Col. IV, 20], and John A. Wilson, trans., in *ANET,*[3] p. 214), a person is said to incur violent death if he utters Amun's mysterious name. Further, in so far as this tale is considered Märchen, anonymity is characteristic. In Märchen, if a hero or heroine has a name, it is something like John, Mary, or Ivan (*Standard Dictionary of Folklore, Mythology, and Legend,* one volume edition, Marie Leach, ed. [New York: Funk & Wagnalls, 1972], p. 66).

25. Kurt Sethe, *Zur altägyptischen Sage vom Sonnenauge,* UGAÄ 5, 3 (1912), p. 35.

26. Ibid., p. 36.

27. The content of this tale is summarized by Lichtheim, *AEL* III, pp. 156–57. The story itself is available in W. Spiegelberg, *Der ägyptische Mythos vom Sonnenauge* (Straßburg, 1917), from the Demotic Papyrus Leiden T 384.

28. Sethe, *Sonnenauge,* p. 36.

29. E. Otto, "Augensagen," *LÄ* I, col. 565, where Otto also discusses briefly the well-known equation of Hathor and the Sun-eye as well as the equation of the Sun-eye and the Uraeus. To the objection that these tales are late, as they are, note Hathor's early appearance as the Sun-eye in *Pyr.* 705*a* as well as the return of the Sun-eye in *CT* IV, 238ff. (Spell 335) and *BD* Chap. 17a, Sec. II (Allen, *Book of the Dead,* 1974, p. 29).

30. Charles Maystre, "Le Livre de la vache du ciel dans les tombeaux de la valée des rois," *BIFAO* 40 (1941), pp. 153–215. Trans. in Lichtheim, *AEL* II, pp. 197–99, and by H. Brunner in *Near Eastern Texts Relative to the Old Testament,* ed. Walter Beyerlin, trans. John Bowden, SCM Press (Philadelphia: The Westminster Press, 1978), pp. 8–11.

31. J. Osing, "Gottesland," *LÄ* II, col. 815–16.
32. *CT* I, 204*c*–205*a* tells how Hathor of Punt gives myrrh.
33. E.g., Gardiner-Peet-Cerny, *Sinai,* pl. XIII. A discussion occurs in *Sinai,* vol. 2, pp. 41–45.
34. *CT* I, 262*b*.
35. Helck, *Die Beziehungen*², p. 22.
36. *Urk.* IV, 1443, 19. See Helck, *Die Beziehungen*², p. 444.
37. Helck, *Die Beziehungen*², p. 64, n. 7 referring to XXVIII, 5.
38. pChester Beatty I, 4, 1–3.
39. *CT* II, 386*d*–387*a*.
40. B. Altenmüller, *Synkretismus,* p. 135.
41. S. Allam, *Beiträge zum Hathorkult bis zum Ende des Mittleren Reiches,* MÄS 4 (1963), pp. 67–68.
42. *CT* II, 387*a*.
43. B. Altenmüller, *Synkretismus,* p. 133.
44. Allam, *Hathorkult,* p. 22. It is interesting to recall that Anubis bore the epithet *nb smywt* in the Early Dynastic and Old Kingdom periods. Many examples can be found in Maspero, *Les Mastaba.*
45. *CT* V, 38*d* and 32*j*.
46. F. Daumas, "Hathor," *LÄ* II, col. 1029, citing *CT* VII, § 939, a text I cannot find and which does not appear in de Buck's copies. The title is present in Graeco-Roman times (Bonnet, *RÄRG,* p. 280).
47. F. Daumas, "Hathor," col. 1029, notes that this etymology emphasizes her role as mother of the king.
48. Westendorf, "Medizinischen Texten," p. 134.
49. Hermann, *Altägyptische Liebesdichtung,* p. 15.
50. Jacobsohn, *Die dogmatische Stellung,* p. 18.
51. *CT* IV, 76*g*. See B. Altenmüller, *Synkretismus,* p. 131. Note that *CT* IV, 76*g* occurs at the end of Spell 331, a text titled BECOMING HATHOR, which describes her in depth.
52. George Reisner, *Mycerinus: The Temple of the Third Pyramid at Giza* (1931), pp. 109–110, 123–24.
53. Jacobsohn, *Die dogmatische Stellung,* p. 20. As representatives of the king, priests could also handle the sistra.
54. Allam, *Hathorkult,* p. 14. See also Marianne Galvin, *The Priestesses of Hathor in the Old Kingdom and First Intermediate Period.* Dissertation, Brandeis, 1981, UMI.
55. Allam, *Hathorkult,* p. 62. Allam speaks of the wife of "Mentuhotep Reichseiniger," whom I take to be Mentuhotep II after W. C. Hayes, "The Middle Kingdom in Egypt," *CAH* I/2, pp. 479–81.
56. Sin. B 185.
57. Sin. B 172.
58. Sin. B 270. For a fuller discussion, see H. Brunner, "Das Besänftigungslied im Sinuhe (B 269–279)," *ZÄS* 80 (1955), p. 10. *Nb.t pt* appears as a title of Hathor in *CT* VI, 298*c*. See also *CT* VI, 403*a*.
59. *Urk.* IV, 21,3. See Lana Troy, *Patterns of Queenship in Ancient*

Egyptian Myth and History, BOREAS 14 (1986), p. 196, D/12, D/13, and D/14 for specific queens bearing this and related titles (*nb.t tꜣw,* Mistress of the Lands and *nb.t tꜣwy,* Mistress of the Two Lands).

60. Wolfgang Schenkel, "Königin," *LÄ* III, col. 464.

61. Wolfgang Schenkel, "Königsmutter," *LÄ* III, col. 538. *Pyr.* 466*a,* cited above, is an Old Kingdom example of the need for this legitimacy. Her role in legitimation will be discussed below in treating the birth of Bata.

62. Siegfried Herrmann, "Isis in Byblos," *ZÄS* 82 (1957), pp. 48–55, especially p. 54.

63. R. Stadelmann, *Syrisch-Palästinensische Gottheiten in Ägypten,* PdÄ 5 (1967), pp. 88–123.

64. Gardiner, *LES,* pp. 76–81. For a translation see John A. Wilson, trans., "Astarte and the Tribute of the Sea," in *ANET*[3], pp. 17–18.

65. pChester Beatty I, 3,4.

66. Hermann, *Altägyptische Liebesdichtung,* p. 15; Daumas, "Hathor," cols. 1025 and 1029.

67. Jan Bergman, *Ich bin Isis: Studien zum memphitischen Hintergrund der griechischen Isisaretalogien,* Acta Universitas Upsaliensis: Historia Religionum, 3 (1968), p. 153. For Hathor, see *CT* IV, 176*g.*

68. Jan Bergman, "Isis," *LÄ* III, col. 187. In col. 187–88, Bergman discusses the relationship of Isis and the throne, noting that the connection may be based on a defective writing, and on this basis it may thus be more apparent than real.

69. Bergman, *Ich bin Isis,* pp. 128–29. See also, above, Excursus: Osiris in Byblos.

70. This concept is treated in more detail in Chap. 6, "Kamutef," below.

71. Bergman, *Ich bin Isis,* pp. 132–33; 143, n. 3; and 147–48.

72. This type of knowledge is characteristic of Märchen. See Max Lüthi, *The European Folktale: Form and Nature,* trans. John D. Niles (1982), p. 60.

73. When Maspero discussed this passage, he felt that it was "an allusion to the Bride of the Nile and her immersion in the river." (Maspero, *Popular Stories,* p. 12, n. 4, a note which does not occur in any of his other editions, and I have not been able to find other references to this idea. I wonder, therefore, if he is alluding to L. Sommer, *Das Haar in Religion und Aberglauben der Griechen* [1912], pp. 37–38, where Sommer refers to a bridal bath that is taken to signify a unification with the flood god. This practice occurs first in the Hellenistic period or is first reflected at that time.) His second comment was an observation that the ancient Egyptians called the Nile *iaûmâ,* just as the modern Egyptians refer to it as *bahr* (Maspero, *Popular Stories,* p. 12, n. 4); presumably it was the Nile that posed the threat to Bata's wife.

74. R. Grieshammer, "Jam (Meer)," *LÄ* III, col. 242.

75. Francis Brown, S. R. Driver, and C. A. Briggs, *A Hebrew and English Lexicon of the Old Testament* (Oxford: Clarendon Press, 1974), pp. 410–11.

76. W. Helck, "Meer," *LÄ* III, col. 1277, and D. Arnold, "Fajjum," *LÄ* II, col. 87. These references, along with Grieshammer, "Jam (Meer)," col. 242 f. and R. Herzog, *Punt,* ADAIK 6 (1968), pp. 79–80, provide a fairly full discussion of the uses of *w3ḏ-wr* and *p3 ym* as terms for bodies of salt and fresh water among the ancient Egyptians.

77. See n. 64 above and William Kelly Simpson, *The Literature of Ancient Egypt,* pp. 133–36.

78. Helck, "Meer," col. 1277, perceives this tale to be a translation and adaptation of the Canaanite story of the battle between Baal and Yam. R. Stadelmann, "Astartepapyrus," *LÄ* I, col. 510, has noted, however, that in the Canaanite myth, for which see Michael Coogan, ed. and trans., *Stories from Ancient Canaan* (1978), pp. 75–89, text pp. 86–89, Yam is supported by El and the gods. The focus is then actually on the personal conflict between Yam and Baal for lordship. In the Egyptian tale of Astarte, on the other hand, the gods are against the sea and its predatory behavior.

79. Lefèbvre, *Romans,* p. 108.

80. Brunner-Traut, "Ägypten," *EM* I, p. 191.

81. E. Brunner-Traut, "Der Skarabäus," *Antios* VI (1955), pp. 570–80, rpt. in E. Brunner-Traut, *Gelebte Mythen* (1981), p. 11.

82. *RÄRG,* p. 536.

83. O. Kaiser, *Die mythische Bedeutung des Meeres in Ägypten, Ugarit, und Israel,* Beiheft ZAW 78 (1959), p. 34.

84. Dieter Kurth, "Nilgott," *LÄ* IV, cols. 485–89.

85. The sense that Seth did so by means of his voice is derived from the evidence of two medical texts, the "Contendings of Horus and Seth," and the "Report of Wenamun." The medical texts can be found in *GMAÄ* IV, p. 258 (pHearst 170) and 153 (Berlin) for translation and *GMAÄ* V, pp. 440 and 268 respectively, for the hieroglyphic transcription. They read as follows:

> *mi sn.n Stš p3 w3ḏ-wr*
> *šn tn Stš m-mitt t3-nt-ʿ3mw* (pHearst 170, 13–14)
> as Seth cursed the sea,
> so Seth curses this, the Asiatic villain (for you).

and

> *mi sḏm p3 ym ḫrw Stš* (pBerlin 189, 21, 2–3)
> as the Sea heard the voice of Seth,

asserting the use of a particular cure for the sick. The other two texts read:

mtw.f hrw m t3 pt
mtw.tw snd n.f (pChester Beatty I, 16,4)
he (Seth) shall be thunder (lit., "a voice in the sky")
and he shall be feared,

and

mk irw Imn hrw m t3 pt
iw di.f Sth m rk.f (Wenamun 2,19)
See, Amun makes a voice in the sky,
having put Seth beside him.

86. Assmann, "Textanalyse," p. 14, n. 45.

Chapter 6

1. See Lüthi, *The European Folktale,* p. 29, and Max Lüthi, *Das Volksmärchen als Dichtung: Ästhetik und Anthropologie* (1975), p. 67f, for discussion.

2. This episode is catalogued in Thompson's *Motif-Index* as T 11.4.1 and H 1213.1.1, Love through Sight of Hair. As the following discussion will show, this typology is not wholly accurate for this narrative, since the love originated with the odor.

3. Hermann, *Altägyptische Liebesdichtung,* pp. 94–95, observes the important part odor played for all Egyptians, mentioning the odor of Punt that appears in Nephthys' lamentation of Osiris and the various love songs which refer to the odor of the beloved or a part of him or her.

4. Brunner-Traut, *Märchen,*[5] p. 291, #29, discusses this search motif in connection with the story of the "Shoe of Rhodopis," found in Strabo, mentioning both the "Tale of Two Brothers," #5 and "Hi-Hor, the Magician," #36 in this volume, another late story.

5. Brunner, *Die Geburt,* pp. 50–51.

6. Sethe, "Seeverkehrs mit Byblos," p. 13, n. 2. Brunner-Traut, *Märchen,*[5] p. 259, likens the lust of the king for Bata's wife to the Old Testament episode of David lusting for Bathsheba (II Sam. 11: 2–4).

7. Georges Posener, "La Légende de la tresse d'Hathor," in *Egyptological Studies in Honor of Richard A. Parker, Presented on the Occasion of His 78th Birthday, December 10, 1983,* ed. by Leonard H. Lesko (1986), pp. 111–12.

8. Ibid., p. 114.

9. E.g., Lichtheim, *AEL* II, pp. 184–85.

10. Sethe, *Sonnenauge,* p. 36.

11. For example, see Norman de Garis Davies, *The Tomb of Rekh-mi-Re* (1943), plates XVII–XXIII.

12. Budge, *Book of the Dead,* Text Vol., p. 445, lines 14–15; Allen, *Book of the Dead,* p. 179, S 2.

13. This use of the *wpwt*-messenger is typical of the New Kingdom.

They frequently served as royal couriers and were often part of the royal entourage, for which see M. Vallogia, *Recherche sur les 'Messagers' (wpwtyw) dans les sources égyptiennes profanes* (Genève-Paris: Librairie Droz, 1976), pp. 230 and 241.

14. Elke Blumenthal, "Königsideologie," *LÄ* III, col. 529; D. Wildung, "Erschlagen des Feinde," *LÄ* II, col. 14–17; and W. Barta, "Königsdogma," *LÄ* III, col. 491.

15. Lichtheim, *AEL* II, pp. 60–72.

16. Desroches-Noblecourt, *Life and Death of a Pharaoh,* plates XVI and XVIIa and b.

17. Maspero, *Les Contes populaires,*[2] p. 22, n. 1; *Les Contes populaires,*[3] p. 13, n. 2; *Les Contes populaires,*[4] p. 14, n. 1; and *Popular Stories,* p. 13, n. 2.

18. See the discussion on sympathetic magic in Chap. 1, "The Egyptian Context," and n. 124.

19. The text includes a divine determinative after *tw,* referring to the king.

20. For *dhn,* as Gardiner, *LES* 22a. 12.3a, notes.

21. Lisa Manniche, "The Wife of Bata," *GM* 18 (1975), p. 36, n. 13. According to Rolf Krauss ("Merneptah," *LÄ* IV, col. 71–72), there were at least two women named Isnofret, *ꜣst-nfrt,* in this period, the mother of Merneptah and his main wife. Eugene Cruz-Uribe, "On the Wife of Merneptah," *GM* 24 (1977), pp. 23–31, argues for four royal women named Isisnofret during the Ramesside period, one of whom bore this title, though he does not designate which one.

22. Manniche, "Wife," p. 34. See also W. Helck, "Kiya," *LÄ* III, col. 422.

23. Such practices include the queen going forth in a chariot (d'Orb. 17, 5), the queen pouring drink for the king (d'Orb. 16, 2–3; 17, 9), and the king's appearance in garlands at the palace window (d'Orb. 17, 4). See Manniche, "Wife," p. 34 for discussion.

24. Manniche, "Wife," p. 34.

25. The Amarna letters report at least three such women: Artatama sent one of his daughters to the king (EA 24, iii, 52ff; 29, 21ff); Shuttarna sent Gilu-kheba to Amenhotep III late in the latter's reign (EA 17, 26ff; 29, 21ff); and Tushratta sent his daughter Tadukheba to the king (EA 19, 17ff; 22, iv, 43ff). W. Schenkel, "Konigin," *LÄ* III, col. 41, states that Ramesses II appointed a Hittite princess as Great Royal Wife and that the mother of Siptah was of Asiatic origin.

26. Jacobsohn, *Die dogmatische Stellung,* pp. 14–15.

27. This kind of time lapse occurs in the transition period in several of the life-cycle rites of passage, most notably that of death, during which time the corpse undergoes preparations for burial, cremation, or whatever practice is specific to the individual culture (cf. van Gennep, *Rites of Passage,* Chap. VIII).

28. B. Altenmüller-Kesting, *Reinigungsriten,* pp. 76, 92, 174, 185, 208ff., and Otto, *Mundöffnungsritual,* II, p. 39.

29. Pyramid Utterance 32 is especially interesting in that it includes cold water, efflux, and the refreshing of the heart (*Pyr.* §§ 22*a*–23*a*):

qbḥ.k ipn Wsir	This cold water of yours, Osiris,
qbḥ.k ipn h3 RN	this cold water of yours, O King,
prw ḫr s3.k	has gone forth to your son,
prw ḫr Ḥr	has gone forth to Horus.
iw.n in n.k irt Ḥr	I have come and I bring the eye of Horus
qb ib.k ḫr.s	that your heart may be refreshed possessing it;
in.n n.k s ḫr kbw.k	I have brought it to you under your sandals.
m n.k rḏw pri im.k	Take the efflux which goes from you;
n wrḏ ib.k ḫr.s	your heart will not be weary possessing it.

30. E.g., the Tomb of Senedjem (nineteenth dynasty) and the papyrus of Anhai (twentieth dynasty). See also Erik Hornung, *Tal der Könige: Die Ruhestätte der Pharaonen* (1982), pl. 30 and 67 and fig., p. 87.

31. See above, Chap. 2, "Anubis, the Ancient Mortuary God," and Chap. 4, "Bata's Heart and Egyptian Beliefs about the Heart." A succinct example of the search may be seen in *Pyr.* 612*b* and *Pyr.* 648*c,* both of which read:

gm.n ṯw Ḥr
Horus has found you.

32. Moret, "La Légende d'Osiris," p. 741.

33. Henri Frankfort, *Kingship and the Gods* (1948), p. 135.

34. Brunner-Traut, "Papyrus d'Orbiney," col. 702, n. 12.

35. See also *Pyr.* 585*b–c.*

36. The translation is Faulkner's *AEPT,* p. 121. The scene is graphically depicted in Hornung, *Tal der Könige,* pl. 151 and 152.

37. See Hornung, *Tal der Könige,* pl. 53 and 150.

38. See R. T. Ridley, *The Unification of Egypt* (Deception Bay, Australia: Shield Press, 1973), for a collection of examples.

39. Kenneth A. Kitchen, "The Titularies of the Ramesside Kings as Expression of their Ideal Kingship," *ASAÉ* LXXI (1987), pp. 131–41; Erik Hornung, "Die Bedeutung des Tieres im alten Ägypten," *Studium Generale,* 20, 2 (1967), p. 78. The thought behind this, as was seen in the discussion of Narmer's name above, is that by appearing as an animal, bearing its name, wearing its skin or parts, the king assumed the power of the animal. Again, it is a case of sympathetic magic.

40. Erik Hornung, "Seth. Geschichte und Bedeutung eines ägyptisches Gottes," *Symbolon* N.F. 2 (1975), p. 53.

41. Eberhard Otto, *Beiträge zur Geschichte der Stierkulte in Ägypten,* UGAÄ 13 (1938), p. 1.

42. Ibid., p. 11.

43. Ibid., pp. 34–35.

44. Ibid., p. 47.

45. Mannhardt, "Das älteste Märchen," p. 10; Maspero, *Contes populaires,*[1] p. 22, n. 2; *Les Contes populaires,*[2] p. 25, n. 2; *Les Contes populaires,*[3] p. 15, n. 3; *Les Contes populaires,*[4] p. 16, n. 2; and *Popular Stories,* p. 15, n. 3, where he sees the bull as Apis because Bata as the doubled-headed bull was the bull par excellence, i.e., Apis.

46. Erman, *The Ancient Egyptians,* p. 158, n. 1.

47. Griffiths, *Plutarch's "De Iside et Osiride",* p. 403.

48. Otto, *Stierkulte,* p. 15. Cf. also Maspero, *Contes populaires,*[1] p. 23, n. 1; *Les Contes populaires,*[2] p. 26, n. 1; *Les Contes populaires,*[3] p. 16, n. 2; *Les Contes populaires,*[4] p. 17, n. 3; and *Popular Stories,* p. 16, n. 3.

49. Brunner-Traut, "Altägyptische Literatur," p. 41; Maspero, *Popular Stories,* pp. xlvi–xlix. P. Walcot, *Hesiod and the Near East* (1966), pp. 78–79, like others before as cited in Chap. 1 of this study, viewed the divine creation of Bata's wife and its result as similar to that of Pandora in Hesiod's *Theogony* and *Works and Days.* The appropriate references to Hesiod can be found in H. G. Evelyn-White, trans., *Hesiod, the Homeric Hymns and Homerica,* Loeb Classical Library 57 (1914), pp. 121–23, ll. 561–612 (*Theogony*) and pp. 7–9, ll. 60–105 (*Works and Days*). See the discussion above in Chap. 1, "One or Several Tales?" and n. 61, concerning Leonard Lesko's interpretation in "Three Late Egyptian Stories Reconsidered."

50. Lichtheim, *AEL* I, pp. 135–39, especially p. 137.

51. A. H. Gardiner, *Egypt of the Pharaohs* (1961), pp. 289–92.

52. Lichtheim, *AEL* I, pp. 222–35, especially pp. 223–24.

53. Lichtheim, *AEL* II, pp. 197–99.

54. Lichtheim, *AEL* I, p. 195. Banquets form part of the funerary activities, and sharing food at a meal typically occurs at the end of funerals in many cultures (cf. van Gennep, *Rites of Passage,* Ch. VIII). See also Ursula Verhoeven, "Totenmahl," *LÄ* VI, cols. 677–79.

55. Peter Kaplony, "Eid," *LÄ* I, col. 1191–1193, explains the oath as a mutual binding of two parties to each other, the breaking of which incurs corporeal punishment. Bonnet, *RÄRG,* p. 164, states that in the case of abrogation, the god and/or king will see to the revenge. The oath in wisdom literature is rarely mentioned, and when it is, as in "The Instruction of Amenemope" (Ch. 6, VII, 18–19; Ch. 11, XIV, 9–10; Ch. 17, XIX, 8–9; Ch. 19, 12), the concern lies primarily with false oaths.

56. pChester Beatty I, 6, 12–13. This type of situation, with an oath and the destructive effect of carrying it out, recalls the story of how John the Baptist was beheaded in Matt. 14:6–11 and Mark 6:22–24 at the behest of the daughter of Herodias, when she was promised anything for which she asked, a parallel noted by Petrie in 1895 (cf. Chap. 1, n. 8 above). It is also pertinent to note that episodes such as the self-judgement by Seth are common in the modern-day folktale.

57. This is a common folktale motif, and one recalls immediately that the first magical objects in the Grimms' "Two Brothers" (KHM 60) are the heart and liver of the golden bird.

58. W. Westendorf, "Leber," *LÄ* III, col. 958, in which he refers to *GMAÄ* VI, 223–25. A reference to not taking the person's liver for Osiris is found in Papyrus Edwin Smith, XIX 2–9, the fifth of eight incantations against pests (James Henry Breasted, *The Edwin Smith Surgical Papyrus,* OIP 3 [1930], vol. 1, pp. 479–81). Presumably there is some obscure mythical reference here, perhaps of the type found in the Cannibal Hymn, Pyr. Utt. 273–74, with an emphasis on the negative side of Osiris.

59. Winfried Barta, *Die altägyptische Opferliste,* MÄS 3 (1963), p. 49, No. 50; p. 118, No. A 51; p. 122, No. C 18; p. 125, No. C 16, p. 137, No. 22; p. 141, No. 16; p. 145, No. E 16, and p. 150.

60. Otto, *Mundöffnungsritual,* p. 26; Otto, "An Ancient Egyptian Hunting Ritual," pp. 165–69. Peter Kaplony (*Kleine Beiträge zum den Inschriften der ägyptischen Frühzeit,* Äg.Ab. 15 [1966], p. 187) suggests that Pyr. Utt. 580 in which a bull, identified with Seth, is slaughtered, is related to Bata's slaughter in the form of a bull.

61. Otto, *Stierkulte,* p. 7.

62. Ibid.; see above Chap. 2, "Contexts of the Ramesside Examples."

63. Otto, *Stierkulte,* pp. 9–10.

64. H. Grapow, *Urk.* V, p. 13, n. 6, of his translation for *BD* Chap. 17, drew this parallel.

65. Although many earlier scholars have postulated cultic tree worship (e.g., Blumenthal, "Papyrus d'Orbiney," p. 4), Hermsen states categorically that the worship is not of the tree but of the tree as the embodiment of a deity (*Lebensbaumsymbolik,* p. 7), an idea apparently, though not specifically, expressed in relation to trees, by Hornung, *Conceptions of God,* Chap. 4. However, the latter asserts that "tree cults . . . are certainly well attested in Egypt" (p. 41).

66. Allam, *Hathorkult,* pp. 103–109; I. Gamer-Wallert, "Baum, heiliger," *LÄ* I, col. 656–58.

67. Ibid., col. 655–60.

68. Philippe Derchain, "Le Lotus, la mandragore, et le persea," *CdÉ* 50 (1975), p. 85.

69. Ibid., p. 85. Maspero, *Contes populaires,*[1] p. 25, n. 1; *Les Contes populaires,*[2] p. 28, n. 1; *Les Contes populaires,*[3] p. 17, n. 1; *Les Contes populaires,*[4] p. 18, n. 1; and *Popular Stories,* p. 18, n. 1, states that the persea was devoted to Osiris, noting in the last three references that one was found on each side of the entrance to Deir el-Bahri. Mannhardt, "Das älteste Märchen," p. 240, n. 1, connects the sun cat and the persea tree in Heliopolis.

70. Derchain, "Le Lotus," pp. 84–85, notes there is generally little or no distinction made between the hieroglyph for the tree and for its fruit.

71. *RÄRG,* p. 83.

72. *Wb* I, p. 136. The *išd.t* is the older form and *išd* is the New Kingdom writing, each defined as "a holy tree."

73. *CD,* p. 31.

74. Lászlo Kákosy, "Ischedbaum (*išd*)," *LÄ* III, col. 182–83.

75. Jum. XII, 11 states that the *išd* is the sacred tree in *Dwnʿwy,* and Jum. XXI, 20, specified the same for *Mn-ʿnẖ,* a town in the eighteenth nome.

76. Kákosy, "Ischedbaum," col. 182; *RÄRG,* p. 84; Gamer-Wallert, "Baum, heiliger," col. 658–59.

77. Ursula Rößler-Köhler, *Kapital 17 des ägyptischen Totenbuches,* GOF 10 (1979), p. 224; *RÄRG,* p. 84.

78. *Urk.* V, p. 50. The text is *BD,* Ch. 17 (Allen, *Book of the Dead,* p. 30) and *CT* Spell 335. See also Rößler-Köhler, *Kapital 17,* p. 224.

79. Kákosy, "Ischedbaum," col. 183, and Goyon, *Rituels funéraires,* p. 82.

80. Gamer-Wallert, "Baum, heiliger," col. 659; Kakosy, "Ischedbaum (*išd*)," col. 183; *RÄRG,* p. 84.

81. Gamer-Wallert, "Baum, heiliger," col. 659. Gamer-Wallert's identification raises the question whether Maspero's mention of the perseas at Deir el-Bahri refers to the *išd* or to the *šwb.*

82. See Hermsen, *Lebensbaumsymbolik,* pp. 122–23 for discussion.

83. Gamer-Wallert, "Baum, heiliger," col. 655.

84. Hermsen, *Lebensbaumsymbolik,* p. 123.

85. pChester Beatty I, 11, 12.

86. Maspero, *Les Contes populaires,*[3] p. 18, n. 2; *Les Contes populaires,*[4] p. 20, n. 1; *Popular Stories,* p. 19, n. 2; and G. Maspero, "Les Hypogées royaux de Thèbes," in G. Maspero, *Études de mythologie et d'archéologie,* BÉ 2 (1893), p. 25.

87. Maspero, "Les Hypogées," p. 26.

88. Piankoff, *The Tomb of Ramesses VI,* I, p. 383ff.

89. The whole appears as time-lapse photography, for there are twelve suns, counting the one she swallows and the one she bears, representing the twelve hours of the night.

90. Piankoff, *The Tomb of Ramesses VI,* I, p. 386, shows attenuated versions of the head and leg areas. More detailed, complete figures can be seen in fig. 130 (opp. p. 389), fig. 131 (opp. p. 392), and fig. 133 (opp. p. 399) as well as in the corresponding plates of vol. II.

91. Dieter Kurt, "Nut," *LÄ* IV, col. 535–36.

92. For example, Hornung, *Ägyptische Unterweltsbücher,* p. 485.

93. See *Pyr.Über,* V, p. 337.

94. Hopfner, *Plutarch,* II, pp. 100–101; Jacques Vandier, *La Religion égyptienne,* 2d ed. (1949), p. 142.

95. This is Faulkner's translation of *ḥꜣḏ.* *Wb* III, 237 gives no translation, only noting the word stands in parallel with *bḥs n nbw.*

96. Jacobsohn, *Die dogmatische Stellung;* H. Jacobsohn, "Der altägyptische, der christliche, und der moderne Mythos," *Eranos Jahrbuch*

(1968), pp. 411–48; Hopfner, *Plutarch,* II, pp. 100–101; Vandier, *La Religion égyptienne,* pp. 142–143. See also H. Jacobsohn, "Kamutef," *LÄ* III, col. 308–309.

97. Griffiths, *Plutarch's "De Iside et Osiride",* p. 343.

98. Within the royal texts of the New Kingdom, the birth narratives of Hatshepsut and Amenhotep III provide the clearest evidence of the idea. In them the god Amun enters into the palace, becoming united into one form with the present king:

> *[. . . nṯr pn Imn šps nb nswt tꜣwy]*
> *[ir].n.f ḫpr.f [m] ḥm [n] hy.s pn*
> *nsw-bit ʿꜣ-ḫpr-kꜣ-Rʿ* (*Urk.* IV, 219, 10–11)
> [. . . this god Ămun, lord of the thrones of the two lands,]
> [made] himself [into] the majesty [of] her husband
> Tuthmosis I.

99. In the birth scene of Hatshepsut, her mother, Ahmes, is described as follows:

> *nfr.s r ḥm.t nb.t*
> *ntt m tꜣ pn r ḏr.f* (*Urk.* IV, 219, 2)
> she is more beautiful than any woman
> who is in the whole land,

which recalls the similar description of Bata's wife:

> *iw.st nfr<.ti> m ḥʿwt.st*
> *r st-ḥm.t nb.t*
> *nty m tꜣ ḏr<.f>* (d'Orb. 9, 7–8)
> she is more beautiful in her body
> than any woman
> who is in the whole land,

a parallel noted by Jacobsohn, "Der altägyptische . . . Mythos," p. 446, n. 21.

100. Jacobsohn, "Der altägyptische . . . Mythos," p. 422.

101. Ibid., p. 413.

102. Jan Assmann, "Das Bild des Vaters im alten Ägypten," p. 47.

103. Jacobsohn, "Der altägyptische . . . Mythos," p. 425.

104. Assmann, "Das Bild des Vaters," p. 47.

105. Ibid., p. 46. In this article, Assmann contrasts the Horus succession myth, representing culture, with Kamutef, representing nature, as follows: Kamutef embodies the nonrational traits of fathership, the natural mystery, and the Horus idea encompasses the rational, the cultural, and community phenomena (p. 32). The Osiris-Horus succession encompasses world lordship, the one in the Otherworld over the spirits, the other in this world over the living (p. 34). (Interestingly, Assmann does not follow this up or in any way relate it to Lévi-Strauss's ideas of binary

opposition in mythology.) The Osiris-Horus succession also concerns the abolition of a lack: at the death of a king, there is a lack which the triumph of Horus liquidates (pp. 38–39). In this Assmann incorporates the Proppian approach in its simplest form: in a tale a lack exists which must be liquidated (see above Ch. 1, n. 186). Furthermore, the myth of Osiris is the paradigm for every act of a son for his father: the son acts as Horus, being the personification of Horus, not the image (p. 40). In the pious acts of Horus for his deceased father, the two are drawn together, contrasting the generations, while Kamutef, in comparison, contrasts the sexes (p. 31).

106. Assmann, "Das Bild des Vaters," p. 32.

107. Otto, "Ein Beitrag zur Deutung der ägyptischen Vor- und Frühgeschichte," pp. 431–52. It must be noted that Griffiths (*The Origins of Osiris,* pp. 151–72) has argued quite strongly and persuasively that Osiris's link with vegetation is a later development, thus forming a secondary characteristic (p. 170). Nevertheless, the association of Osiris with vegetation cannot be discounted and certainly was valid at the time of the d'Orbiney.

108. Jacobsohn, "Kamutef," col. 309.

109. The concept is that for a man to impregnate a woman makes her his wife.

110. Vandier, *La Religion égyptienne,* p. 142. One might view this idea in the same light as the idea of inheriting the alter-ego by the son from the father held by various preliterate peoples, e.g., the Yąnomamö (Napoleon Chagnon, *Yąnomamö: The Fierce People*[3] [1983], p. 104). There are certain parallels also to be seen with the people of the Andes (Irene Silverblatt, *Moon, Sun, and Witches: Gender Ideology and Class in Inca and Colonial Peru* [Princeton, 1987], especially Chap. III).

111. Jan Assmann, "Das Bild des Vaters im alten Ägypten" in *Das Vaterbild in Mythos und Geschichte: Ägypten, Griechenland, Altes Testament, Neues Testament,* ed. H. Tellenbach (1976), p. 32.

112. Jacobsohn, *Die dogmatische Stellung,* p. 17, cites the following text with regard to Hatshepsut:

> *s3.t pw nt k3-mwt.f*
> *[Ḥw.t-Ḥr] mrr.t* (*Urk.* IV, 249, 4–5)
> It is the daughter of Kamutef,
> beloved of Hathor.

The restoration of *Ḥw.t-Ḥr,* made on the basis of LD III, 20*c* in the first edition of *Urk.* IV, was changed by Sethe in the 1927 edition to read *nṯrw.*

113. Waddell, *Manetho,* pp. 4–5.

114. Franz Joseph Lauth, *Aegyptische Chronologie,* Strassburg: Karl J. Trübner (1877), pp. 30–31; Gardiner, "Hero," p. 185; Helck, *Manetho,* p. 6, and Chap. 2 above, n. 161.

115. Assmann, "Das Bild des Vaters," p. 46, states that the idea of Kamutef appears to derive from astral myths, but he does not discuss it.

116. The lunar Kamutef gives the king an additional link with the cosmological realm, adding the moon (Jacobsohn, "Der altägyptische . . . Mythos," p. 419) to the king's ancient relation with the sun.

117. Jacobsohn, "Kamutef," col. 308.

118. Most often the cycle is expressed as tripartite: the first quarter or fecundity, the full moon, and the new moon or conception of the moon for the next month. It is observed that the waning or decline (that is, the third quarter) is omitted. Derchain states that this period is equal to the castration of the bull (Philippe Derchain, "Mythes et dieux lunaires en Égypte," in *La Lune: Mythes et Rites,* Sources Orientales V [1962], p. 27). It is not surprising to find this omission in accordance with the regular proscription of potentially threatening ideas or depictions. In this case, when applied to cosmological and political areas, the loss of fecundity and fertility represents the threat of general chaos.

119. Jacobsohn, "Kamutef," col. 308.

120. Jacobsohn, *Die dogmatische Stellung,* pp. 22–24. See also Barta, *Götterkreis der Neunheit,* p. 36.

121. Jacobsohn, *Die dogmatische Stellung,* p. 22, and "Der altägyptische . . . Mythos," pp. 418–19.

122. Maspero, *Popular Stories,* p. 19.

123. Ibid., p. 19, n. 4. The significance of name-giving as giving personhood has strong anthropological basis, for which see Van Gennep, *Rites of Passage,* Chap. V.

124. *LES,* p. 28a, note to 18, 10a.

125. Adolf Erman, *Neuägyptische Grammatik* (1933), p. 273, §§569–70.

126. Ibid., note to §570 with reference to §499.

127. *Wb* II, p. 436, 4. See *Urk.* IV, 1060, 13, for its use, along with that of *ẖnm.t* (see below) by a nonroyal person. Note that Leonard H. Lesko does not take into account the *Wörterbuch*'s translation in his definition of *rnn* in *A Dictionary of Late Egyptian,* vol. 2, p. 65, using there Gardiner's definition.

128. *CD,* p. 150.

129. Lichtheim, *AEL* II, p. 210.

130. Brunner-Traut, *Altägyptische Märchen,*[5] p. 39.

131. Brunner-Traut, *Altägyptische Märchen,*[5] p. 258, n. 7.

132. Brunner, *Die Geburt,* p. 114ff. It is Scene X at Luxor.

133. Ibid., p. 114.

134. Ibid., p. 118.

135. Ibid., p. 111, XLb, n.a.

136. Ibid., pl. 10.

137. See Brunner, *Die Geburt,* pp. 205–206 for a less comprehensive comparison.

138. Brunner, *Die Geburt,* p. 112.
139. Ibid., p. 112, n. 3.
140. H. Brunner, "Erzieher," *LÄ* II, col. 20.
141. Erik Hornung, *Das Buch von den Pforten des Jenseits. I. nach der Versionen des Neuen Reichs,* Aeg.Hel. 7 (1979), pp. 397–98, and Hornung, *Ägyptische Unterweltsbücher,* p. 303.
142. I am postulating that *ḫnm* and *ẖnm* can both designate the same function. *Wb* III, 378, 14 gives two eighteenth-dynasty examples in which *ḫnm* apparently means "to touch," and there is no question in III, 381, 8 that *ḫnm.t* designates a nurse, commonly next to *rnn.t.* Correspondingly, *Wb* III, 293, 9 clearly defines *ẖnm* as "to nurse a child," and III, 293, 11–13 shows that *ẖnm.t* is a nurse, especially for the divine child.
143. Paul Barguet, "Le Livre des Portes et la transmission de pouvoir royal," *RdÉ* 27 (1975), p. 34.
144. Brunner, *Die Geburt,* p. 206.
145. Bettina Schmitz, *Unterschungen zum Titel s3-njswt "Königsohn",* Habelts Dissertationsdrucke, Reihe Ägyptologie, 2 (1976), p. 267ff.
146. Labib Habachi, "Königssohn von Kusch," *LÄ* III, col. 630–40. Documents attest to approximately thirty-two of these officials during the eighteenth through twentieth dynasties, many of them sons of their predecessors. Four additional persons also served, including the first two, who may have been royalty. See also Edmund Meltzer, "A Funerary Cone of Merymose, Viceroy of Kush," *SSEA Newsletter,* December 1974, pp. 9–11.
147. Schmitz, *Titel s3-njswt,* p. 327.
148. Wolfgang Helck, *Der Einfluss der Militarführer in der 18. ägyptische Dynastie,* UGAÄ 14 (1939), p. 78ff.
149. A. H. Gardiner, "The Tomb of General Haremhab," *JEA* 39 (1953), p. 10. See also *AEO* 14*–19*.
150. Gardiner, "The Tomb of General Haremhab," p. 10.
151. W. Helck, "*Rpꜥt* auf dem Thron der *Gb,*" *Orientalia* 19 (1950), pp. 416–34.
152. Ibid., pp. 430–32.
153. *rpꜥt* is a variant writing of *r-pꜥt,* and both signify "hereditary noble" or "heir" (Lesko, *A Dictionary,* vol. 2, pp. 49 and 60).
154. Hermann te Velde, "Geb," *LÄ* II, col. 428.
155. Thompson motif E 670, Repeated Reincarnation; motif S 401, Unsuccessful attempt to kill with repeated revival; and motif E 607.2, Person transforms self, is swallowed and reborn in new form. See also Lefèbvre's article, cited in Chap. 1, "Postwar Egyptologists," on the Russian parallel.
156. pChester Beatty I, 5, 7.
157. pChester Beatty I, 6, 4–5.
158. pChester Beatty I, 6, 13–14.

159. pChester Beatty I, 8, 9.

160. The Pyramid Texts and the *Book of the Dead* also contain such spells, often introduced by "I am. . . ."

161. Lord, *Singer of Tales,* pp. 97, 250–54.

Chapter 7

1. See Brunner-Traut, "Altägyptische Literatur," pp. 31 and 42; also E. Brunner-Traut, "Märchenmotive," *LÄ* III, col. 1124, and Blumenthal, "Papyrus d'Orbiney," p. 3.

2. As Dan Ben-Amos has stated ("Analytical Categories and Ethnic Genres," *Genre* 2, no. 3 [Sept. 1969], 275–301, rpt. in *Folklore Genres,* ed. Dan Ben-Amos, Publication of the American Folklore Society 26 [1976], p. 217), "to refer to similar subjects in biblical and Greek traditions as examples of the genre Märchen is sheer anachronism."

3. See especially A. Spalinger's review of Miriam Lichtheim, *Ancient Egyptian Literature,* vol. 2 in *OLZ* 74, #6 (1979), cols. 525–27.

4. Edmund Meltzer, review of *Egyptology and the Social Sciences. Five Studies,* ed. Kent R. Weeks (1979), *The SSEA Journal,* XI (1981), p. 111. The ambiguity and difficulty of literary classification of the works of ancient Egypt are amply illustrated by J. Assmann, "Die literarische Text im alten Ägypten," *OLZ* 69 (1974), col. 117–26; A. Spalinger, in his review of Miriam Lichtheim's *Ancient Egyptian Literature,* vol. 2 (1976), *OLZ* 74 (1979), col. 525–27, shows that such attempts are far from conclusive. H. Brunner, "Literatur," *LÄ* III, col. 1068, has stated that some texts belong to obvious literary types, such as prayers and hymns, but others do not. He has also pointed out that there is no possible way of judging the effect of the literature in Egypt itself (col. 1070).

5. Brunner-Traut, "Altägyptische Literatur," pp. 40–43, mentions the traditional Egyptian forms: "'Es war einmal', 'es begab sich einmal', 'viele Tage danach', 'als die Erde hell wurde und der nächste Tag begann' oder 'sagt man'."

6. Lüthi, *The European Folktale,* pp. 19–20, 33, 38.

7. Ibid., p. 16.

8. Ibid., pp. 17–18.

9. Brunner-Traut, "Ägypten," *EM,* I, col. 179.

10. Brunner-Traut, "Märchenmotive," col. 1124–1127, "Altägyptische Literatur," pp. 36–40, and "Ägypten," col. 178–79, and Brunner, "Literatur," col. 1067–1072, present the most readily available and detailed discussions of Egyptian literature, especially those relative to Märchen.

11. Lüthi, *The European Folktale,* p. 66.

12. Ibid., p. 6.

13. Ibid., p. 11.

14. Ranke, *Die Zwei Brüder,* p. 39.

15. Lüthi, *The European Folktale,* p. 12. For an excellent example, see Grimm tale #31, "The Maiden Without Hands," AaTh 706.

16. Lüthi, *The European Folktale,* pp. 13, 16.

17. Ibid., p. 15.

18. Ibid., p. 58.

19. Ibid., pp. 15–16.

20. Perhaps its closest relative is the New Egyptian tale of "The Doomed Prince" from Papyrus Harris 500, Verso, dating to the early nineteenth dynasty, a tale set in the real world with the intervention of the fantastic at numerous points. In fact, one might draw an analogy between it and a number of tales from the modern European corpus that have a girl in a tower and a young man from far away who does marvelous feats to gain her in marriage. The Middle Egyptian narratives of Sinuhe and the Westcar Papyrus also show such motifs, but the total structure removes them from the folktale classification.

21. See Bettleheim, *The Uses of Enchantment;* Carl G. Jung, "Approaching the Unconscious," in Carl G. Jung, et al., *Man and his Symbols* (1964), pp. 18–103; Joseph L. Henderson, "Ancient Myths and Modern Man," in Jung, *Man and his Symbols,* pp. 104–57; and Albert B. Lord, *Singer of Tales* (1977), and A. B. Lord, lectures for Humanities 9a, spring term, 1980 at Harvard University, Cambridge, Mass. Bettleheim, *The Uses of Enchantment,* pp. 90–96, specifically discusses the Egyptian tale, but, as indicated in the section on psychoanalytic approaches in Chap. 1, "Psychoanalytical Approaches," in this study, his exposition is far from clear.

22. Assmann, "Zweibrüdermärchen," pp. 23–24.

23. Ibid., p. 24. Assmann's "unrecognized return" is not truly an aspect of the rite of passage but rather a feature of some narrative presentations of it, as I mentioned in Chap. 6, "Bata's Birth."

24. See Victor Turner, *The Ritual Process* (1969), pp. 97–102; also van Gennep, *Rites of Passage,* though he does not outline royal rites to speak of; and Mircea Eliade, *Rites and Symbols of Initiation* (1958).

25. te Velde, *Seth, God of Confusion,* p. 108.

26. Erik Hornung, "Seth. Geschichte und Bedeutung eines ägyptischen Gottes," *Symbolon,* N.F. 2 (1975), p. 52; te Velde, *Seth, God of Confusion,* p. 108.

27. Köhler, *Das Imiut,* p. 386; Brunner, *Die Geburt des Gottkönigs,* p. 27ff, especially p. 28, n. 2; Blumenthal, *Untersuchungen zum ägyptischen Königtum,* pp. 35–36.

28. The actual words used by the scribe to describe what he did are *ir n sš,* "made into writing," which suggest contemporary composition. This phrase was used frequently in the scribal introductions to the love poems from pChester Beatty I, for which see Ulrich Luft, "Zur Einleitung der Liebesdichtung auf Papyrus Chester Beatty I, r* XVI 9ff," *ZÄS* 99 (1973), pp. 108–16.

Appendix

1. The English rendition follows Vandier's translation with some minor changes that were made in order to bring it closer to the hieroglyphic text. Further consultation was made with Heike Sternberg, *Mythische Motive und Mythenbildung in den Ägyptischen Tempeln und Papyri der Griechisch-Römischen Zeit.* GOF IV, 14 (1985), pp. 144–52. The Roman numeral headings reflect their appearance in the Papyrus itself, being rearranged here for an orderly presentation.

Selected Bibliography

Albright, William F. *The Vocalization of the Egyptian Syllabic Orthography.* American Oriental Series, vol. 5. New Haven, Conn.: American Oriental Society, 1934.

———, and Thomas O. Lambdin. "New Material for Egyptian Syllabic Orthography." *JSS* 2 (1957): 113–27.

Allam, S. *Beiträge zum Hathorkult bis zum Ende des Mittleren Reiches.* MÄS 4. Berlin: Verlag Bruno Hessling, 1963.

Allen, T. G. *The Book of the Dead or Going Forth by Day.* SAOC 37. Chicago: Univ. of Chicago Press, 1974.

Altenmüller, Brigitte. *Synkretismus in den Sargtexten.* GOF IV/7. Wiesbaden: Otto Harrassowitz, 1973.

Altenmüller, Hartwig. "Die Bedeutung der 'Gotteshalle des Anubis' im Begräbnisritual." *JEOL* 22 (1971–72): 307–17.

———. "Bemerkungen zum Hirtenlied des Alten Reichs," *CdÉ* 48 (1973): 211–31.

———. *Die Texte zum Begräbnisritual in den Pyramiden des Alten Reiches.* Äg.Ab. 24. Wiesbaden: Otto Harrassowitz, 1972.

Altenmüller-Kesting, Brigitte. *Reinigungsriten im ägyptischen Kult.* Hamburg: Lüdcke bei der uni, 1968.

Assmann, Jan, trans. *Ägyptische Hymnen und Gebete.* Zürich und München: Artemis Verlag, 1972.

———. "Das ägyptischer Zweibrüdermärchen (Papyrus d'Orbiney)." *ZÄS* 104 (1977): 1–25.

———. "Das Bild des Vaters im alten Ägypten." In *Das Vaterbild in Mythos und Geschichte: Ägypten, Griechenland, Altes Testament, Neues Testament.* Ed. H. Tellenbach, 12–49. Stuttgart-Berlin-Köln-Mainz: Verlag W. Kohlhammer, 1976.

———. "Die literarische Text im alten Ägypten." *OLZ* 69 (1974): 117–26.

———. *Liturgische Lieder an den Sonnengott.* MÄS 19. Berlin: Verlag Bruno Hessling, 1969.

———. "Textanalyse auf verschiedenen Ebenen: zum Problem der Einheit des Papyrus d'Orbiney." In *XIX Deutscher Orientalistentag vom 28. September bis 4. Oktober 1975,* 1–15. ZDMG Suppl. III, 1. Wiesbaden: Franz Steiner Verlag GMBH, 1977.

Astour, Michael C. *Hellenosemitica: An Ethnic and Cultural Study in West Semitic Impact on Mycenaean Greece.* Leiden: E. J. Brill, 1965.

Attridge, H., and R. Oden, eds. *The Syrian Goddess (De Dea Syria).* Texts and Translations 9, Graeco-Roman Series 1. Missoula, Montana: Scholars Press, 1976.

Badawi, Ahmed Mohamad. *Der Gott Chnum.* Glückstadt: Verlag von J. J. Augustin, 1937.

Baines, John. "Interpreting *Sinuhe.*" *JEA* 68 (1982): 31–44.

Bakir, Abd el Mohsen. *The Cairo Calendar, No. 86637.* Cairo: n.p., 1966.

Barta, Winfried. *Aufbau und Bedeutung der altägyptischen Opferformel.* Äg.For. 24. Glückstadt: J. J. Augustin, 1968.

———. *Untersuchungen zum Götterkreis der Neunheit.* MÄS 28. München-Berlin: Deutscher Kunstverlag, 1973.

———. *Untersuchungen zur Göttlichkeit des regierenden Königs.* MÄS 32. München-Berlin: Deutscher Kunstverlag, 1975.

Beckerath, Jürgen von. "Die 'Stele der Verbannten' im Museum des Louvre." *RdE* 20 (1968):7–36.

Begelsbacher-Fischer, Barbara. *Untersuchungen zur Götterwelt des Alten Reiches im Spiegel der Privatgräber der IV. und V. Dynastie.* OBO 37. Freiburg (Schweiz): Universitätsverlag; Göttingen: Vanderhoeck & Ruprecht, 1981.

Bergman, Jan. *Ich bin Isis: Studien zum memphitischen Hintergrund der griechischen Isisaretalogien.* Acta Universitatis Upsaliensis: Historia Religionum, 3. Uppsala: n.p., 1968.

Bettelheim, Bruno. *The Uses of Enchantment: The Meaning and Interpretation of Fairy Tales.* New York: Vintage Books, 1977.

Birch, Samuel. *Select Papyri in Hieratic Character from the Collections of the British Museum.* Pt. ii. London: Woodfall and Kinder, 1860.

Bissing, F. W. F. von, and H. P. Blok. "Eine Weihung an die Sieben Hathoren." *ZÄS* 61 (1926):83–93.

Blumenthal, Elke. *Untersuchungen zum ägyptischen Königtum des Mittleren Reiches I: Die Phraseologie.* ASAW 61, 1, 1970.

———. "Die Erzählung des Papyrus d'Orbiney als Literaturwerk." *ZÄS* 99 (1972):1–17.

Bolte, J., and G. Polivka. *Anmerkungen zu den Kinder- und Hausmärchen der Brüder Grimm.* Vol. 4. Leipzig: T. Weicher, 1930.

Bonnet, Hans. *Reallexikon der ägyptischen Religionsgeschichte.* Berlin: Walter de Gruyter & Co., 1952.

Borghouts, J. F. *Ancient Egyptian Magical Texts.* Nisaba 9. Leiden: E. J. Brill, 1978.

Breasted, James Henry. *The Edwin Smith Surgical Papyrus.* Vol. 1. OIP 3. Chicago: Univ. of Chicago Press, 1930.

Brunner, Helmut. "Das Herz als Sitz des Lebensgeheimnis." *AfO* 17 (1954–56): 140–41.

———. "Das Herz in ägyptischen Glaubens." In *Das Herz im Umkreis des Glaubens.* Biberach an der Riß: Dr. Karl Thomae, 81–106. GMBH, 1965.

———. *Die Geburt des Gottkönigs.* Äg.Ab. 3. Wiesbaden: Otto Harrassowitz, 1964.

———. *Grundzüge einer Geschichte der altägyptischen Literatur.* 1966; rpt. Darmstadt: Wissenschaftliche Buchgesellschaft, 1978.

Brunner-Traut, Emma. "Ägypten." *EM* 1.

———. "Altägyptische Literatur." In *Altorientalische Literaturen.* Ed. Wolfgang Röllig. Vol. I, 25–99. *Neues Handbuch der Literaturwissenschaft.* Ed. Klaus von See. Wiesbaden: Akademische Verlagsgesellschaft Athenaion, 1978.

———. *Altägyptische Märchen.* 5th ed. Düsseldorf und Köln: Eugen Diederichs Verlag, 1979.

———. *Altägyptische Tiergeschichte und Fabel: Gestalt und Strahlkraft.* Darmstadt: Wissenschaftliche Buchgesellschaft, 1968.

———. *Die alten Ägypter: Verborgenes Leben unter Pharaonen.* Stuttgart-Berlin-Köln-Mainz: Verlag W. Kohlhammer, 1971.

———. *Gelebte Mythen. Beiträge zum altägyptischen Mythos.* Darmstadt: Wissenschaftliche Buchgesellschaft, 1981.

———. "Papyrus D'Orbiney." *LÄ* IV (1982): 697–704.

Buck, Adriaan de, and Alan H. Gardiner, eds. *The Egyptian Coffin Texts.* 7 vols. OIP 34, 49, 64, 67, 73, 81, 87. Chicago: Univ. of Chicago Press, 1935–1962.

Burchardt, Max. "Das Herz des Bata." *ZÄS* 50 (1912): 118–19.

———. "Parallelen zum Papyrus d'Orbiney und zum Mythus von des 'Vernichtung des Menschengeschlechts.'" *ZÄS* 53 (1917): 148.

Calverley, A. M., and M. F. Broome. *Temple of King Sethos I at Abydos.* Ed. A. H. Gardiner. Vol. 2. London: Egyptian Exploration Society, 1933–1938.

Capart, Jean. "Cultes d'el Kab et préhistoire." *CdÉ* XIV (1939): 213–17.

Coats, G. *From Canaan to Egypt: Structural and Theological Context for the Joseph Story.* CBQMS 4; Washington, DC: Catholic Biblical Association, 1976.

Coogan, Michael, ed. and trans. *Stories from Ancient Canaan.* Philadelphia: The Westminster Press, 1978.

Cruz-Uribe, Eugene. "On the Wife of Merneptah." *GM* 24 (1977): 23–31.

Daumas, François. "Quelques remarques sur les représentations du pêche à la ligne sous l'ancien empire," *BIFAO* 62 (1964): 67–85.
Dawson, W. R., and T. E. Peet. "The So-called Poem on the King's Chariot." *JEA* 19 (1933): 167–74 and plates 25–29.
Dégh, Linda. "Folk Narrative." In *Folklore and Folklife: An Introduction.* Ed. Richard M. Dorson, 53–83. Chicago and London: Univ. of Chicago Press, 1972.
Derchain, Philippe. "La Perruque et le cristal." *SÄK* 2 (1975): 55–74.
———. "Le Lotus, la mandragore, et le persea." *CdÉ* 50 (1975): 85.
———. "Le Rôle du roi d'Égypte dans le maintien de l'ordre cosmique." In *Le Pouvoir et le sacré.* Annales du Centre d'Étude des Religions, 1 (1962): 61–73.
———. "Mythes et dieux lunaires en Égypte." 17–68. In *La Lune: mythes et rites.* Sources Orientales V. 1962.
———. Rev. of "Die fünfte Variante des Hirtenlieds" by Peter Kaplony. 87–88. In *Annual Egyptian Bibliography,* 1969.
———. Rev. of *Le Papyrus Jumilhac* by J. Vandier. *Bi.Or.* 20 (1964): 34.
———. "Snéfrou et les rameuses." *RdÉ* 21 (1969): 19–25.
Duell, Prentice. *The Mastaba of Mereruka.* OIP 39. Vol. 2. Chicago: Univ. of Chicago Press, 1938.
Dundes, Alan, ed. *The Study of Folklore.* Englewood Cliffs, N.J.: Prentice-Hall, 1965.
Ebers, Georg. *Aegypten und die Bücher Mose's: sachlicher Commentar zu den aegyptischen Stellen in Genesis und Exodus.* Vol. 1. Leipzig: Verlag von Wilhelm Engelmann, 1868.
Edel, Elmar. *Altägyptische Grammatik.* 2 vols. An.Or. 34/39. Rome: Pontificum Institutum Biblicum, 1955/64.
Edwards, I. E. S. "A Relief of Qudshu-Astarte-Anath in the Winchester College Collection." *JNES* 14 (1955): 49–51.
Egypt's Golden Age: The Art of Living in the New Kingdom, 1558–1085 B.C., Catalogue of the Exhibition. Boston: Museum of Fine Arts, 1982.
Enzyklopädie des Märchens. Vol. 1. Ed. Kurt Ranke. Berlin and New York: Walter de Gruyter, 1978.
Erman, Adolf. *The Ancient Egyptians: A Source Book of their Writings.* Trans. Aylward M. Blackman. New York: Harper Torchbooks, 1966.
———. "Denksteine aus der thebanischen Gräberstadt." *SPAW* 1911: 1086–1110.
———. *Die Märchen des Papyrus Westcar.* Berlin: W. Spemann, 1890.
———. *Neuägyptische Grammatik.* Leipzig, 1933; rpt. Hildesheim: Georg Olms Verlag, 1979.
———. *Reden. Rufe. und Lieder auf Gräberbilden des Alten Reichs.* APAW 1918.
Fairman, H. W. "The Kingship Rituals of Egypt." In *Myth, Ritual and Kingship: Essays in the Theory and Practice of Kingship in the Ancient Near East and in Israel.* Ed. S. H. Hooke, 47–104. Oxford: Clarendon Press, 1958.

Faulkner, R. O. *The Ancient Egyptian Coffin Texts.* 3 vols. Warminster: Aris & Phillips, 1973–1980.
———. *The Ancient Egyptian Pyramid Texts.* Oxford: Oxford Univ. Press, 1969.
Federn, Walter. "*Ḥtp (r)di(w) (n) 'Inpw*: zum Verständis der vor-osirianischen Opferformel." *MDAIK* 16 (1958): 120–30.
Fischer, H. G. "Bat." *LÄ* I: 630–32.
———. "*B3.t* in the New Kingdom." *JARCE* 2 (1963): 50–51.
———. "The Cult and Nome of the Goddess Bat." *JARCE* 1 (1962): 7–23.
Friedrich, Wolf-Hartmut and Walther Killy, eds. *Das Fischer Lexikon: Literatur* 2/1. Frankfurt am Main: Fischer Taschenbuch Verlag, 1965.
Funk and Wagnalls Standard Dictionary of Folklore, Mythology and Legends. One volume ed. rev. Ed. Maria Leach. New York: Funk and Wagnalls, 1972.
Gaillard, Claude. *Recherches sur les poissons.* MIFAO 51. Le Caire: Imprimerie de l'Institut français d'Archéologie orientale, 1923.
Gamer-Wallert, I. *Fische und Fischkulte im alten Ägypten.* Äg.Ab. 21. Wiesbaden: Otto Harrassowitz, 1970.
Gardiner, Alan H. *Ancient Egyptian Onomastica.* 3 vols. Oxford: Clarendon Press, 1948.
———. "The Astarte Papyrus." 74–85. In *Studies Presented to F. Ll. Griffith.* London: Egyptian Exploration Society, 1932.
———. *Die Erzählung des Sinuhe und die Hirtengeschichte.* Hieratische Papyrus aus den Königlichen Museen zu Berlin, 5. Ed. A. Erman. *Literarische Texte des mittleren Reiches.* Leipzig: J. C. Hinrichs, 1909.
———. "The Hero of the Papyrus d'Orbiney." *PSBA* 27 (1905): 185–86.
———. "Hymns to Amun," *ZÄS* 42 (1905): 12–42.
———. "Hymns to Sobk in a Ramesseum Papyrus." *RdÉ* 11 (1957): 43–56.
———. *Late Egyptian Stories.* BAe I. 1932; rpt. Bruxelles: Édition de la fondation égyptologique reine Élisabeth, 1980.
———. *The Library of A. Chester Beatty. Descriptions of a Hieratic Papyrus with a Mythological Story, Love-Songs, and Other Miscellaneous Texts. Chester Beatty Papyri, No. I.* London: Oxford Univ. Press, 1931.
———. *The Wilbur Papyrus.* 4 vols. London: Oxford Univ. Press, 1948–1952.
———, T. Eric Peet, and J. Cerny. *The Inscriptions of Sinai,* 2d ed. 2 vols. London: Egyptian Exploration Fund, 1952/55.
Gauthier, Henri. *Dictionnaire des noms géographiques.* 7 vols. Kairo, 1925–1931.
———. *Temples immergés de la Nubie. Le Temple d'Amada.* Le Caire: Institut français d'Archéologie orientale, 1913.
Gennep, Arnold van. *Rites of Passage.* Trans. Monika B. Vizedom and Gabrielle L. Caffee. Chicago: Univ. of Chicago Press, 1960.

Godron, Gerard. "A propos du nom royal  ." *ASAÉ* 49 (1949): 217–20.
Goedicke, Hans. "Eine Variante des 'Hirtenliede'." *WZKM* 54 (1957): 46–50.
———. "The Story of the Herdsman." *CdÉ* 90 (1970): 244–66.
Goyon, Jean-Claude. *Rituels funéraires de l'ancienne Égypte*. Paris: Les Éditions du Cerf, 1972.
Grapow, Hermann, et al. *Grundriß der Medizin der alten Ägypter*. 8 vols. Berlin: Akademie Verlag, 1954–73.
———. *Urkunden V. Ausgewählte Texte des Totenbuches*. Leipzig, 1915–1917.
Grenier, Jean-Claude. *Anubis alexandrin et romain*. ÉPRO 57. Leiden: E. J. Brill, 1977.
Griffiths, J. Gwyn. *The Conflict of Horus and Seth from Egyptian and Classical Sources: A Study in Ancient Mythology*. Liverpool: Liverpool Univ. Press, 1960.
———. *The Origins of Osiris and his Cult*. Supplement to Numen XL. Leiden: E. J. Brill, 1980.
———. "Osiris and the Moon in Iconography." *JEA* 62 (1976): 153–59.
———, ed. and trans. *Plutarch's "De Iside et Osiride"*. Cardiff, Wales: Univ. of Wales Press, 1970.
Guglielmi, W. *Reden, Rufe, und Lieder auf altägyptische Darstellungen der Landwirtschaft, der Viehzucht, des Fisch- und Vogelfangs vom Mittleren Reich zur Spätzeit*. TÄB I. Bonn: Rudolf Habelt Verlag, GMBH, 1973.
Habachi, Labib. "Amenwahsu Attached to the Cult of Anubis, Lord of the Dawning Land." *MDAIK* 14 (1956): 52–62.
———. *The Second Stela of Kamose and His Struggle against the Hyksos Ruler and his Capital*. ADAIK 8. Glückstadt: J. J. Augustin Verlag, 1972.
Harris, J. R. "Kiya." *CdÉ* 49 (1974): 25–30.
Helck, Wolfgang. *Die altägyptische Gaue*. Beiheft TAVO, Reihe B, no. 5. Wiesbaden: Dr. Ludwig Reichert Verlag, 1974.
———. *Die Beziehungen Ägyptens zu Vorderasien im 3. und 2. Jahrtausend v. Chr.* 2d ed. Äg.Ab. 5. Wiesbaden: Otto Harrassowitz, 1971.
———. "Herkunft und Deutung einiger Züge des frühägyptischen Königsbildes." *Anthropos* 49 (1954): 961–91.
———. "*R-pꜥt* auf dem Thron des *Geb*." *Orientalia* 19 (1950): 416–34.
———. *Urkunden IV. Urkunden der 18. Dynastie, 17–22*. Berlin: Akademie Verlag, 1955–61.
———. "Zur Frage der Entstehung der ägyptisches Literatur." *WZKM* 63/64 (1972): 6–26.
Hermann, Alfred. "Das steinharte Herz." *Jahrbuch für Antike und Christentum* 4 (1961): 77–107.
Hermsen, Edmund. *Lebensbaumsybolik im alten Ägypten: Eine Untersuchung*. Köln: in commission with E. J. Brill, 1981.

Herrmann, Siegfried. "Isis in Byblos." *ZÄS* 82 (1957): 48–55.
Hillers, Delbert. "The Bow of Aqhat: The Meaning of a Mythological Theme." In *Orient and Occident: Essays Presented to Cyrus H. Gordon on the Occasion of his Sixty-fifth Birthday.* Ed. Harry A. Hoffner, 71–81. AOAT 22. Neukirchen-Vluyn: Neukirchner Verlag, 1973.
Hintze, Fritz. *Untersuchungen zu Stil und Sprache neuägyptischer Erzählungen.* VIO 2 and 6. Berlin: Akademie Verlag, 1950–52.
Hollis, Susan. "On the Nature of Bata, the Hero of the Papyrus d'Orbiney." *CdÉ* LIX, No. 118 (1984): 248–57.
———. "The Woman in Ancient Examples of the Potiphar's Wife Motif, K2111." *Gender and Difference in Ancient Israel.* Ed. by Peggy L. Day, 28–42. Minneapolis: Augsburg Fortress Press, 1989.
Horálek, Karol. "Brüdermärchen: Das ägyptische B." *EM* I.
Hornung, Erik, trans. *Ägyptische Unterweltsbücher.* Zürich und München: Artemis Verlag, 1972.
———. *Conceptions of God in Ancient Egypt: The One and the Many.* Trans. John Baines. Ithaca, NY: Cornell Univ. Press, 1982.
———. *Das Amduat.* 2 vols. Äg.Ab. 7. Wiesbaden: Otto Harrassowitz, 1963.
———. *Das Buch von den Pforten des Jenseits, I, nach der Versionen des Neuen Reichs.* Aeg.Helv. 7. Basel-Genf: n.p., 1979.
———. *Der Eine und die Vielen: Ägyptischen Gottesvorstellungen.* Darmstadt: Wissenschaftliche Buchgesellschaft, 1973.
———. "Seth. Geschichte und Bedeutung eines ägyptischen Gottes." *Symbolon* N.F. 2 (1975): 49–63.
———. "Zur geschichtlichen Rolle des Königs in der 18. Dynastie." *MDAIK* 16 (1957): 120–33.
———, trans. *Das Totenbuch der Ägypter.* Zürich und München: Artemis Verlag, 1979.
Jacobsohn, Helmut. "Der altägyptische, der christliche, und der moderne Mythos." *Eranos Jahrbuch* 1968: 411–48.
———. *Die dogmatische Stellung des Königs in der Theologie der alten Ägypter.* Äg.For. 8. Glückstadt-Hamburg-New York: Verlag J. J. Augustin, 1939.
Jacquet-Gordon, H. K. *Les Noms des domaines funéraires sous l'Ancien Empire égyptien.* BdÉ 34. Le Caire: Imprimerie de l'Institut français d'Archéologie orientale, 1962.
Jesi, F. "Il tentato adulterio mitico in Grecia e in Egitto." *Aegyptus* 42 (1962): 276–96.
Junker, H. *Auszug der Hathor-Tefnut aus Nubien.* APAW 1911. Anhang Abh. III.
———. *Die Onurislegende.* DAWW 59, 1917.
Kadish, Gerald. "Eunuchs in Ancient Egypt." In *Studies in Honor of John A. Wilson, September 12, 1969,* 55–62. SAOC 35. Chicago: Univ. of Chicago Press, 1969.
Kaiser, O. *Die mythische Bedeutung des Meeres in Ägypten, Ugarit, und*

Israel. Beiheft ZAW 78. Berlin: Verlag Alfred Töpelmann, 1959.
Kákosy, Lászlo. "Ischedbaum (*išd*)." *LÄ* III.
Kaplony, Peter. "Bata." *LÄ* I:632–36.
———. "Das Hirtenlied und seine fünfte Variante." *CdÉ* 44 (1969): 27–59.
———. "Die Definition der schönen Literatur im alten Ägypten." *Fragen an die altägyptische Literatur: Studien zum Gedanken an Eberhard Otto.* Ed. Jan Assmann, Erika Feucht, and Reinhard Grieshammer, 289–314. Wiesbaden: Dr. Ludwig Riechert, 1977.
———. *Die Inschriften der ägyptischen Frühzeit.* Äg.Ab. 8/9. 3 vols. and suppl. Wiesbaden: Otto Harrassowitz, 1963/64.
———. "Hirtenlied, Harfnerlieder und Sargtext-Spruch 671." *CdÉ* 45 (1970):240–45.
———. *Kleine Beiträge zu den Inschriften der ägyptischen Frühzeit.* Äg.Ab. 15 Wiesbaden: Otto Harrassowitz, 1966.
Kees, Hermann. "Anubis, Herr von Sepa und der 18. oberägyptische Gau." *ZÄS* 58 (1923):79–101.
———. "Der Gau von Cynopolis und seine Gottheit." *MIO* 6 (1958): 157–75.
———. *Der Götterglaube im alten Ägypten.* 2d ed. Leipzig, 1956; rpt. Berlin: Akademie Verlag, 1980.
———. "Kulttopographische und mythologische Beiträge." *ZÄS* 71 (1935):150–55.
———. *Totenglauben und Jenseitsvorstellungen der alten Ägypter.* 2d ed. Leipzig, 1956; rpt. Berlin: Akademie Verlag, 1980.
Kitchen, K. A. "The Titularies of the Ramesside Kings as Expression of their Ideal Kingship." *ASAÉ* LXXI (1987):131–41.
Köhler, Ursula. *Das Imiut.* GOF IV, 4. Wiesbaden: Otto Harrassowitz, 1975.
Leca, A.-P. *The Egyptian Way of Death.* Trans. Louise Asmal. New York: Doubleday & Co., 1981.
Lefèbvre, Gustave. "Bata et Ivan." *CdÉ* 25 (1950):17–26.
———, trans. and comm. *Romans et contes de l'époque pharaonique.* 1949; rpt. Paris: Librairie d'amérique et d'orient, 1976.
Lesko, Leonard H. "Three Late Egyptian Stories Reconsidered." In *Egyptological Studies in Honor of Richard A. Parker Presented on the Occasion of His 78th Birthday December 10, 1983.* Ed. Leonard H. Lesko, 98–103. Hanover and London: Brown University Press by University Press of New England, 1986.
Lexikon der Ägyptologie. 6 vols. Ed. Wolfgang Helck and Eberhard Otto. Wiesbaden: Otto Harrassowitz, 1972–86.
Leyen, Friedrich von der. *Die Welt der Märchen.* Vol. 1. Dusseldorf: Eugen Diederichs Verlag, 1953.
Lichtheim, Miriam. *Ancient Egyptian Literature.* 3 vols. Berkeley-Los Angeles-London: University of California Press, 1973–80.

Lopez, J. "Inscriptions de l'Ancien Empire à Khor el-Aquiba." *RdÉ* 19 (1967):51–66.

Lord, Albert B. *Singer of Tales.* Cambridge, Mass., 1960, rpt. New York: Atheneum, 1977.

Loret, Victor. "Quelques notes sur l'arbre âch." *ASAÉ* XVI (1916): 33–51.

Lucas, A. *Ancient Egyptian Materials and Industries,* 4th ed. rev. and enlarged by J. R. Harris. London: Edward Arnold, Ltd., 1962.

Lüddeckens, Erich. *Untersuchungen über religiösen Gehalt, Sprache und Form der ägyptischen Totenklagen.* MDAIK 11. Berlin: Reichsverlagsamt, 1943.

Luft, Ulrich. "Zur Einleitung der Liebesdichtung auf Papyrus Chester Beatty I, r* XVI 9ff." *ZÄS* 99 (1973):108–16.

Lüthi, Max. *The European Folktale: Form and Nature.* Trans. John D. Niles. Philadelphia: Institute for the Study of Human Issues, 1982.

Manniche, Lisa. "The Wife of Bata." *GM* 18 (1975):33–38.

Mariette, Auguste. *Les Mastaba de l'ancien empire.* Paris: F. Viewegs Libraire Editeur, 1884.

Maspero, Gaston. "Conte des deux frères." *Revue Archéologique* XXXV (March 1878), 164–79. Rpt. BE 8:44–73.

———. *Contes populaires de l'Égypte ancienne.* Les littératures populaires de toutes les nations, IV. Paris: Maisonneuve et Cie, 1882.

———. *Études égyptiennes.* Vol. 2. Paris: Imprimerie Nationale, 1888.

———. "Le Conte des deux frères: récit égyptien d'il y à trois mille ans." *Revue de Cours Littéraires* 7 (Feb. 28, 1871):780–84.

———. *Les Contes populaires de l'Égypte ancienne.* 2d ed. Les littératures populaires de toutes les nations, IV. Paris: Maisonneuve, Editeur, 1889.

———. *Les Contes populaires de l'Égypte ancienne.* 3d ed. Paris: Librairie orientale et américaine, 1906.

———. *Les Contes populaires de l'Égypte ancienne.* 4th ed. Paris: Librairie orientale et américaine, 1911.

———. "Les Hypogées royaux de Thèbes." In *Études de mythologie et d'archéologie,* BÉ 2 (1893).

———. *Popular Stories of Ancient Egypt.* Trans. A. S. Johns from the 4th French ed. with revisions by Gaston Maspero. 1915; rpt. New Hyde Park, N.Y.: University Books, 1967.

Maystre, Charles. "Le Livre de la vache du ciel dans les tombeaux de la valée des rois." *BIFAO* 40 (1941):53–115.

Meltzer, Edmund. Rev. of *Egyptology and the Social Sciences. Five Studies.* Ed. Kent R. Weeks. *The SSEA Journal,* XI, 2 (1981):111–14.

Montet, Pierre. *Everyday Life in Ancient Egypt in the Days of Ramesses the Great.* Trans. A. R. Maxwell-Hyslop and Margaret S. Drower. New intro. David B. O'Connor. Philadelphia: Univ. of Pennsylvania Press, 1981.

———. *Géographie de l'Égypte ancienne.* 2 vols. Paris: Librairie C. Klincksieck, 1957–61.
———. "Le Fruit défendu." *Kemi* 11 (1950):85–116.
———. "Le Pays de Negau, près de Byblos, et son dieu." *Syria* IV (1923):181–92.
———. *Les Scènes de la vie privée dans les tombeaux égyptiens de l'Ancien Empire.* Strasbourg: Publication de la Faculté des Lettres de l'Université de Strasbourg, 1925.
———. "Notes et documents pour servir à l'histoire des relations entre l'Égypte et la Syrie." *Kemi* 16 (1962):76–96.
Morenz, Siegfried, "Anubis mit dem Schlüssel." *Wiss. Ztschr. de Karl Marx Univ.* 1953–54, 79–83; rpt. *RGAÄ,* 510–30.
———. *Egyptian Religion.* Trans. Ann E. Keep. Ithaca, N.Y.: Cornell Univ. Press, 1973.
———. *RGAÄ. Gesammelte Aufsätze.* Köln Wien: Böhlau Verlag, 1975.
———. "Wortspiele in Ägypten." Festschrift Johannes Jahn zum 22. November 1957, 23–32; rpt. *RGAÄ,* 328–42.
———. and J. Schubert. *Der Gott auf der Blume.* Artibus Asia Supplementum XII. Ascona, Schweiz: Verlag Artibus Asia, 1954.
Moret, A. "La Légende d'Osiris à l'epoque thébaine d'après l'Hymne à Osiris du Louvre." *BIFAO* 30 (1931):725–50.
———. *La Mise à mort du dieu en Égypte.* Paris: Librairie orientalist Paul Geuthner, 1927.
Müller, Dieter. "Der gute Hirte: Ein Beitrag zur Geschichte ägyptischer Bildrede." *ZÄS* 86 (1961):126–44.
———. "Die Zeugung durch das Herz in Religion und Medizin der Ägypter." *Orientalia* 35 (1966):247–74.
Münster, Maria. *Untersuchungen zur Gottin Isis vom Alten Reich bis zum Ende des Neuen Reiches.* MÄS 11. Berlin: Verlag Bruno Hessling, 1968.
Nagel, Georges. "Set dans la barque solaire." *BIFAO* 28 (1929):33–39.
Otto, Eberhard. "An Ancient Egyptian Hunting Ritual." *JNES* 9 (1950): 164–77.
———. *Beiträge zur Geschichte der Stierkulte in Ägypten.* UGAÄ 13. Leipzig: J. C. Hinrichs Verlag, 1938.
———. *Das ägyptische Mundöffnungsritual.* 2 vols. Äg.Ab. 3. Wiesbaden: Otto Harrassowitz, 1960.
———. "Ein Beitrag zur Deutung der ägyptischen Vor- und Frühgeschichte." *WdO* 1 (1952):431–53.
———. "Legitimation des Herrschers im pharaonischen Ägypten." *Saeculum* 20 (1969): 385–411.
Piankoff, Alexandre. *Le "Coeur" dans les textes égyptiens.* Paris: Librairie orientaliste Paul Geuthner, 1930.
———. *The Tomb of Ramesses VI.* Ed. N. Rambova. Bollingen Series XL, 1. New York: Pantheon Books, 1954.
Pieper, Max. "Aegyptischer Literatur." In *Handbuch der Literaturwissen-*

schaft. Ed. Oskar Walzel, 78–81. Wildpark-Potsdam: Akademische Verlagsgesellschaft Athenaion MBH, 1927.

———. "Aegyptische Motive." In *Handwörterbuch des deutschen Märchens.* Eds. Johannes Bolte und Lutz Mackensen. Vol. 1. 24–46. Berlin und Leipzig: Walter de Gruyter & Co., 1930–33.

———. "Das ägyptische Märchen." *Morgenland* 27 (1935): 33–40.

Posener, Georges. *De la Divinité du pharaon.* Paris: Imprimerie National, 1960.

———. "La légende de la tresse d'Hathor." *Egyptological Studies in Honor of Richard A. Parker: Presented on the Occasion of His 78th Birthday December 10, 1983.* Ed. Leonard H. Lesko, 111–17. Hanover and London: Brown Univ. Press, 1986.

———. "La Légende égyptienne de la mer insatiable." *Annuaire de 'Institut de Philologie et d'Histoire orientales et slaves* 13 (1953): 461–78.

———. "La Piété personelle avant l'âge amarnien." *RdÉ* 27 (1975): 195–210.

———. "Literature." In *The Legacy of Egypt.* 2d ed. Ed. J. R. Harris, 220–56. Oxford: Clarendon Press, 1971.

———. *Littérature et politique dans l'Égypte de la XIIe dynastie.* Paris: Librairie ancienne Honoré Champion, Editeur, 1956.

Propp, V. *Morphology of the Folktale.* Trans. L. Scott. 2d edition. Rev. and ed. Louis Wagner. New intro. Alan Dundes. Austin and London: Univ. of Texas Press, 1968.

Quaegebeur, J. "Anubis, fils d'Osiris, le vacher." *Studien Aegyptiaca* III (1977): 119–30.

Radwan, Ali. "Der Königsname: Epigraphisches zum göttlichen Königtum in alten Ägypten." *SAK* 2 (1975): 231.

Ranke, Hermann. *Die ägyptische Personennamen.* 2 vols. Glückstadt: J. J. Augustin, 1935/52.

———. "Zum Wiedergeburtsglauben der alten Ägypter." *ZÄS* 79 (1954): 52–54.

Ranke, Kurt. "Brüder: Die zwei B. (AaTh 303)." *EM* I.

———. *Die zwei Brüder.* FFC 114. Helsinki: Soumalainen Tiedeakateimia Scientiarum Fennica, 1934.

Redford, D. B. *A Study of the Biblical Story of Joseph.* Supplements to *Vetus Testamentum* 20. Leiden: E. J. Brill, 1970.

Reiser, Elfriede. "Der königliche Harim im alten Ägypten und seine Verwaltung." Dissertationen der Universität Wien. Wien: Verlag Notring, 1972.

Renouf, Sir Peter Le Page. "Parallels in Folklore." *PSBA* XI (Apr. 1889): 177–89. Rpt. in *The Life Work of Sir Peter Le Page Renouf.* Eds. Gaston Maspero and Harry Rylands, 311–27. Vol. 3. Paris: Ernest Leroux Editeur, 1902–1905.

Röhrich, Lutz. "The Quest of Meaning in Folk Narrative Research." In *The Brothers Grimm and Folktale.* Ed. James M. McGlathery with Larry W.

Danielson, Ruth E. Lorbe, and Selma K. Richardson, 1–15. Urbana and Chicago: Univ. of Illinois, 1988.
Rößler-Köhler, Ursula. *Kapital 17 des ägyptischen Totenbuches.* GOF 10. Wiesbaden: Otto Harrassowitz, 1979.
Rougé, Emmanuel de. *Notice sur un manuscrit égyptien en écriture hiératique écrit sous le règne de Merienphthah, fils du grand Ramses vers le XVe siècle avant l'ère chrétienne.* Extrait de *Revue archéologique.* Paris: A. Leleux, Librairie, 1852.
Sasson, Jack. *Ruth: A New Translation with a Philogical Commentary and a Formalist-Folklorist Interpretation.* Baltimore: Johns Hopkins Univ. Press, 1979.
Sauneron, S. *The Priests of Ancient Egypt.* Trans. Ann Morrissett. New York: Grove Press, 1980.
Schäfer, Heinrich. *Principles of Egyptian Art.* Ed. Emma Brunner-Traut. Trans. and ed. John Baines. Oxford: Clarendon Press, 1974.
Schlögl, Hermann. *Der Sonnengott auf der Blüte.* Aeg. Hel. 5. Basel, 1977.
Schmitz, Bettina. *Unterschungen zum Titel s3-njswt "Königsohn".* Habelts Dissertationsdrucke, Reihe Ägyptologie 2. Bohn: Rudolf Habelt Verlag, GMBH, 1976.
Seeber, Christine. *Untersuchungen zur Darstellung des Totengerichts in Alten Ägypten.* MÄS 35. München-Berlin: Deutscherkunstverlag, 1976.
Seibert, Peter. *Die Characteristik: Untersuchungen zu einer altägyptischen Sprechsitte und ihren Auspragungen in Folklore und Literature, I.* Äg.Ab. 17. Wiesbaden: Otto Harrassowitz, 1967.
Sethe, Kurt. *Die altägyptischen Pyramidentexte.* 4 vols. Leipzig, 1910. Rpt. Hildesheim: Georg Olms Verlagsbuchhandlung, 1969.
———. "Die Sprüche für das Kennen der Seelen der heiligen Orte." *ZÄS* 57 (1922): 1–50.
———. "Osiris und die Zeder von Byblos." *ZÄS* 47 (1910): 71–73.
———. *Übersetzung und Kommentar zu den altägyptischen Pyramidentexten.* 6 vols. Glückstadt: J. J. Augustin, 1935–62.
———. *Urgeschichte und älteste Religion der Ägypter.* AKM, 1930.
———. *Urkunden I. Urkunden des Alten Reiches.* Leipzig: J. C. Hinrichs'sche Buchhandlung, 1904.
———. *Urkunden IV. Urkunden der 18. Dynastie, 1–16.* Leipzig: J. C. Hinrichs'sche Buchhandlung, 1914.
———. *Zur altägyptischen Sage vom Sonnenauge.* UGAÄ 5,3. Leipzig: J. C. Hinrichs'sche Buchhandlung, 1912.
———. "Zur ältesten Geschichte des ägyptischen Seeverkehrs mit Byblos und dem Libanongebiet." *ZÄS* 45 (1908): 7–14.
———. "Zur Geschichte der Einbalsamierung bei den Ägypten." *SPAW* (1934): No. 13, 211–39.
———. "Zur Vorgeschichte der Herzskarabäen." In *Mélanges Maspero.* MIFAO LXVI. Le Caire: Imprimerie de l'Institut français d'Archéologie orientale, 1935.

Settgast, Jurgen. *Untersuchungen zu altägyptischen Bestattungsdarstellungen.* ADAIK 3. Glückstadt: J. J. Augustin, 1963.
Simpson, William Kelly. *The Offering Chapel of Sekhem-Ankh-Ptah in the Museum of Fine Arts, Boston.* Boston: Department of Egyptian and Ancient Near Eastern Art, Museum of Fine Arts, 1967.
Smith, G. Elliot. *The Royal Mummies.* Catalogue Général des Antiquités du Égyptiennes du Musée du Caire, Nos. 61051–61100. Cairo: Service des Antiquités de l'Égypte, 1912.
Spalinger, A. Rev. of *Ancient Egyptian Literature,* Vol. 2, by Miriam Lichtheim. *OLZ* 74 (1979):525–27.
Speiser, E. A. *Genesis: A New Translation with Introduction and Commentary.* 3d ed. AB I. Garden City, NY: Doubleday, 1987.
Spiegel, Joachim. *Die Götter von Abydos.* GOF IV, 1. Wiesbaden: Otto Harrassowitz, 1973.
———. "Göttergeschichte, Erzählungen, Märchen, Fabeln." *HO*² I. Abt; I. Band; 2. Abschn., 147–67. Leiden: E. J. Brill, 1970.
Spiegelberg, W. "Das Herz als zweites Wesen des Menschen." *ZÄS* 66 (1930):35–37.
———. "Der Gott Bata." *ZÄS* 144 (1907):98–99.
Stadelmann, Rainer. *Syrisch-Palästinenische Gottheiten in Ägypten.* PdÄ 5. 1967; rpt. with corrections, Leiden: E. J. Brill, 1977.
Standard Dictionary of Folklore, Mythology, and Legend. One volume ed. Ed. Marie Leach. New York: Funk & Wagnalls, 1972.
Théodoridès, A. "De le Prétendue Expression juridique *pn ʿr mdt.*" *RdÉ* 19 (1967):111–21.
Thompson, D'Arcy Wentworth. "On Egyptian Fish Names Used by Greek Writers." *JEA* 14 (1927):22–33.
Thompson, Stith. *The Folktale.* New York, 1946; rpt. Berkeley and Los Angeles and London: Univ. of California Press, 1972.
Troy, Lana. *Patterns of Queenship in Ancient Egyptian Myth and History.* BOREAS 14. Uppsala, 1986.
Turner, Victor. *The Forest of Symbols: Aspects of Ndembu Ritual.* Ithaca: Cornell Univ. Press, 1967.
———. *The Ritual Process.* Ithaca, NY: Cornell Univ. Press, 1969.
Vallogia, M. *Recherche sur les 'Messagers' (wpwtyw) dans les sources égyptiennes profanes.* Genève-Paris: Librairie Droz, 1976.
Vandier, Jacques. "Bata, maître de Saka." *RHR* 136 (1949):5–9.
———. "La Légende de Bata, maître de Saka." *Actes du XXI Congrès International des Orientalistes* (1949):54–55.
———. *Le Papyrus Jumilhac.* Paris: Centre Nationale de la Recherche Scientifique, 1961.
Velde, H. te. *Seth, God of Confusion.* PdÄ 6. 1967; rpt. with corrections. Leiden: E. J. Brill, 1977.
Vergote, J. *Joseph en Égypte.* Orientalia et Biblica Louvaniensia III. Louvain: Publications Univ., 1959.

Vries, Jan de. *Betrachtungen zum Märchen.* FFC 150. Helsinki: Soumalainen Tiedeakateimia Scientiarum Fennica, 1954.

Weill, R. *Recherches sur la Ire dynastie et les temps prépharaoniques.* BdÉ 38. Le Caire: Imprimerie de l'Institut français d'Archéologie orientale, 1961.

Westendorf, W. "Beiträge aus und zu den medizinischen Texten." *ZÄS* 92 (1966).

Wild, Henry. *Le Tombeau de Ti.* MIFAO 65, 2. Le Caire: Imprimerie de l'Institut français d'Archéologie orientale, 1963.

Williams, R. J. "Ancient Egyptian Folktales." *University of Toronto Quarterly* 27 (1958):256–72.

———. "Literature as a Medium of Political Propaganda in Ancient Egypt." In *The Seed of Wisdom: Essays in Honor of T. J. Meek.* Ed. W. S. McCullough, 14–30. Toronto: Univ. of Toronto Press, 1964.

Wolf, Walther. *Kulturgeschichte des alten Ägypten.* Stuttgart: Alfred Kroner Verlag, 1962.

Yohannan, John D. *Joseph and Potiphar's Wife in World Literature.* New York: New Directions Books, 1968.

Yoyotte, Jean. "Sur Bata, maître de Sako." *RdÉ* 9 (1952):157–59.

Index